COACHING:
A Management Skill for Improving Individual Performance

Arthur X. Deegan II, Ph.D.

Reading, Massachusetts • Menlo Park, California • New York
Don Mills, Ontario • Wokingham, England • Amsterdam
Bonn • Paris • Milan • Madrid • Sydney • Singapore
Tokyo • Seoul • Taipei • Mexico City • San Juan

To my wife,
PATRICIA,
whose patience, understanding,
and love
make this book
and all my work
possible.

The publisher offers discounts on this book when ordered in quantity for special sales.
For more information please contact:
Corporate & Professional Publishing Group
Addison-Wesley Publishing Company
One Jacob Way
Reading, Massachusetts 01867

Library of Congress Cataloging in Publication Data

Deegan, Arthur X
  Coaching.

  1. Organizational change. 2. Management.
3. Employee counseling. I. Title.
HD58.8.D43   658.31'4   79-619
ISBN 0-201-01266-9

Tenth Printing, August 1991

Copyright © 1979 by Addison-Wesley Publishing Company, Inc. Philippines copyright 1979 by Addison-Wesley Publishing Company, Inc.

All rights reserved. No part of this publication may be reproduced, stored in a retrieval system, or transmitted, in any form or by any means, electronic, mechanical, photocopying, recording, or otherwise, without the prior written permission of the publisher. Printed in the United States of America. Published simultaneously in Canada. Library of Congress Catalog Card No. 79-619.

ISBN 0-201-01266-9
10 11 12 –AL–9594939291

PREFACE

Determining the appropriate audience for a message you wish to deliver is always important. I have been delivering the message in this book in workshops for almost ten years to managers at varying levels of authority in their respective organizations. I personally believe it is a message which can be important to anyone who manages people, no matter at what level.

In discussing the message with middle or upper level managers *face to face,* I have found excitement about the importance of the topic and appreciation for the assistance in reducing a nebulous responsibility to a series of practical procedures. I have also been warned by other senior managers who reviewed this text that the *written* message may get only to first level supervisors because of the tendency of some to say, "Oh, I heard all about the need to coach, and I approve of it," as though it is something they can delegate to others.

I sincerely hope this does not happen. I'm convinced of the universal need for this skill. Hence, this message is addressed to managers at all levels in your organization.

Given the situation of many organizations today—rapid overall growth, necessitating unusually rapid movement of key personnel from one position to another with the feeling that all of them are not ready for it—this message is especially important for higher level managers. For it is they who are typically responsible for controlling the growth of the organization. And no organization can grow any faster than its key people.

Clearwater, Florida A.X.D.
July 1979

CONTENTS

Introduction vii

1 **People Development: Option or Policy** 1

The simple words on a job description, "Responsible for the development of people in the department" are analyzed in detail. After a self-test is taken to determine your preconceived notions about the seriousness of this responsibility, a set of company-wide policies is recommended. Linear charting is then used to indicate both the detailed nature of the various action steps involved in the function of developing people and the many other individuals in the organization who share that duty.

2 **Coaching as a Communications Skill** 17

After a quick summary of recent theories of organizational communications, one is offered in detail as the framework for studying what happens when the manager seeks to help an individual develop. Six steps in the process are identified and potential pitfalls at each step are discussed. Interviewing techniques are then reviewed.

3 **Who Needs to Develop?** 43

The universality of development is stressed through identifying three types of people who need development. Development needs are broken down into knowledge, skills, or attitudes needing change. Technical growth, management growth, and total human growth needs are discussed. A convenient checklist is offered to assist in identifying growth needs.

4 **Personal Development Plan** 65

A simple form is offered as a way to document a plan for personal growth. Development needs, measurable objectives to denote growth has taken place, and a time/action plan to achieve that growth are all recorded.

5 Preparing for Development Interview 75

The need to prepare for people development interviews is stressed. What you know about five categories of background characteristics of your people is challenged. Strategies are suggested for handling seven common kinds of reactions on the part of people you are trying to develop.

6 The Annual Performance Preview 97

The annual performance evaluation interview is suggested as the vehicle for gaining commitment to personal development objectives. Changing the focus of this interview from salary administration to people development is stressed. The pros and cons of the traditional approach to performance review versus the recommended approach are reviewed.

7 Profile of an Effective People Developer 125

Background traits and behavior characteristics proven to be effective in the developing of people are discussed. Situations calling for people development are cited.

8 Day-to-Day Coaching Opportunities 147

Because coaching is an ongoing responsibility, the opportunities presented by many day-to-day situations are important to recognize and be prepared for. A few important such occasions are discussed in detail, such as giving orders, making corrections, delegating authority, and group problem-solving.

9 Transactional Analysis for the Coach 169

After a brief review of the theory of transactional analysis, the parent, adult, and child parts of the manager's personality are examined in terms of their impact on attempts to develop people.

10 Practice Cases 193

A series of ten cases is offered as a means of practicing the people development interview. Checklists and observer forms are included to assist in role playing.

INTRODUCTION

"Management by C.P.R.O.E.S.M." was the unintelligible title of a *Harvard Business Review* article some time ago. The author was spoofing the many attempts periodically in vogue to capture the essence of management in a catchall "Management by . . ." phrase. We have had Management by Communication, Management by Persuasion, Management by Results, Management by Objectives, Management by Motivation, and so on. Despite the claims by many that a particular Management by . . . is synonymous with the entire management process, it would seem that no single tool or technique really is coextensive with the entire job of managing, if only because the whole is greater than the sum of its parts.

For this reason, the title of this book is not "Management by Coaching," in order not to claim that this particular management skill is the end-all and be-all of good management. But it might come pretty close to that! For more and more today it seems that the successful manager, like the successful coach, is the one who can *unleash the full potential of individuals.* Study after study shows that leadership is a process of unleashing energy in the rank and file by means of personal impact, whether in a government, an army, a corporation, a college, a hospital, or any other business or team effort.

This has led to a series of new definitions of management away from the traditional "a manager is a person who plans, organizes, directs, motivates, and controls." Instead, this book emphasizes the role of an environment creator or facilitator, giving strength and enthusiasm to others, reinforcing their desire to do well, to grow as they are successful, to do their thing. We are currently witnessing quite a new and different concept of leadership. The leader's role today is not so much to make all key decisions himself or herself, but to develop an organization and a process by which decisions can be made by others. Today we cannot get very far with one-person companies or organizations any better than we can with one-person football teams.

In the face of difficulties, many leaders in business, as in other endeavors, have the urge to take the ball and run with it, leaving others to follow along as best they can. Today such action would be impulsive and imprudent. In the industrial field it will almost certainly result in losses; in other contexts, it will at least cause chaos. Instead, the leader must develop others with a variety of administrative talents, professional skills, scientific and technical disciplines. The challenge is to spark such people with such widely differing points of view to release their creative enthusiasm, imparting to them a feeling of pride not only in their own efforts but in the organization-wide efforts as well.

What we come down to in the end is a confrontation between a manager's vigorous style—the natural impulse to lead—and the all-important need to unleash the power of making creative decisions to others in the organization. If the two horns of this dilemma are not properly balanced, the mission of the organization is in jeopardy, for no organization can develop any faster than its key people.

MAJOR THESIS

This may explain the encompassing nature of what is meant here by the word *coaching,* and its use to describe the battery of managerial skills I have in mind—despite some of my friends who have told me in all candor, "I have no desire to learn anything about sports."

The overall thesis of this book has several parts which are interrelated as follows:

1. The way to achieve results in any organization is through individual achievements of its key people; hence, no organization can develop any faster than its key people. Developing people is the best way to maximize the bottom line.

2. Just as organizational results do not simply happen by themselves, but must be carefully planned and tracked, so the development of people must be professionally planned and monitored.

3. Individual managers, especially senior executives, get to the point where their success and personal advancement depends on the ability to develop people more than their professional or technical knowledge or skills.

No organization can develop any faster than its key people. This is more than just a pious platitude. It is an axiom, yes—but also a practical reality. If the organization's successful achievement of results depends on the development of people and their individual achievements, then the manager who is conscious of being measured by organizational results will see the overriding importance of people development.

This is, therefore, a text on People Development, not in the narrow sense of only career planning (though this is part of it), but in the broader context of the many occasions the busy manager of today faces, calling for the attitudes, skills, and style of unleashing the potential of others. Style is pace, flair, commitment. Anything less, when it comes to the development of people, will make it a part-time job, and that it is not.

Some texts and workshops treat Coaching or Counseling as the specific Personnel function of Employee Counseling; that is, helping employees solve personal problems, whether on or off the job. The focus here will be much broader than this. Still, recognizing the trend for such organized employee counseling programs to decrease, the individual manager might recognize where such an approach might be beneficial.

People development must be planned and monitored. Managing by crisis or reactionary management has primarily given way to anticipatory management or some sort of management by objectives involving a carefully laid out plan of action to achieve carefully stated desired results. Being accountable for the results achieved or not achieved has led any manager deserving of the title to some results-oriented system of management with documented commitments as to *job-related* results.

Many organizations also profess belief in *personal development* objectives. The understanding of what that means and the level of expertise in stating such objectives or gaining commitment to achieve such objectives lags by light years. The literature on how to develop personal development objectives is almost nonexistent.

This will therefore also be a text on Personal Development Objectives—how to state them in words, how to gain commitment on them, and how to measure successful accomplishment of them. The continuing emphasis will be the development of the skills of planning and measuring the development of people. This will include a formal overall development plan entered into periodically, as well as discussion of the many opportunities that present themselves to modify/embellish that plan on a day-to-day basis.

Senior managers are eventually measured more by people development than anything else. Here is the special focus which will distinguish efforts in this text from other texts, handbooks, or seminars entitled Coaching or Counseling. The thrust of most of these seems to be on the need for managers to train, motivate, and/or otherwise influence the behavior of their workers in overcoming something unsatisfactory on their part. It's as though coaching means "find out what's wrong with the other person and change it." The worker is either performing below standard, refusing to accept a promotion opportunity, showing signs of complacency, or otherwise standing in the way of the team's progress. So, coaching is a matter of changing someone else's behavior.

Further, since such unsatisfactory conditions are thought to exist much more often at the lowest level in the organization, it is usually the supervisors of the lowest level persons in the organization who find themselves being signed up by their superiors to take courses on Coaching. I have consistently tried to take a different approach and advise client organizations to adopt a different focus on coaching. I believe it is a lot easier to change one's own behavior than it is to change someone else's. Therefore, the manager is advised to examine/improve his or her own skills in the people development interface, which will also include the ability to identify development needs on the part of others.

Therefore, this is also a text on communication skills—the techniques or process of transmitting information from one person to another, including allowance for the social psychology of both the sender and receiver of the transmission, and the organizational relationships they obtain. Since these skills are at least as important for the senior executive of an organization as for first line supervisors, Coaching ought to be an organization-wide commitment to people development, starting at the top—not a remedial program for correcting the weak.

STYLE

This text is the fruit of almost ten years of seminars on Coaching conducted with practicing managers in a wide variety of organizations. While the words are mine, the thoughts they express have been refined over the years by the many types and levels of supervisory personnel who have worked with me in these workshops.

At times this has undoubtedly led me to a more conversational style than some expect to find in a textbook. I would like to neither boast nor apologize for this. I simply ask you to accept it as the style I find most convenient to use in addressing you on this subject.

For this reason, it might be more appropriate to say this is a workbook rather than a text. It contains descriptive material, diagrams, charts, forms, and worksheets to be used by you. All have been tested through much use in both profit-making and nonprofit-making organizations. The full benefit from this volume will be obtained only if you practice with the worksheets as recommended in the text.

There is a logical development of ideas intended as you move from chapter to chapter. So, while some may wish to look up a particular topic, most of you will prefer to use the text as a self-teaching tool to acquire or develop the coaching skills discussed.

The organization by chapters suggests a logical progression

from: 1. defining and accepting the responsibility to develop people
to: 2. communicating with another person
about: 3. identifying development needs
and: 4. documenting needs, activities, resources, and measurements

in: 5-6. the context of a formal performance evaluation or other interview
or: 7-8. on the occasion of day-to-day coaching opportunities
by: 9. two persons transacting with each other
as in: 10. case situations presented for discussion.

This flow of material covered can be seen as answering the following questions:

Chapter
1. Do you accept the responsibility to coach, i.e., to develop people? Who might assist you in this responsibility and how?
2. Are you aware that this will require communications skills? What are the steps in a simple communications process?
3. Who needs to develop? In what ways do people need to develop?
4. How do you measure personal development? How do you make a formal plan for personal growth?
5. How do you prepare for a performance appraisal interview? What can you anticipate during such an interview?
6. How do you get people to commit themselves to personal growth? What should be the focus of such a discussion?
7. What are the traits of an effective people-developer? On which occasions will these traits be used?
8. What day-by-day opportunities present themselves for the development of people?
9. How does your ego state or that of your people affect attempts at developing them?
10. What are some real case situations presenting opportunities for unleashing the potential of others?

1 PEOPLE DEVELOPMENT: OPTION OR POLICY

Full many a gem of purest ray serene
  The dark unfathom'd caves of ocean bear;
Full many a flower is born to blush unseen
  And waste its sweetness on the desert air;

THOMAS GRAY
Elegy Written in the Country Churchyard

The comment, "A manager is responsible for the development of his or her people," is one of those universal statements, rarely questioned by anyone. It is reinforced over and over by being incorporated just about verbatim on every manager's job description or list of principal accountabilities. But, beyond the rhetoric, just what does it mean? What specifically does such a responsibility entail for you? Go ahead. Use the space below to write down exactly what you think it means to be responsible for the development of your people.

> **Q** What does it mean to be responsible for the development of your people?
>
> **A**

If you are like most people, your answer mentions something about providing training, in-service, or motivating workers to do their best or to get ahead, and guiding them in becoming career-oriented. If you are further ahead in your thinking than most people, you might have written something about trying to get your workers to live up to their potential. But after such generalizations, you probably quit.

SELF-INVENTORY

Here is a second way to test your perceptions about people development as you begin to study this book. Figure 1-1 is a self-test. Right now, before you read any further, take a pencil and in column A, mark each statement either true or false. Leave column B alone for the moment.

Figure 1-1   Self-Inventory on People Development

Statement	A	B
1. Planned people development should be one of the basic concepts of any organization's professional management system.		
2. The development of my people should be planned professionally just as sales or budgeting programs should be.		
3. It is my responsibility to review individual plans for development at least annually.		
4. Each of my subordinates should work out a specific plan of personal development.		
5. I should require individual development plans from each of my subordinates.		
6. Periodic instructions/assistance on the job is a major part of any individual's development.		
7. Correcting mistakes/errors is a part of any individual's development.		
8. I should encourage my subordinates to take advantage of job rotation opportunities in order to grow.		
9. I am expected to provide time for people to pursue development activities consistent with the workload.		
10. I am expected to recommend and help develop at least one replacement candidate for my own job.		

In marking these statements true or false, you undoubtedly reflected conditions as you know them to exist at the present time in your particular organization. You probably indicated what you should or should not do, or what you are or are not expected to do in your own company. And you are most likely correct because you know the policies and procedures of your organization.

But now let's discuss each of those ten statements in the Self-Inventory as though each were being presented for ratification as a policy statement. The suggestion is that each and every one of them be made a policy in your organization and every organization which is interested in achieving results. These statements then become possible ways of helping managers in your organization to come to a more practical grasp of exactly what it means in the job description when it says to be responsible for the development of your people.

1. Planned people development should be one of the basic concepts of any organization's professional management system. This is an attempt to state a broad policy which removes any option about people development by stipulating that developing people is a pillar of whatever system of management your organization espouses. This people development should be planned, not given mere lip service or expected to happen by itself.

Adoption of this policy would guard against the simplistic way in which some managers consider themselves to be results-oriented as opposed to people-oriented, thus absolving themselves from people development. The major thrust of people development will be to emphasize that the development of people is the best means available to achieve results of the organization. Hence, rather than choose between one or the other, they are seen to be two sides of the same coin.

2. Development of my people should be planned professionally just as sales or budgeting programs should be. What is suggested here is not the hiring of outside staff specialists who become "professional" people managers. Rather, the comparison with sales or budgeting programs is to remind individual managers that they are personally responsible for planning people development, just as they are personally responsible for planning sales and budgets. This responsibility should not be taken lightly, but carried out professionally with the same care, training, and assistance that is necessary in any other important responsibility they have.

Admittedly most managers have not had training to be a professional in this field. All too often they have yielded to the internal "experts," usually in personnel, to do this. In turn, this causes many personnel people to resent such passing of the buck even when they understand what causes it. One personnel manager put it:

> The bane of my life are those managers who think we are here to talk to their people for them because they don't feel comfortable doing it,

especially the ones that come from school, or our trainee programs, rather than up through the ranks. They come with lots of training and confidence about the technical job, but not much on people building. Then it takes six months to get comfortable with their job and learn to take care of themselves, and then they can turn their attention to developing others. During this time they run to personnel and ask for help in talking to their people. They just never were one of them and so don't know what the relationship should be from that experience which they lack.

3. It is my responsibility to review individual plans for development at least annually. Three new thoughts are intended by this policy recommendation. First, because development is different for everyone, there should be *individual* development plans. While there may always be areas of growth or development common to many at the same time, these ought not to be the sum total of the people developing taking place. It is often an easy excuse for managers to point to plant-wide or company-wide "people" programs as a way of absolving themselves of their people development responsibility.

The second operable word in this policy statement is *review*. The manager is required to follow up on the people development plans. They are not to be spoken of enthusiastically for a brief period and then forgotten. If documented on company forms, they ought not to be forwarded to some staff office as though floating off into never-never land. They require monitoring so that progress may be checked periodically.

Third, individual plans should be reviewed at least annually. This is an attempt to offer some time frame for periodic review, so as not to make the task overly time-consuming. Furthermore, a lot can happen in twelve months, so that this span of time is not too soon for considering new situations that might warrant change or updating the plan. Many practicing manners indicate a twelve-month time frame as a very practicable one, especially when the development plan is discussed in the context of the annual performance evaluation, as we shall discuss in detail in chapter six.

4. Each of my subordinates should work out a specific plan of personal development. A word on semantics here first. Etymologically the word *subordinate* is devastating, especially when used in the context of helping develop all the positive things in people. Literally it means someone who is lower in rank, often thought to automatically mean lesser in worth. And this is farthest from what you would like to connote here. Still, the word has been accepted in organizational jargon since the days of Max Weber. We are addressing managers in this text, and we are speaking of the manager's responsibility as a key link in the organization to foster the development of certain other members of the organization, specifically those who report to him or her administratively. While there is much each manager can do to assist in developing peers and superiors in the organization, the manager is typically held accountable for developing subordinates only.

Two thoughts are incorporated in this policy statement. First, *each* subordinate is to have a development plan. Again we speak of the universality of development. This isn't only for the weak, or only for those identified as shining stars, or only for the chief executive's relatives, or only for any select lucky or unlucky few. Everyone has developmental needs in order to help achieve the mission of the organization. Chapter three will go into this in great detail, showing how every job tends to grow, if only in becoming more complex, necessitating the incumbent to at least keep up with that kind of development.

Then there is the question of who works out this plan for development. Some of you will immediately think of some subordinates who do not appear capable of working out a plan for their own personal development, hence this may prompt a negative vote (or "false" mark) on this statement. Clearly there will be some individuals less qualified than others to work out such a plan. But the intent is not to expect people to do it alone—quite the contrary. As we go on, we shall be identifying together the many individuals who might assist somehow in this responsibility. The real point of this statement is to fix on the subordinate a sharing of the development responsibility for which the manager is accountable. It becomes then a shared responsibility between manager and subordinate.

5. *I should require individual development plans from each of my subordinates.* This statement is a reinforcement of the previous one. Many readers take exception to the word *require*. In earlier versions of this Self-Inventory, the word *demand* was used but was found to be unnecessarily harsh sounding. Perhaps what the word *require* connotes is closer to the mark. If it is to be a policy that all be challenged to develop to their fullest potential, if the option is not to be left to the manager to pick and choose which individuals benefit from development opportunities, then it ought to not be a matter of choice to the subordinate either.

Again many managers can point to individuals who might state, or who have actually stated, they are not interested in development. We've all encountered people like that. They readily aver that they have no interest in getting promoted; they don't want any administrative or managerial headaches: they know their job, they do it well, they simply want to work from 9 to 5 or whatever and leave the jockeying for new positions to someone else, etc. This is precisely why the universality of the need for development needs reinforcing. It ought not to be an option. The organization cannot afford to let people maintain that attitude. It is not that we want to force people to think of promotion or becoming managers or anything they truly do not want to become, but in order to continue to perform well in the present areas of responsibility, people must keep pace with developments in their field. Because no job stays the same, no jobholder can stay the same. "Future shock" is a concept with which we are all familiar. So much happens in the developing world around us that no job remains the same very long. Hence, if a worker is doing the job the same way he or she did a year ago, that person is at least ineffective, if not completely wrong.

6. *Periodic instruction/assistance on the job is a major part of any individual's development.* The hope here is that the manager will feel at home. Periodic instruction or assistance on the job is an everyday occurrence. No one will deny the need for giving instruction or assistance on the job to those who need it, and some need it more than others. If we can begin to see this as part of the warp and woof of individual development, then the universal change envisioned in these statements will not be so threatening to some.

Further, this statement begins to move us away from the planning of individual development to actually participating in that process. The best plan in the world is going to have holes in it and will require amendment from time to time. This is one way in which the manager will move from talk to action, from moral support to personal involvement. As in work-oriented objectives, you plan the work, then work the plan; the same is true for personal development.

7. *Correcting mistakes/errors is a part of any individual's development.* This is very much like the preceding statement, in that opportunity for this kind of development activity is likely to occur on a day-to-day basis, and ought to be seen as an integral part of helping people grow. This makes correcting mistakes an opportunity to learn and profit rather than a matter of chastisement or shame.

Both this and the last statement should even be considered a part of a person's plan for development. The manager and the subordinate should envision that there will be times when giving instructions or giving corrections will be necessary. Engaging in these kinds of communications ought not to be seen as indicative of problems or failure or anything necessarily negative. They are a part of the workaday world. Accepting such facts ahead of time, welcoming the occasions when they occur as a chance to grow and develop, should bring more beneficial results than often happens.

8. *I should encourage my subordinates to take advantage of job rotation opportunities in order to grow.* This is intended as another example of a possible kind of developmental activity that might be appropriate for many

individuals. Everyone should be encouraged to consider whether job rotation might be appropriate. Clearly not all individuals will find it appropriate. It will depend on the nature of the job and so on. This statement is intended to indicate that this will not equally apply to all people performing all jobs, but only to those where there is an opportunity.

9. *I am expected to provide time for people to pursue developmental activities consistent with the workload.* Again, recall that we are talking about this statement as a proposed policy, not as things actually exist in your present organization. Your organization is encouraged to adopt this statement as a policy, removing much of the option from the individual manager. All managers would then be expected to provide time for people to engage in whatever the appropriate developmental activities will turn out to be for each individual.

It really is not a laughing matter when a worker asks to attend a workshop, for example, and is told by the manager: "OK, you can go; but remember while you're gone the work is going to pile up on your desk, so be ready to burn some midnight oil when you return to make up for it." It's as though the worker grows or develops on his or her own time, and should not be stealing company time to become a better worker.

Still, the exigencies of the job cannot be ignored, and that is why the statement includes mention of being consistent with the workload. This policy provides an obvious chance to cop-out, but it is not reason enough to delete reference to it, because the fact is that development can often be scheduled around work exigencies, to the detriment of neither the work or the people growth, if only an honest attempt be made to balance one with the other.

10. *I am expected to recommend and help develop at least one replacement candidate for my own job.* There are a couple of important words here which are often overlooked and which sometimes lead some managers to mark this one false. Notice it is a matter of *recommending* a replacement, not promising anything to anyone. The last thing you want to do is identify an "heir apparent" when there may be several persons in the organization who might be possible candidates in their own minds, if not in yours.

Then it is a matter of helping develop someone to be a candidate for the job, not just selecting a person who might already be qualified and dropping the subject at that point. The manager that realizes his or her chances for further upward movement may be enhanced by having someone already developed to take over the position to be vacated tends to take people developing seriously.

Some have interpreted this as a promise to move upward as soon as someone is developed. That is not the intent. Rather the intent is to have someone qualified if and when the manager moves up (or out). Some refer to this as the concept of "organizational surplus." As more and more organizations report they are "growing by leaps and bounds," "bursting at the seams," and "doubling and tripling in size overnight," there are more and more complaints that the one thing slowing down further growth is the lack of qualified personnel to move into key positions that open up by virtue of this growth. This policy statement can prevent delays in organizational growth, can prevent the need for constantly hiring from outside whenever a nice plum of a job opens up (thereby ruining morale), and can literally provide a surplus of people qualified to move into positions before there is even need for it. Some argue that having too many qualified people is also a way to hurt morale. While that has to be admitted as a possibility, it would seem to be a much happier fate, not to mention that the record seems to indicate that generally speaking we are so far in arrears the other way that it will be a long time before we do any serious damage by having too many overqualified people.

Policy summary

Here is how the president of one business firm put across the ideas set forth in the preceding policy statements when introducing planned people development in his company:

- Our organization is proud of the professional approach we take in all aspects of conducting our business.
- Having on-hand qualified managers to meet growth opportunities is a valid and basic concept to which we are committed just as we realize the need for other resources like capital, land and ideas.
- A professional approach to helping development of our people in order to maximize their full potential will have a direct impact on the "bottom line."
- Professionalism in people development is as important a responsibility for line managers as any other program they pursue to achieve results. We are a "people" business.
- A professional approach to people development is the responsibility of every manager in the company. We are dedicated to Planning for Individual Achievement and Organizational Results.

Self-inventory again

Assuming you can accept the ten policy statements as operable in your organization, whether or not they are actually made a formal matter of written policy, how many of them are you now putting into practice to your own satisfaction? You might want to now go back to Figure 1-1 and make a notation under column B about each of the ten statements. A simple Yes or No will indicate which of them you now practice and which you don't. Clearly the statements you do not practice might be areas in this workbook to which you will wish to pay special attention.

SHARING THE RESPONSIBILITY FOR PEOPLE DEVELOPMENT

The preceding discussion of policy statements has hopefully added a lot of specificity to the bland charge that a manager is responsible for the development of people. But let us not be guilty of overkill. The responsibility is not awesome—it is in many ways shared with others in the organization. As a matter of fact, there are often those in the firm or group who are sometimes prone to think that professional or formal people development is their private poaching ground; for example, a Training Director, a Management Development Manager, or a Manpower Planning Supervisor. There is also a manager's own superior who often makes the final decisions about people development or movement.

The purpose of Figure 1-2 is to help you realize the number of others who work with you on people development and the many ways in which they share this duty with you. This figure is called a linear responsibility chart because it seeks to graph, line by line, the many activities involved in people development and to show on each line the type of collaboration you may expect from different persons.

Let's literally fill in the chart as we review how it can help you better comprehend what it means to be responsible for the development of your people.

Begin by calling to mind the identity of one of your key people, one who deserves the kind of attention you will be paying to this individual as we continue to work through this text together. There will be a series of exercises like this one which you will engage in, so choose someone on whom you wish to devote a good deal of time. It can be your strong right arm or the sour apple in your group who needs help, or anyone at all for that matter, given the universality of people development needs.

Write in that person's name and title where called for in Figure 1-2. Then, of course, write in your name and title where it states "Prepared by," since you are the one primarily accountable for these responsibilities. Also, it helps to date the form, as what is true today may not be true tomorrow.

Now pause for a moment and look at how the remainder of the figure is laid out. Down the left side of the sheet is a series of activities having to do with people development. Across the top is room to insert the titles of several persons in the organization, including your title and that of your sub-

10 PEOPLE DEVELOPMENT: OPTION OR POLICY

Figure 1-2 Linear Responsibility Chart

For the development of:

(Name) _____

(Title) _____

(Prepared by) _____

(Title) _____

(Date) _____

a. Identify development needs

b. Identify development resources

c. Prepare written dev. plan

d. Plan job rotation experience

e. Give day-to-day instructions

f. Make appropriate corrections

g. Plan appropriate course work

h. Give formal instructions in class

i. Plan upward career path

j. Provide time for dev. activities

k. Periodic review of dev. progress

l. Identify promotion potential

m. Recommend personnel actions

ordinate. Write in those two titles immediately. Then in the other spaces write in the titles of other persons who are going to share with you in one way or another the responsibilities for developing your chosen subordinate. Figure 1-3, which has already been completed for a hypothetical worker, may be helpful as a reference for this and other steps.

Next you will note in the completed example (Figure 1-3) different symbols have been drawn in under the several titles to show the different kinds of collaboration to be given by the respective individuals in the development of our fictitious John or Jane Doe. A quick glance at any activity line will indicate how many people will be involved in that single por-

Figure 1-3 Linear Responsibility Chart

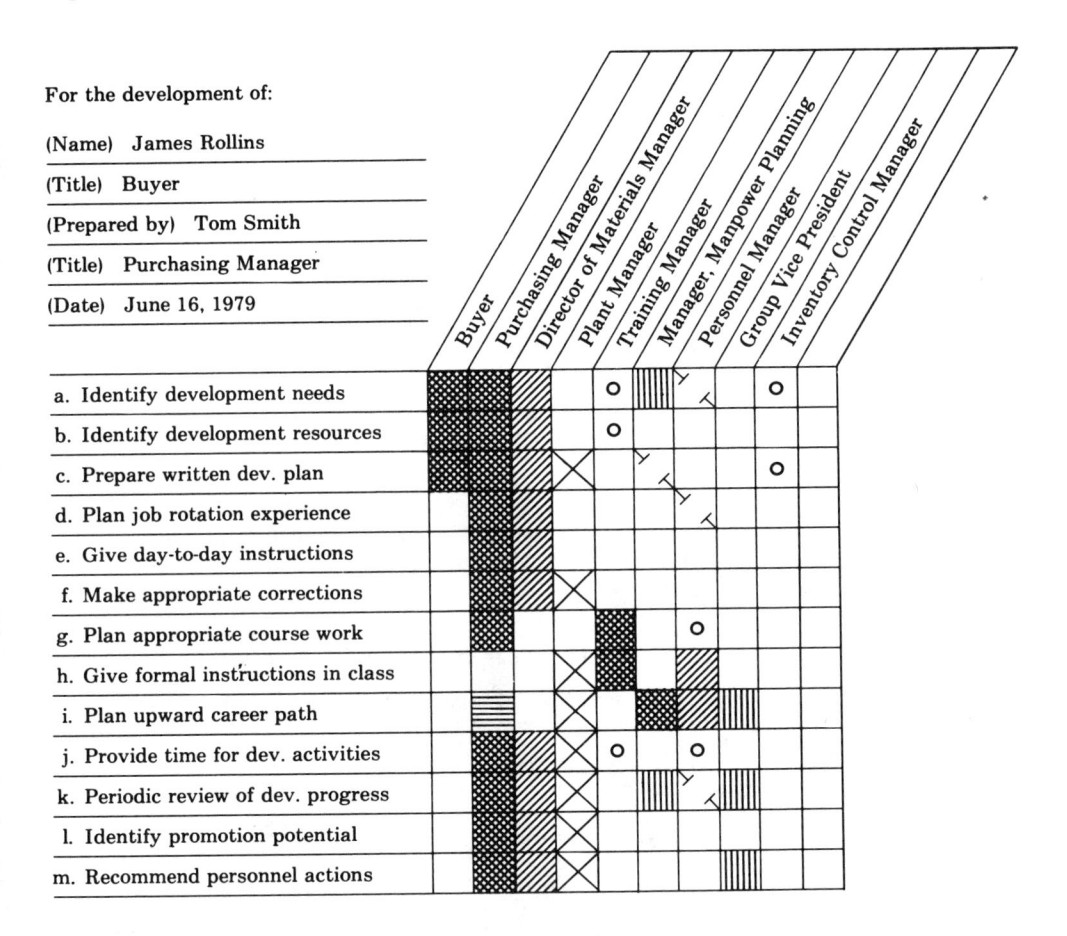

For the development of:

(Name) James Rollins
(Title) Buyer
(Prepared by) Tom Smith
(Title) Purchasing Manager
(Date) June 16, 1979

Columns (left to right): Buyer, Purchasing Manager, Director of Materials Manager, Plant Manager, Training Manager, Manager, Manpower Planning, Personnel Manager, Group Vice President, Inventory Control Manager

Rows:
a. Identify development needs
b. Identify development resources
c. Prepare written dev. plan
d. Plan job rotation experience
e. Give day-to-day instructions
f. Make appropriate corrections
g. Plan appropriate course work
h. Give formal instructions in class
i. Plan upward career path
j. Provide time for dev. activities
k. Periodic review of dev. progress
l. Identify promotion potential
m. Recommend personnel actions

tion of J. Doe's development, and exactly what each of these persons' role will be. This chart delineates exactly who is responsible for what when it comes to the development of your employee. The sum total of the entire list is a much clearer definition of what the job description means when it says the manager is responsible for the development of people.

The different symbols which might be used are found in Figure 1-4. Beside each symbol you will find a description of the type of responsibility it represents. As you can see, they range from actually doing the work, to command or decision-making responsibility, to being asked for advice on a given matter. It is even possible for a couple of individuals to have the same kind of involvement in a given activity. Take a few moments to study Figure 1-4, so you are familiar with the eight definitions. You don't have to commit them to memory, for you will keep this chart in front of you as you work on Figure 1-2. And you will have the sample in Figure 1-3 to serve as a guide also.

Figure 1-4. Definition of Symbols for Linear Responsibility Charting

Symbol	No.	Description
▦	1.	Work is Done. The activity described is to be performed by the individual whose position is shown on the chart.
▨	2.	Direct Supervision. The activity described is to be overseen/approved by the individual shown on the chart.
⊠	3.	General Supervision. The activity is to be checked by way of administrative approval "once removed" by the individual shown on the chart.
▽△	4.	Coordinative Supervision. The activity described falls within the purview of the individual shown by virtue of that person needing to insure a unified approach where activities require the cooperation of several persons.
◩	5.	Decision on Ad Hoc Basis. Applied to making a decision on special points where specific technical knowledge is called for.
≡	6.	Person Must be Consulted. Means the individual shown must be consulted on the point, though the advice need not to be followed.
‖‖‖	7.	Person Must be Notified. Means the individual shown must be advised, verbally or in writing, so as to be able to function properly.
○	8.	Person May be Called in for Exchange of Ideas or Advice. Self-explanatory.

All that remains now is for you to draw in the appropriate symbols on Figure 1-2 for your chosen employee. Let's do that now, taking each of the activity lines one at a time.

a. Identifying development needs for your subordinate. Who literally has to do the work, to sit down and put on paper the areas in which John or Jane Doe should develop? (Hint: you probably are the one, so put symbol number 1 under your title; and the subordinate should also be charged with this work, so put symbol number 1 under the subordinate's title also.) Then, who might have to approve or double check your ideas on this? (Perhaps your own superior? If so, put symbol number 2 under your superior's title.) Does someone coordinate this kind of activity in the organization? Must someone

SHARING THE RESPONSIBILITY FOR PEOPLE DEVELOPMENT   13

be notified at this point? Are there individuals whom you might call in for consultation? If so, put the appropriate symbols under these persons' title.

b. Identifying development resources to help meet those needs. Who should actually do this activity? Might it again be you and John Doe or Jane Doe? Will someone approve that work? Can anyone offer assistance like referring you to catalogs of courses, workshops, etc.? Put the appropriate symbols under each person's title.

c. Preparing the written development plan for John Doe or Jane Doe. Who should physically write the plan? Who must approve it? Is there anyone assigned in a staff office, for example, to coordinate this type of activity throughout the organization? Is there someone who perhaps relates closely to the individual's work on a frequent basis who might be helpful in giving advice? Will some higher level manager give supervision once removed? Find the appropriate symbol for each of these and write them in on the chart.

d. Planning job rotation experience, where this might be helpful for the development plan. Who should make the judgment as to whether this would be appropriate or not? Must this decision be verified once or twice removed? Does anyone coordinate all the job rotating inside and outside of the department? Be sure to show the correct symbol for each person, so as to clarify the degree and type of involvement for this activity.

e. Giving day-to-day instructions to your John Doe or Jane Doe. Will you actually do this yourself? Might someone else also be expected to do this regularly? (This will be important for your subordinate to know and expect.) Who checks on your instructions?

f. Making appropriate corrections. Are you the one to do this for John Doe or Jane Doe? Might someone else have occasion to do this, again due to the nature of the job? Is there someone to verify that the corrections were helpful? Is there a court of appeal once removed?

g. Planning appropriate course work. Who literally will be expected to determine which courses might help in the development of your subordinate? Often there is a staff person available to do this with you, or at least to give advice; or maybe to ask advice from, even if not followed.

h. Giving formal classroom instruction. Here is one where you often will not get symbol 1, for you may very well not do any formal teaching of this sort. Maybe no one will, for that matter. Then again you may have a whole staff engaging in this kind of activity, but probably under someone's supervision, notification, coordination, or whatever. Find the appropriate symbol designating the degree of involvement deemed suitable in your particular organization so you and all parties will know what is expected of whom.

i. Planning upward career path possibilities for your subordinate. Even if the judgment is that there may be none in the foreseeable future for this particular individual, who literally does that? Who must be asked for advice? Who must be notified? Who is involved in approving the plans? This activity is very crucial in terms of who makes decisions, who advises, and who approves.

j. Providing time for developmental activities, always in recognition of the exigencies of the workload as discussed earlier. Isn't this really your personal responsibility? But won't someone supervise how well you are doing your scheduling? And is someone even higher up than that taking an interest in seeing that this is being done? Are there staff persons who can be consulted on an ad hoc basis in order to find the most convenient times for all?

k. Periodic review of development progress. Who has the official formal responsibility to do this? Does your superior review your judgment? Does his or her superior want to be notified or to approve the judgment, or be asked for advice, or just what? Will anyone have to be notified once the judgment is made? Is there an office "in charge" of seeing that this is done, in a coordinative or facilitative manner?

l. Identifying promotion potential of John Doe or Jane Doe. Much the same questions should be asked: Who is supposed to decide about the potential (not actual readiness)? Is that judgment supposed to be approved? Does anyone have to be notified, etc.?

m. Recommending personnel actions like transfer, promotion, probation, discharge. Do you initiate those motions? Does anyone have to approve your judgment? Does anyone expect to be notified, or consulted, or asked for advice? Find the correct symbol for each of these and place under the person's title on the chart.

Once you get the hang of this, you will add or substitute your own list of activities to this chart. With or without such improvements, the completed form should give you and John Doe or Jane Doe a much better idea of the work involved in fostering personal development, and a healthier regard for the sharing of this responsibility with others.

SUMMARY

This chapter has attempted to define the meaning of the responsibility to coach. A coach is a people developer. But because these terms are so nebulous, they have been defined here as including all the activities involved in developing business resources. A coach, therefore, is a person who:

- plans the development of people
- reviews development plans annually
- requires that people develop
- gives instructions on the job
- corrects mistakes when they occur
- considers job rotation opportunities
- provides time for development activities
- develops replacement candidates
- identifies people development needs
- works with other development resources
- places formal and informal resources
- plans upward career paths
- identifies promotion potential

These and many similar behavior characteristics are to be understood in the term *coach* as it will be used over and over in the following chapters. But the emphasis, the main new material presented in this book, concerns the detailed procedure of preparing for and conducting an interview with a subordinate regarding specific plans for personal growth.

2 COACHING AS A COMMUNICATIONS SKILL

Word is not crystal, transparent and unchanged; it is the skin of a living thought and may vary greatly in color and content according to the circumstances and the time in which it is used.

                    JUSTICE OLIVER WENDELL HOLMES

So far we have seen that being responsible for the development of people can be understood as entailing a whole series of individual activities dealing with identifying developmental needs, selecting appropriate courses of action, scheduling events efficiently, checking on progress periodically, playing an active part in the actual developmental progress, and many more. Each of these in turn is generally shared with many other individuals in terms of varying types and degrees of involvement. To carry them off well, a lot of communicating is going to have to take place—so much so that we like to consider coaching (the cluster of all the aforementioned activities) as basically a communications skill.

For this reason we are going to interrupt our work on the development of John Doe or Jane Doe and remind ourselves of some very important points about communicating as it takes place in the organizational setting.

COMMUNICATIONS THEORIES

Recent explanations of organizational communications theory might be classified into three main approaches: (1) those which see the communications task as an engineering problem in solving the difficulties of transmitting information from one point to another; (2) those which explain communications in terms of social psychology, wherein the human properties of the sender and the receiver receive most consideration; and (3) those which concentrate on administrative communications as the study of organizational relationships.

Mechanics

The first group is more concerned with the mechanics of the process of communications. Defining communications as the transmission of information or understanding from one person to another, they posit six steps or stations in the complete procedure. This is exemplified in the Shannon-Weaver analog where we find the sender, the encoding, the transmission, the decoding, the receiver, and feedback to the origin. Problems or barriers may arise in any or all of these points, and good communication involves overcoming obstacles in each of these stations. Attention must be paid to the proper timing, the frequency, the right media, the quantity, the accuracy, the channels, the format, and all other mechanical aspects of communicating. (We shall return to this analog in greater detail after identifying the other theories.)

Another illustration of this school would be the work of C. G. Browne, who, together with Shore, described the work of the leader in communications as a task of "predictive abstracting." They felt that empathy as spoken of by Likert and others was too broad; that all the communicator really had to do was to abstract from his or her knowledge of others those particulars which well determine their behavior or attitude and communicate accordingly. They conducted studies which showed that the higher you go in an organization, the better you are at predicting the behavior of others.

Another example of this school is the "map" and "territory" analogy of Browne. He said words are like maps; they are symbols for territories. The possibility that my map and your map, though they look alike, might represent different territories for each of us, causes the semantic problems in communications.

Again, William Scott speaks of *entropy* in communications. This is a term borrowed from the natural sciences, where it refers to a tendency of natural bodies to seek the condition of greatest randomness. Scott says it may be applied to communications theory to indicate that without control, communications also seeks greatest randomness and disintegration, so that the communications problem is really one of control.

Perhaps the ultimate in this approach to communications is known as information theory. Founded on the general principles of cybernetics, which is the theory of a system feedback whereby complex (especially electronic) systems check on their own performance to correct behavior as necessary, communications is thought to be incomplete when the complete circle is not closed. Like the thermostat (the usual example given to explain cybernetics), communications must have feedback in order to properly regulate itself. Alex Bavelas and others have performed experiments to show the efficacy of feedback. A popular example is the exercise where the communicator attempts to explain verbally how to lay out a pattern of dominoes to listeners who are not allowed to show in any way whether they are receiving the message. Invariably their ability to comprehend (by actually laying out the dominoes) lags far behind another group of listeners who are permitted, as the instructions are being given, to ask questions, to show whether they are keeping up, or otherwise provide feedback so the sender can amend the message.

Psychology

The second school of communications theories explains communications as a matter of assuring proper attention to perception, motivation, and the other psychological factors present in the sender and receiver. The British social scientist Higham, for instance, comments on studies made by Lorenz on dogs, as well as others on hens and monkeys, showing how human perceptions follow closely what we so easily observe in animals. The Lorenz study of two adult male dogs is a classic, showing how a dominance-submission relationship follows initial sizing up exercises. The same is said to be true of human interactions. We cannot separate the communications process from the likes and dislikes we build up. The process of communications then becomes a task of fitting our messages into the existing structure of perceptions of the receiver.

Higham's example of how a picture brought to mind by the words *man . . . knife . . . table . . . cloth* can be easily changed by association with additional words *surgeon . . . blood . . . anesthetic* explains the context factor. (Or, we have more fun with *bottle . . . blonde . . . instrument . . . coat*, finding we have one mental picture until we add the word *rat* and get a different association.) He also gives the example of telling an incident to a group of students about hypothetical students in a real-life situation, and how this is more easily understood than the same story couched in a setting foreign to the students' own behavior experiences.

Mason Haire also has a good example of how earlier states of mind color our reception of information. You might try this one yourself. In this example you will see nine dots arranged in three rows of three dots each with a little space between the rows and the dots. Now connect all nine dots by only four lines. You may not lift your pencil off the paper once you begin to draw, and every time you change direction you start a new line. Try it.

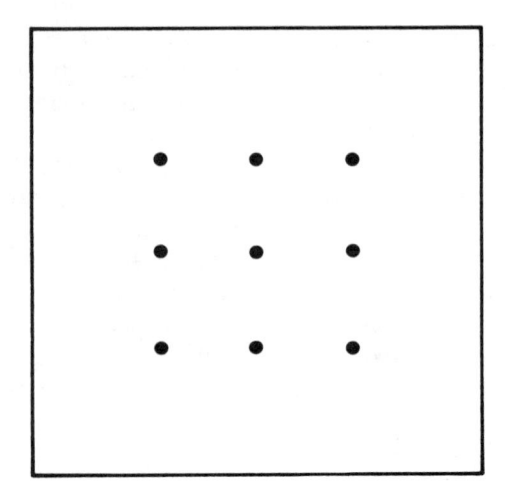

The correct answer is shown in Figure 2-1. As soon as you see it, you will be prompted to say: "Oh, I thought I had to stay within the square made by nine dots." But nothing was said about that; you *assumed* additional rules, probably because of your earlier indoctrination to doing things neatly, staying within bounds, and the like. Thus, we can see the point Haire is trying to make: we receive information and color it by virtue of previous experience.

Roethlisberger's oft-used Hart and Bing case is another example of how interpersonal relationships require some basic skills. The natural "bad" tendency to evaluate as we give and receive communications (one of the barriers to effective communications) must be cured by a conscious attempt to see things from the other person's point of view.

Rensis Likert has also reported many studies showing the value of good communications in motivating subordinates. He has shown how superiors and subordinates do not agree on whether the superiors understand the problems of subordinates, or if they estimate performance goals correctly, etc. These and similar findings of his studies on organization performance highlight the importance of communications.

Management

The third school follows Barnard in almost equating the entire managerial process with the task of effective communications. For Barnard, communications is one of three essential elements in the existence of any organization (along with a willingness to cooperate and a common purpose). For him, communications is the same as the coordinative function of the executive. The ability to communicate limits the size of any unit of an organization.

Authority is the most general phase of communications, as Barnard sees it, so that the system of communications is a system of objective authority, almost synonymous with lines of responsibility in the organization. Barnard states that it is precisely the need for centers of communications that brings about the need for executives, whose first function is to serve as a channel of communications.

It was Barnard, too, who suggested that an organization chart really should be shown as a circle or a sphere rather than the usual pyramid, in order to more accurately show all the directions of good communications. An interesting elaboration on this point is the work of McMurray who talks of a beehive organization chart. In this scheme, the top executive is at the middle center. Pie-shaped segments go out from the center to depict the various functions (manufacturing, accounting, marketing, personnel, engineering, etc.). Concentric circles represent different layers of the organization (vice-presidencies, directorships, managers, etc.). Squares representing executives are placed with the circles and wedges so to pictorially describe relationship (close or far) from layers above and below and from peers to each side. This shows the informal communications net as well as the formal. The squares can also be color coded to show stages of development or promotability.

This opens the door to the whole area of informal lines of communication, and many authors talk about the importance of using this means of communicating. Beginning with the principles of sociometry (Moreno calls it static; Lewin, dynamic), people like Bavelas and H. J. Leavitt especially have shown experimentally how social choices within the group lead to the informal structure of the group, which become communication nets.

Many studies of these nets show how communications can or cannot be restricted in direction, and may have different effects on morale, productivity, speed, accuracy, leadership, etc. Bavelas developed the concept of "centrality" of communications, that is, the amount of focusing on one member of a net. He showed the correlation between centrality and morale to be strongly negative, yet a strongly positive correlation between centrality and production. He also worked on a concentric organization chart to show these relations. Another important concept contributed by Bavelas is "distance" in communications, and the significance of distance on the number of layers in the organization.

Leavitt has done the same kind of studies, showing the importance of content, noise, network, and direction (feedback) on communications. Besides the domino exercise, he tells of the usefulness of feedback to an artillery team (through the Forward Observer), and the importance of providing for this two-way communications in the organization.

Kenneth Boulding and H. Simon have also shown, in studying networks and their efficiency in the organization pattern, how the traditional pyramid

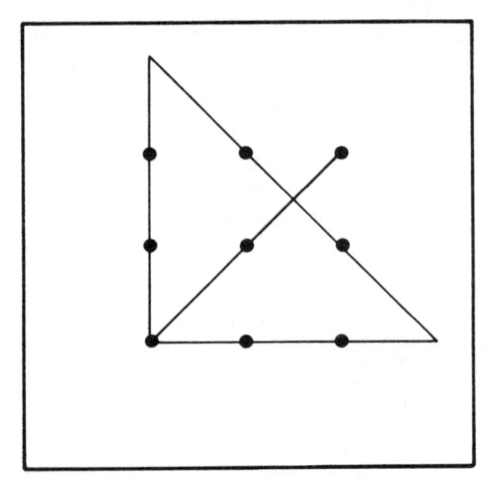

Figure 2-1

pattern is not as good as a star pattern. Also, with respect to this matter of direction, we have the work of Cartwright Jackson and others at the Research Center for Group Dynamics. Communications is said to be like a piece of driftwood—subject to all the forces that can come into play (not really aimless or misdirectional). Still, people prefer upward communications because they want to improve their status; they want to address their communications where needs will be gratified. So the effect of communications will depend on the relationships that exist; for example, whether support is or is not received from peers.

All three of these schools have important messages for us to recall if we are to be successful in assisting in the development of our people. The rest of this chapter concentrates on the process method and what it means for us practically in helping John or Jane Doe develop. In chapters seven, eight, and nine, we shall discuss the other two schools.

COMMUNICATIONS AS A PROCESS

The six steps involved in communicating are shown in Figure 2-2. There is (1) a sender who has an idea he or she wants to get across somehow to another human. So the sender (2) encodes the idea in some symbol, word, gesture, or whatever, which is then (3) transmitted to the other individual. Upon receipt, the message is (4) decoded by (5) the receiver, so that it now is a thought in the receiver's mind, awaiting some kind of (6) feedback mechanism which will verify that the thought now in the head of the receiver corresponds to the idea originally intended by the sender.

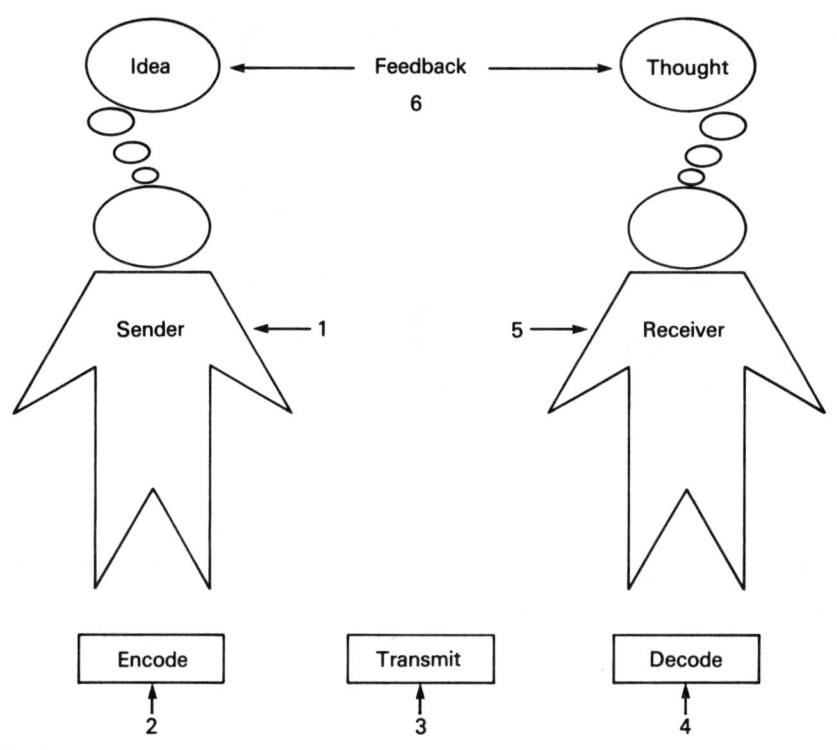

Figure 2-2 The Communication Process

On the surface, this is simple enough to grasp as a process. But each step in the process is fraught with a myriad of potential pitfalls, any one of which can vitiate the entire communications. Let us examine some of the most significant of these possible danger points. And let's make the application to our topic as we go along. You are a sender of some communication about personal development to your John Doe or Jane Doe. In particular, you are going to attempt to gain his or her commitment to your ideas about a formal development plan which we shall be working out in the next couple of chapters. Imagine yourself with some ideas about development which you wish to discuss with your subordinate. Now how and where can this kind of communicating break down?

The first station is you, the sender, and the idea you wish to communicate. The whole process can break down right here if the idea you wish to send to John or Jane Doe is in any way inappropriate. How clear is the idea in your own mind? If it is not clear or precise in your mind, there is little likelihood that it will be very clear by the time it gets over to the receiver's head. One of the first rules you may remember from early courses on composition in elementary school says to clarify your ideas in your head before you pick up a pencil to write. That's still a good rule here. Be sure the idea you wish to discuss with your subordinate is clear.

Learn to challenge your own ideas before beginning to transmit them. If they are not clear, concise, or precise, or just plain not worth communicating to start off with, you can be sure that John or Jane Doe will challenge them. Especially in our context now, since the ideas will concern John or Jane's development, and since he or she will have been encouraged to think about the same things ahead of time, chances are John or Jane will be likely to challenge anything that is not well thought out. For all of these reasons, we are going to dedicate the next two chapters to helping you work out for yourself what it is you wish to share with John or Jane Doe by way of the development plan before you ever begin to think of a discussion with that subordinate.

The second station in the process is the encoding step. This refers to the selection of appropriate words, diagrams, statistics, (and in our case, a completed form), to faithfully convey the idea which has now been clarified. There are a number of things you should be wary of in this step. What are some of them? This time perhaps you should try to make a list for yourself. Do so now in the space below.

> Q How can the communicating process break down in the encoding step?
>
> A

You could have mentioned first of all that the spoken or written word is not the only method of encoding. Sometimes pictures, diagrams, charts, or statistics can be as useful, or more useful, than mere words.

You will want to be sure the picture or gesture cannot be misinterpreted, either because it doesn't reinforce the words used, or because of interference in the transmission. The following story may serve as an example of a communications breakdown. One day an air force pilot had a trainee up for an orientation flight in one of the new planes to be used in flight school. As they were flying over the Gulf of Mexico on a bright sunny day, they passed over the beaches where people were enjoying themselves sun bathing. The pilot could not be heard very well over the din of the motor, but he pointed down to the people on the beaches while saying, "Look at the fantastic day down there." The trainee could not hear the words, but did see the gesture pointing (he thought) frantically to the beach below, so he quickly stood up and jumped with his parachute, thinking he had been told to jump!

When it comes to selecting words, hopefully you will remember that the code you chose to use must be decoded on the other end; hence, it will be important to select words which are intelligible to the receiver and which make maximum use of what we saw about association earlier in this chapter. You should therefore avoid jargon (and acronyms, a special form of jargon), which seems to creep into the language of all of us so easily.

An example of this might help make the point. I was conducting a seminar not too long ago with a group of hospital personnel. Reference was made on the printed organization chart and in casual conversation about the DON and some assistant DON's. I knew I wasn't working with the Mafia, but still had to have it explained to me that this meant the Director of Nursing. I subsequently checked with a number of other health care institutions and have yet to find any place where DON meant the same thing. Hence, we have an example of strictly local jargon.

Another example: The U.S. Commissioner of Education, Mr. Ernest L. Boyer, recently gave his employees a crash course to improve the quality of writing in his bureaucracy. As part of the course, he showed memos he had been asked to sign, including this one: "This workshop is part of an RFP issued by IOC aimed at helping SEA's better serve LEA's with reference to the LEA-Prime Sponsor agreements called for under the YETP portion of YEDPA."

Here is another caveat: be wary of red-flag words. Depending again on the laws of association, certain words will rub some people's fur the wrong way. (There's a phrase, incidentally, which will be a red flag to some; namely to those who resent the analogy to animals, for humans do not customarily have fur!) Any word which has mainly negative connotations or is likely to elicit unhappy recollections might well be voided. Speaking of a *R.I.F.* (reduction in force) in a governmental unit is an example; the term *lay-off* in a union setting; the mention of *quotas* to salespersons; the words *superior* and *subordinate* because of their derivations as mentioned earlier; not to mention downright insulting words like *nigger* and other terms for minority members.

There are also a lot of words which unintentionally are discounting to people. A person's very name, for example, might be improperly encoded. To automatically shorten a first name or to use the diminutive may be insulting; some want to be William and not Bill, Charles and not Charlie, Margaret and not Peg, and so on.

Remembering the receiver must decode your message may also keep you from using a vocabulary level above or below the other person's head. Don't use fifty-cent words with someone with a ten-cent command of the language. But neither talk down to someone who typically converses in two-dollar words. Consider not only the level of vocabulary, but what about the receiver for whom English is not the mother tongue? You may really have to watch your choice of words with someone struggling to learn English.

Short of that, one person's interpretation of some word is not always the same as another person's meaning. There was a laboratory professor who was teaching his students how to take care of the lab equipment. Among other instructions he gave them he said, "And when you have been using test tubes with dry powder in them be sure to turn them upside down and give them a tap on the bottom to force out any remaining sediment before you wash them." He was trying to underscore the need for emptying the tubes and not getting chemicals in the wash basin. Following instructions, one football player picked up a test tube, turned it upside down and his "tap" on the bottom broke the tube to smithereens.

In a later chapter we will return to a detailed discussion of gestures, tonal inflections, and body language. These are all part of the encoding mechanism and must be carefully watched so to convey what we wish by way of reinforcing the verbal message.

The actual transmission or sending of the message is the third stage wherein might lie a breakdown in the communication process. Since you probably did very well on the second stage, perhaps you would like to try to itemize some pitfalls at this station. Try it in the space below.

Q How can the communication process break down in the act of transmission?

A

One important consideration you must have mentioned in your answer is the selection of the best medium for the communication. Should the message be given face-to-face, over the telephone, by written memo, or in person with documentation? Each of these is more appropriate for different messages. Generally speaking, the more lengthy the message is, the more complicated the message is, or the more important feedback might be, the less likely are you to succeed by a phone call or memo. For the type of discussion envisioned about a development plan, therefore, there is little chance of being effective without a combination personal interview assisted by written material. For other parts of the coaching process (giving orders, making corrections) you may want to choose other ways to transmit your message.

Timing of the communication is another vital matter. What time of the day will you choose? Some people think better in early morning, some don't even wake up until lunch time. One manager told me in a workshop that he always brought important requests to his boss the last thing in the day because the boss' resistance was low at that time and he would approve almost anything.

Picking a time to communicate when the other person's interest is miles away is undesirable. Examples of poor timing are: (1) shortly before quitting time, when everyone is thinking of fighting the traffic home; (2) payday when everyone is trying to squeeze time to run by the payroll office to pick up a paycheck; (3) Friday afternoon when somone is cleaning off his or her desk in preparation for a long vacation; and (4) the day of the annual Christmas office party when everyone is excited and in a holiday mood.

A lot of transmissions never get through because of static of interference on the line. Distractions of all types fall into this category: picking a place where there are too many things to take away one's attention is bound to lessen the concentration which a serious discussion requires. Picking a place where there can be interruptions (phone, visits, passers-by) will hurt the transmission. Environmental interference can be as damaging: too hot, too cold, too much or too little light, cigarette smoke, unventilated rooms, or noise from neighboring desks, offices, machines, and phones. In general, proper transmitting will consider the questions when to transmit, where to transmit, and how to transmit.

The fourth station in the process shown in Figure 2-2 is the decoding step. This is the process by which the receiver accepts the communique and translates it to a thought in his or her mind, which is the fifth stage. So let's consider these two together. How can the communication break down as it goes into the head of the receiver?—by any and every filter used by John and Jane Doe in attempting to decipher and understand your message.

The receiver invariably screens out an unbelievable percent of any communication—not out of animosity or hostility, but simply because he or she hears, sees, and interprets things through personal life experiences, mental capacities, and emotional states. Earlier discussions in this chapter focused on experiments in which a message as originally delivered is practically unintelligible when repeated by several persons, one to another. TV comedians do a stunt periodically in which a very funny joke is told to one person who repeats it to a second person and so on through six or seven persons, until the last relays it back to the original storyteller only to find this person can find nothing funny in it any more.

So what to do? We must make allowances for that filtering process and attempt to lessen its impact as best we can. We have to take into consideration not only who the receiver is, but all we know about his or her background and interpretative skills and then adjust our communicating accordingly. Interpreting who that person is will be discussed in greater detail in chapter five. For now, we will look at a few examples of how to allow for filtering.

During Christmas a few years ago, a part-time postal truck driver in Washington D.C. made headlines over an instruction he carried out. In the middle of the annual rush to get greeting cards and gifts delivered before the holiday, this man's supervisor said to him at 11:30 P.M., "Deliver that New York mail." About 6:00 A.M. the supervisor received a call from the trucker who was then on the New Jersey turnpike with a flat tire. He was delivering the New York mail literally, when he was supposed to simply drive the truck with the New York mail to the Washington railroad depot.

If the individual is a slow listener, one who grasps ideas very painstakingly (perhaps due to a low mental IQ, a small vocabulary, or newness to the language), then we expect this filtering will block out much of our message unless we slow down the pace of delivering the message. We repeat things slowly and distinctly—I say again, slowly and distinctly. Possibly we even use a few words from another tongue, if need be.

If the person is quick on the up-take, knows what we are going to say by way of conclusion before we've even laid the groundwork for it, we can expect a screen of boredom to set in unless we speed up the delivery, move on from one point to another quickly, and leave a lot of the details for the listener to fill in. Here we might recall that studies indicate a person listens at least five times as fast as someone else speaks, which explains why it is hard to keep anyone's attention for very long.

If the other person has any kind of a complex—say what we call a persecution complex (be cautioned that pinning labels on people is always a danger)—then we can expect that anything we say is going to be filtered through a tendency to hear things as condemnatory even when not intended that way. We would compensate for this filter by giving positive strokes, and by asking for self evaluations and suggestions for development rather than making those judgments initially.

All of this takes us to the absolute necessity for the sixth and final stage of the communication process: the feedback step. When we have reached this stage, there is now a thought in the mind of the receiver; but is it the same as the original idea in the mind of the sender? Have enough precautions been taken to minimize interferences and screening? Did the sender succeed in properly encoding? Did the receiver operate on the same wavelength so that the message was decoded properly? If we *assume* a positive answer to all these questions, we are liable to later find the receiver saying, "Oh, I thought you meant..." How often has someone said that to you?

So there has to be some way of comparing the thought in the receiver's head with the idea in the sender's head. Someone must determine that they are sufficiently the same, meaning the message was successfully completed. Now, and this is important, *who is the only one who can make that determination?*

> **Q** Who is the only one who can tell whether the thought in the receiver's mind corresponds to the idea in the sender's mind?
>
> **A**

If you answered "the sender" you go to the head of the class. If you did not, you probably do what most of us do: we ask our listeners, "Is that clear?" "Do you understand?" "Any questions?" We are expecting the receiver to read our minds to guess whether his or her thought corresponds with the idea we started out with. Only the sender knows the idea in his or her head. So only the sender is in a position to judge whether all or part of that idea got over to the receiver.

To make that judgment, however, the sender will need what we call feedback, something positive from the receiver which feeds back to the sender what is now lodged in the receiver's mind. To get this feedback is quite simple. First, we can ask a question, provided it is not a leading question, or a question calling for a simple yes or no. This is because if all you get back is a yes, you cannot be sure; you're asking the receiver to make a judgment. If you get back a no, you still cannot be sure that's true; and if it is, you haven't learned anything to help you remedy things. The question must be an open-ended question, gaining enough information back that you can safely make a determination. Such questions might include, "Now what are you going to do first?" "How would you pass along this information to someone else?"

Second, we could ask for a paraphrase of our message, for example, "Would you repeat in your own words what we've just agreed upon?" This is truly an opportunity for the receiver to reflect back to you what is now in his or her head.

Third, we really don't have to say or do anything. If we just stay there with our bare face hanging, the receiver will say or do something to give us feedback. Nature abhors a vacuum; and more so, subordinates abhor a vacuum in the presence of their superior. If you say or do nothing, the receiver will ask you a question, or will automatically summarize, or will get up and start doing something which you can observe to see if the message has gotten through. The trouble with a lot of us is that we are too impatient.

We are very busy about a lot of things, and having divested ourselves of a message we busily bundle ourselves off to the next chore without taking the time to see if the communicating chore was successfully completed.

INTERVIEW TECHNIQUES

Many of the coaching activities you will be employing in the development of your people will entail face-to-face communicating in interviews. There will be the interview to work out a detailed development plan; the annual performance appraisal interview; periodic interviews to review progress; interviews to assign duties, give orders, make corrections, and many more. While the communications process is still fresh in our minds, let us now review some helpful hints about effective interviewing.

There is probably no such thing as a sure thing in terms of how to conduct an interview. More and more as organizations move away from traditional, top-down oriented methods of doing business (and therefore of interviewing), the successful interview is one with a high degree of initiative, spontaneity and exchange of ideas on the part of both individuals. Interviews are not so much *conducted* any more as they are *facilitated*.

Nonetheless, the manager will be the initiator of these interviews most of the time, and will wish to become skillful in interviewing. As with most skills, practice makes perfect. Especially today, the manager will wish, in an interview, to be able to establish and maintain a face-to-face relationship in which the subordinate will feel free to express himself or herself without reserve. This will be brought about with varying degrees of success by persons with natural aptitude and different amounts of hard practice.

Since interviewing is simply talking to another human, possible pitfalls to avoid is thinking there is no need to learn how to conduct or prepare for an interview, or to analyze what happened when such a talk is over. There are certain methods or lines of approach which will prove more successful in achieving such a productive relationship during an interview. Let us review some of these so to provide the manager with a "bag of tools" from which can be selected those most appropriate for individual interviewing needs.

Control

Interviews fit into two general categories in terms of the control exercised by the manager: directive and nondirective. In the coaching environment, a combination of the two types will be found to be appropriate.

The directive interview is characterized by determining in advance the items which are to be covered during the interview. The interviewer has in front of him or her on paper (or in the head) a list of items to be covered. Questions are asked to cover those items either in a set or when they seem pertinent. The interviewee is asked only to give specific information which might have bearing on the problem or given topic.

Those who use this method believe that the necessary information will be obtained in a more rapid and efficient fashion because the interviewer is controlling and directing the course that the interview takes. Many times during a coaching session there are bits of information that can only be gained by direct questioning.

The danger of directive interviews is that they may become, or appear to become, a somewhat mechanical process. The interviewer may become so engrossed in obtaining certain information that the subordinate can be cut short and not given a chance to tell the full story. The interviewer may be thinking more about the next question than about what is being said by the other person. The subordinate in turn is being trained to be more passive and less likely to provide good feedback. Hence, a directive interview also runs the risk of becoming completed when the list of preordained material has been covered, not when it has been thoroughly understood by both parties.

The nondirective interview is done with the assumption that the interviewee should retain full responsibility for explaining the subject at hand. The manager does not ask for any specific information; neither does he or she seek to direct the course the conversation takes. The interviewer encourages, accepts, recognizes, clarifies, and reinforces statements of the interviewee.

One big advantage of this type of interview is that time is going to be spent talking about things which the subordinate feels are most important to him or her. This allows the manager the luxury of being able to sit back and better evaluate the subordinate's statements, note items needing further clarification, and observe the interviewee during the discussion.

This technique cannot be followed entirely during a coaching session because it is necessary for the coach to get across certain points or feret out certain information. It takes a highly skilled person to conduct a nondirective interview and get the information which is needed to guide the worker to a resolution of the coaching need and thereby make a contribution to development.

It is impossible to say whether strictly directive or nondirective interviewing techniques are best. If one or the other were better, experience would probably so indicate since both have been talked about and practiced for a long time. The fact that both techniques are retained would suggest that there is no reason to work exclusively with one technique when common sense indicates that another approach would be better. You will therefore probably wish to practice both types of interviewing and learn when to use which. You will undoubtedly combine the two in the same interview, or occasionally switch from one technique to the other with the same person.

Apropos of switching, it is useful to note that it seems very difficult to go from a directive to a nondirective technique during the same interview session, but the reverse is easy. For some reason, the subordinate, put in the more passive mode by the directive approach, finds it difficult to respond to a sudden invitation to relax or take charge. But the reverse can work. If you start off in a relaxed environment with the reins held very loosely, you can always tighten up on them if circumstances warrant.

Therefore, for most coaching interviews, you might begin by using the nondirective approach, encouraging the subordinate to speak freely, make judgments, evaluate progress, suggest ways to develop, and identify his or her own goal thinking, until you feel you have obtained all the information possible from this approach. Then the directive approach can be used to round out the information.

Setting

Remembering what was said earlier about the possibility of environmental conditions impeding transmissions, you will want to choose an appropriate setting for your discussions. As much as possible, the setting should be a private and comfortable place. (This always elicits a smile from supervisors who think, "Oh sure, we've all got swanky offices or conference rooms around here.") The point is that coaching is a private affair, and if the other person is not reasonably comfortable, you will not have his or her attention.

Think, therefore, of such things as: Must the discussion always be in your office rather than the other person's place of work? After all, which is more comfortable to the subordinate? And what about other symbols of authority? Try not to sit enthroned behind your desk, looking over and down at the other person. Try to arrange the seating so that the subordinate is not staring at the name plate or title sitting on your desk to remind everyone who runs things. Move the chairs side by side, and make sure they are the same style chair. Or, move to a couch or armchair if you have one. (Office furniture manufacturers say they sell as many stuffed chairs and couches as they do desks these days.) Try to move away from any distractions, like all your diplomas and letters of congratulation and awards all over the wall. Also, watch out for glaring light in the other person's eyes. See if you can't keep the door closed for the duration of the interview and avoid telephone interruptions until it's over. And, be sure you have both allocated enough time for this meeting in the first place, which is your responsibilty to gauge when you set it up.

Be sure you refrain from mannerisms which ruin the setting. For example, smoking might annoy the other person; a habit of pacing would tend to be distracting; looking at your watch, signing papers, or flipping through your appointment pad are bound to suggest your mind is somewhere else. Staring at the floor or out the windows or at passers-by give the impression you are not there yet, and therefore creates a poor setting.

Rapport

Following our earlier suggestion of beginning an interview using the nondirective approach, we would suggest here that you attempt a free and easy manner at the start. Rapport is for the purpose of establishing a relationship. You want it to be easy-going, so you must show it yourself. Remember, though, that a relationship is a two-way thing, so you haven't established rapport by a simple, "Hi, John, come on in and have a chair!" That's one way only. You may not do it by moving on to a friendly, "How's everything with the family?" or a reference to the weather or the work in the shop or a recent operation. While these are intended to be personal references and are often thought to invite casualness and relaxation, they often have no effect—you get a one word reply—or the opposite than desired effect. The subordinate asks silently, "I wonder why the sudden interest in my family or my health or my problems in the shop. What am I being set up for?"

There won't be any rapport until the other individual feels at ease. This is best done by starting off with a question or comment about something you both are honestly interested in, and can say at least a couple of sentences about. This could deal with work in the shop, or family, or health, but only if you customarily talk together about those things. Evoking suspicions is not what you're trying to do. That will bring defensiveness and silence. You are trying to open things up. The other person must hear the sound of his or her own voice or rapport is not established. This is not as easy as it sounds, so you should practice establishing rapport any time you have a chance. And in these interviews, stick with it if the first question doesn't get the person relaxed; work at it a little. You might have to say, "John, you seem a little tensed up. Anything you'd care to discuss with me before we get into our topic?"

Opening statement

Now you're ready to get into the reason for the interview. The opening statement outlines the area for discussion, the central issue to be resolved by the two of you. It is actually a brief (few sentences) kick-off by you in which you analyze and explain the problem/issue/suggestion in an effort to bring the understanding, interest, and attitude of the other person to a point where each can contribute freely to the discussion. One to three minutes should do it. More than that and you're giving a speech, and are not going to be nondirective. Too brief a statement, on the other hand, is apt to leave the worker bewildered and unprepared to discuss your leadoff question or point.

Several things can help clarify a topic for discussion. The opening statement can be framed around: (1) a summary of background facts, like reviewing the company's policy on development plans; (2) an example or case, which would be more likely in interviews whose purpose is to correct or discipline; (3) charts or diagrams, like referring to an organization chart when the interview will deal with realigning duties, considerations for promotion, etc.; or (4) brief board work, if the interview is to seek a solution to a problem of a technical nature.

The main thing about this opening statement is that it focuses the subordinate's attention on the reason for the interview. You can often tell it has been effectively communicated when you sense a physical reduction of tension in the air as the subordinate relaxes into his or her chair and breathes almost audibly upon verifying the real reason for the meeting. You can also tell it has not been well summarized at the beginning when you come to the end and find the interviewee asking, "Is that all?"

Phrasing questions

How a question is phrased greatly influences the freedom of the interviewee to discuss the topic. There are several types of questions, some more helpful than others.

The lead-off question is the question used to get the discussion started. The way this question is worded is particularly important. If it is poorly phrased it misleads, confuses, and puts the other person on the defense. To say, for example, "John, why haven't you made progress in your personal development?" is probably going to suggest a tone for the meeting which will only cause John to be antagonistic. If it is well framed, it clarifies the area of the discussion and yet leaves the discussion free and open. For example, "John, now that we've reviewed the company's policy on encouraging all workers toward personal growth, what areas of personal development are important to you?" Such a question is expansive; it is open; it encourages self-interest; and it is thought provoking.

Closed questions are those which invite a one-word answer, usually of the yes or no variety. For example, "Do you feel this is true?" "Have you thought about personal growth?" Closed questions begin with the words: *Is... Do... Has... Can... Will... Shall...* etc. It will take many closed questions to secure any meaningful amount of information and thus fully explore a topic or problem. It's like playing 20 Questions with your subordinate, and it quickly becomes exasperating to both of you.

Open questions are the expansive type, inviting a more lengthy response. They cannot be answered with a single word, especially an affirmation or denial. They usually begin with the words: *What... When ... Who... Where... Which... How...* etc. For example, "Why do you feel that way?" "Which of the areas we mentioned is of more interest to you?" Since the nondirective approach is an attempt to let the other person run with the ball (within bounds), such questions allow the interviewee to direct the discussion at will and are therefore more appropriate.

Leading questions should, if possible, be avoided because they suggest the answer you're looking for and are not going to gain the subordinate's true and unguided response. To say, for example, "Don't you think my suggestion is a sound one?" hardly seems to be expecting a negative answer and in all probability the response will be affirmative whether or not the subordinate really agrees. But if you say, "What do you think of my suggestion?" you give more leeway to state true feelings. Other examples of leading questions might be: "You wouldn't want to work next Saturday, would you?" or "This job we've been discussing calls for considerable planning. Do you like to plan?"

Judgmental questions are a particularly damaging kind of leading question. We are trying to be nondirective—that means we are attempting to let the other person guide the conversation, decide what needs further elaboration and what does not, feel the freedom to let ideas pour forth as he or she deems comfortable. Notice what happens in the following illustration:

Subordinate: "I don't think schooling will do me any good. Anyway I am the type that didn't want to go to school. I wanted to make money so I went to work. Besides..."

Manager: "You didn't like school?"

Subordinate: "Well, yes, but I had to go out and work."

It seems reasonable that the subordinate would have answered many questions in the manager's mind if the latter had permitted the subordinate to tell the story in his or her own words. The manager's question was definitely an interruption of the worker's discussion. Notice how this put the employee on the defensive with a "well, yes, but" answer. From here on the interview is likely to be nothing more than a series of short answers.

Probing

Probing is closely related to asking questions. It is what you do when you wish further elaboration of a key point. The trick is to be listening well enough to pick up key points needing further expansion, to refrain from jumping into the conversation and interrupting, and to be able to go back to the key point with a question that draws attention to this area and invites additional information.

A key point could be any idea, opinion, experience, or example expressed by the other person which is unclear to you, seems to be deserving of more explanation, or for any reason appears to you to have an important bearing on the discussion. It could be hidden in the most casual comment or reference. To draw out that additional information successfully, it might help to remember these guidelines:

1. Listen carefully to the other person. Be sure you thoroughly understand everything being said as well as what is *not* being said.
2. Make mental or written notes of the key thoughts brought up by the subordinate.
3. Refer back to these points at a lull in the discussion. When you find one which is not as clear in your mind as you would like it to be, or which needs reinforcement or further elaboration, use an open question to redirect the attention of the interviewee to that point.

Listening

Listening then becomes an important need for good interviewing. In the nondirective setting listening should be an active positive response, not a passive thing. A listening response is a brief comment or action made in reaction to the other person which conveys the idea that you are interested, attentive, and wish him or her to continue. It must be made briefly and quietly after the employee pauses, so as not to interfere with the train of thought. The major types of listening responses include:

1. The nod. This is nodding the head lightly and waiting. It must not be too vigorous or it will be distracting. Just a gentle nod, with eyes fixed on the speaker attentively, does not necessarily indicate agreement with what is being said, but that you have heard it, grasp it, are ready for the next part. People often wonder if what they say is being understood. The nod tells the other party that it is safe to go ahead, that you have kept pace with what is being said.

2. The casual remark. This is literally a small word or two not intended to have substantial meaning of itself, for example, "I see," "Ah huh," "Is that so," "Really," "That's interesting," "Right on," etc. The words themselves blend into the background of the conversation and contribute nothing of themselves, but do serve to indicate once more that you have caught on to that part and are ready for more. On the part of some listeners it's about all the other party has to tell if the audience has gone to sleep!

3. The pause. This is saying nothing at all, but looking expectantly and encouragingly at the other person. A definite break or pause in the conversation will take place as you neither say nor do anything at all. You can safely maintain this look and expectation for as long as thirty seconds without harm. The whole idea, of course, is that the silence will be an invitation for the subordinate to fill the void with more information. Some people fear that too long a silence will put the other person ill at ease, but this is true only if the silence is not accompanied by a look of encouragement. A more substantial fear should be your own desire to fill the void by speaking too soon. Thirty seconds can feel like a long time, and you will likely feel like blurting something out. (Look at your watch and time a thirty-second interval; it's quite long.) But invariably if you use the pause the other person will have more to say, which you might never hear if you pick up the conversation.

4. The echo. This is literally repeating the last one or two words spoken by the other person. Again, the idea is that if you have been listening well enough to repeat the last two words or so, you must have grasped what has been said, and so the signal is clear for the subordinate to continue. Be careful not to do this repeatedly, or your worker will think that he or she is being mimicked.

5. The mirror. This is often called the reflection technique because it is reflecting back your understanding of what has been said by paraphrasing or summarizing part of what was understood by you. Don't be afraid of a response like, "You feel that . . ." It is not leading, as the other person has already made the statement and you are merely clarifying or asking for more. Again, don't do this repeatedly or it gets to be a game. As a matter of fact, the hope is that you will learn to do all of these different listening responses well enough that you will intersperse the conversation with all of them, mixing them up. And all of these should be done *after* the other party pauses, not as an interruption.

6. Hearing what is not said. Sometimes what is not said is as important as what is said. For this reason, you want to develop a sixth sense to get behind the actual words used by your subordinate. As a rule, it is what is not said that keeps the individual from making a full commitment to what is said. Hence, you want to develop the ability to listen for that less-than-full commitment and interpret what is said for what the person really means, and then turn that to some fruitful purpose.

Suppose, for example, that you are discussing cost savings with John and Jane Doe. Here are some common ways in which the subordinate could respond, showing some kind of resistance. Listen for what is behind the phrase used to find out what attitude the phrase symbolizes. Once you know what the attitude means, you will be in a better position to cope with it.

What is said: "I'm paid to get out the work—not to cut costs."

What it means: He doesn't see how the cost of getting the work out is part of doing the job well. He needs to learn how costs are integral to the work he's paid to get out.

Try this: Use a comparison. "John, your wife tries to feed the family well. Suppose she did it by serving steak and prime roast beef every night. How would you like the effect on the budget? And would her saying that costs didn't matter make a convincing argument to you?"

What is said: "What difference would my saving paper clips make?"

What it means: This woman sees herself as a small cog; she fails to recognize that nothing happens to the team as a whole unless individuals cooperate.

Try this: Point out two things: "Once we've got the habit of making small savings, we're in a stronger position to make big ones. And don't forget, when we work as a team, our contribution is multiplied many times."

What is said: "I've already done all I can."

What it means: She wants recognition for past cost-cutting efforts and a sense that you do count on her for the future.

Try this: Praise her past performance using examples. Point out that you count on her for continuing cost-cutting effort.

What is said: "What's a few pennies to a company that sells in the millions?"

What it means: This person is simply unaware of how profits come about. He assumes that sales means profits.

Try this: Point out that average profits after taxes are only 4.2¢ on the dollar. So for most companies it takes $23.81 in sales to make up for each $1 in excess costs.

What is said: "Why should I worry?"

What it means: This attitude is bad right down the line. The man is uninvolved in the job; he simply doesn't care.

Try this: This one is tough to handle. Tell him he *has* to help cut costs, and you won't tolerate any harping about the matter. It's everbody's job not simply to do the work, but to do it in the best possible way.

What is said: "Your new way might cut costs on paper, but the way we've always done things . . ."

What it means: The attitude is negative, but it disguises positive feelings. Old ways *may* be better—they certainly aren't all wrong. You'll want to respect this person's experience.

Try this: Use this employee to double-check the specific proposed method of cost cutting. Assure the individual that the past has been taken into account, but you're willing to go over the idea, perhaps add some old truths to the new and more efficient methods, if this person will experiment.

What is said: "There is no waste around here that amounts to anything."

What it means: You'll hear this most often from a person who has tried hard, and doesn't really see any more problems. His vision is set, but needs focus. With a new focus, the individual usually cooperates.

Try this: Admit there's no conscious waste. But suggest that there may be waste nobody sees. Ask him to look at his own work as if he were an outsider. What would he see from the new frame of reference? Make him aware of indirect costs; challenge him to come up with ideas for spotting and stopping cost leaks.

7. Avoid bad listening habits. Ralph Nichols cites ten bad listening habits that you want to avoid:

- Listening faster than someone can speak, using the excess time to turn your thoughts elsewhere.
- Listening primarily for facts rather than for ideas.
- Letting certain words, phrases, or ideas prejudice you against the speaker so that you cannot listen objectively to what is being said.
- Interrupting the speaker's train of thought by getting to the bottom of something said which puzzles or annoys you.

- Going out of your way to avoid hearing something which you think would take too much time and effort to understand.
- Deliberately turning your thoughts to other subjects when you believe the speaker will have nothing particularly interesting to say.
- Judging a person by his or her appearance or delivery rather than listening to what is to be said.
- Trying to make someone think you are paying attention when you really are not.
- Being distracted by outside sights and sounds.
- Writing down everything a person says as the conversation progresses.

Conversation stoppers

There are some commonly used phrases which will ruin your interview almost every time they are used. No additional comment is needed as to why they tend to stop the free flow of ideas:

- If I were you . . .
- What you say just isn't so . . .
- This is what we're going to do . . .
- If you did this . . .
- If you did what Jim did . . .
- Fine, but . . .
- When I had your job . . .

Feedback

Your listening techniques have continuously shown the other person that you understand him or her. But sometimes you are trying to communicate an idea in the other direction, so part of good interviewing is getting good feedback. We have discussed earlier how important it is for the sender to verify that the thought in the receiver's mind corresponds to the idea originally in the sender's mind. The interview is a very important time for you as a sender to do this well. Particularly in a developmental interview, when you are discussing ways for the other individual to grow, a good kind of feedback is the use of *feed-forward*. This is forming the major points you've made into commitments for future action. You might say, "John, what steps are we agreeing will be done first?" "Jane, please suggest an appropriate timetable for the steps we just mapped out." Their answers will allow you to determine whether the ideas got through or not and will also be a commitment on their part.

SUMMARY

This quick review of the theory of communications and the practical suggestions for conducting an interview was intended to aid in the preparation of development plans for the people you manage. Keeping them in mind as you work toward gaining commitments to personal growth should help avoid the many pitfalls in sharing important ideas with others. It is these process techniques which are very often the undoing of otherwise excellent plans for growth. It would be a shame to have very good plans vitiated simply for lack of skills in bringing home these ideas to the people who would benefit from them.

We are now ready to return to a consideration of specific development plans for your John or Jane Doe.

3 WHO NEEDS TO DEVELOP?

Unless we foster versatile, innovative and self-renewing men and women, all the ingenious social arrangements in the world will not help us. For the self-renewing man, the development of his own potentialities and the process of self-discovery never end. It is a sad but unarguable fact that most human beings go through their lives only partially aware of the full range of their abilities.

JOHN GARDNER
Self-Renewal

You have a John Doe or a Jane Doe in mind. You identified this person on your linear responsibility chart in chapter one. This is any one of your subordinates: strong, weak, or indifferent. We have suggested that no matter who this person is, he or she needs personal growth, and you now want to prepare a plan for this individual. The first thing to do, and a way of demonstrating the universality of the need for personal development, is to identify your subordinate by type of demonstrated performance and performance capabilities. There are three types, depending on where the individual is on the flow chart of questions you will ask yourself about this person's contributions to the organization. (See Figure 3-1.)

The first question you will ask is, "Is performance satisfactory?" This should always be answered in objectives terms, that is, in terms of meeting standards of performance which were previously mutually agreed upon and verified by documented evidence of some sort as opposed to subjective judgment. The answer must be either Yes or No. If the response is negative, then you already have some valid ways of showing desired improvement, one kind of development need, certainly.

So then you ask the second question, "Is performance correctable?" Here is where you must make a personal judgment. From what you know about the individual's incentive, the person's track record, and the availability of time and other resources to work with this subordinate, does it appear to you that the performance deficiencies can be corrected in a reasonable length of time? For some employees you will simply have to determine, in the light of everything that's been tried to date and all the other environmental considerations, that this person just does not appear to be correctable with your help. So the negative answer must unfortunately lead in some cases to a decision to terminate or ask for a reassignment to other duties. This may be a lateral transfer or an outright demotion to a position which is within the grasp of this person. Be wary of transferring your headaches to some other manager, however. It's too easy a cop-out to suggest transfer simply to avoid the unpleasant, but necessary, task of deciding on demotion or termination. This judgment must be made only after every effort has been made by you and/or others to bring about satisfactory performance. Parenthetically it might be pointed out that this individual has demonstrated development needs, even though you have decided you cannot help with them, and so you are leaving that development up to the individual in a different situation.

If, however, the answer to the second question is Yes (it does seem to you that this person's performance can be improved to reasonable standards in reasonable time), then you have identified a Type I person: one whose performance is unsatisfactory and needs improvement. Development or growth for this individual will mean moving performance up to acceptable levels.

After time, you will review performance again and move to question three, "Is performance now satisfactory?" A negative answer here moves you back to question number two. Here you must to decide once more whether there is reason to believe with another attempt that performance can be corrected. After two or three times, you may either decide to give up (dismiss, transfer, demote) or you will eventually get an affirmative answer: the person is now meeting all performance requirements of the present job.

Either because of a successful development effort on a Type I person, or because the very first question received a positive answer (the performance is satisfactory), you are now ready to go to question four, "Is the person promotable?" Concerning some subordinates, if not most, the answer here will at first be negative. Such workers are quite capable in their present level of responsibility, but are not deemed able to handle higher level responsibilities—not yet anyway. And so, question five must be asked, "Is the person groomable?" This means does there seem to be evidence that the individual can be prepared to take on additional responsibilities at a later time?

A good number of individuals will receive a negative answer here. These are the ones we had in mind back in chapter one when we spoke of those with no desire to "get ahead." They do their job, they come to work when they're supposed to, they follow all the rules and policies, they get the work out, they make no waves, they run a tight ship, they earn their day's pay, and all the rest, but they just are not interested in moving into higher level jobs. There are a lot of these people—they are the backbone of most organizations; there is nothing wrong with this. They have fulfilled their

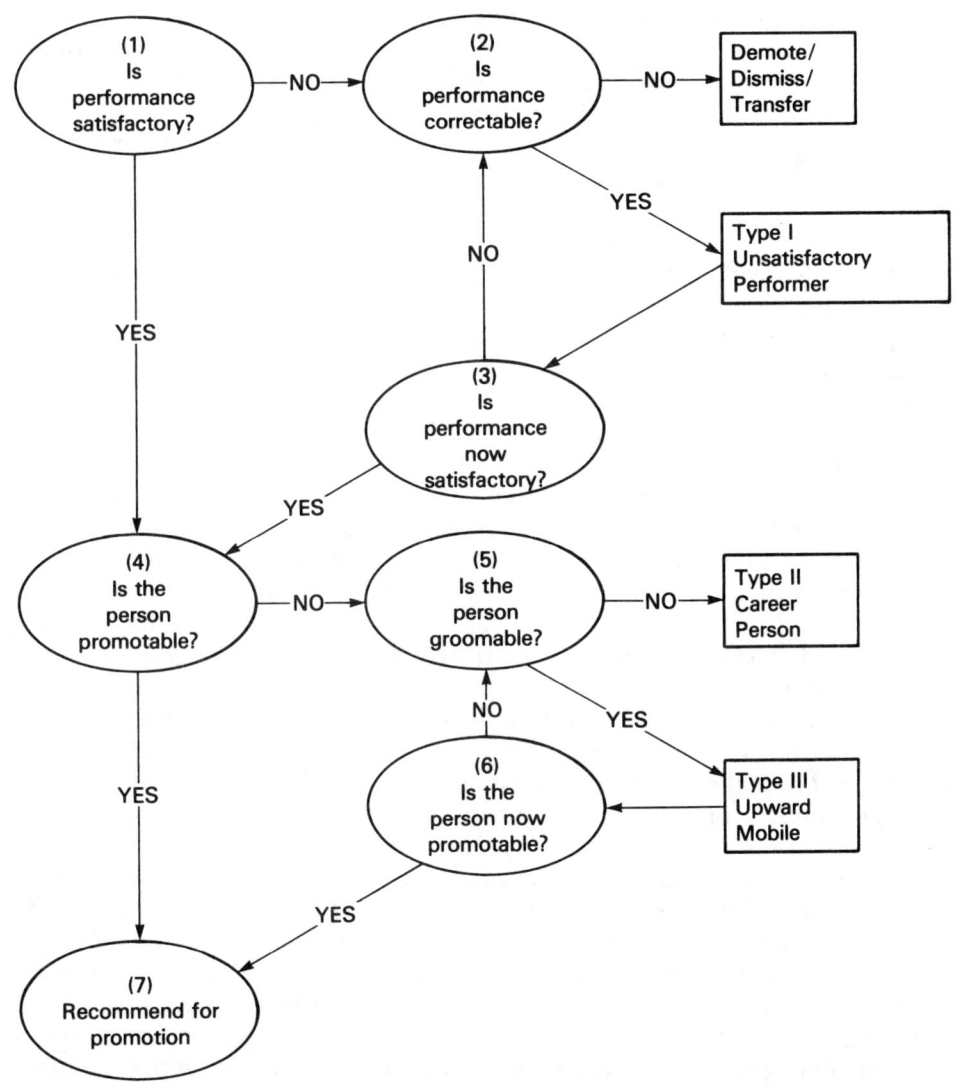

Figure 3-1 Three Types of Development Needs

particular need for achievement in terms of climbing the ladder of success, and they just want to stay where they are because they are comfortable, and are making a valued contribution to the organization.

But, because this person does not wish to "move up" is no reason to conclude that he or she has no need to grow or develop. We call this a Type II person: one whose performance is satisfactory, but needs to develop in order to *maintain* that level of performance. The assumption is that no job remains static. Every job is becoming more difficult, either because of increasing volume, more stringent quality needs, shorter time constraints, tighter cost parameters, or more complex in some way. That being the case, the same level of effort today will not be sufficient tomorrow; hence, the incumbent will have to grow at least to keep pace with the growing nature of the job.

This type person will continue to pursue the type of work he or she is now engaged in for as long as you both can tell. The individual might be called a "career person," that is, one who intends to make a career out of what his or her present job is. A less flattering way of stating the same concept is to say this person has "plateaued," he or she will not rise to any higher level in the organization. No matter what the designation, this person is not going to be groomed to go anywhere higher in the company, but must be encouraged and assisted to keep abreast of developments in the present position.

Your challenge will be to convince this individual that personal growth is not only for those desiring promotion. As long as this person wishes to continue in the present job, he or she will have to work to maintain the already satisfactory level of achievement. Without an effort, performance may begin to slacken. Without being alert, developments in the field may get ahead of the worker. So, growth will be in terms of staying on top of things, so to speak.

A reminder here about the findings of motivation research. Everyone needs to be motivated. And what is it which seems to really motivate workers? A challenging job which allows a feeling of achievement, a sense of responsibility, opportunities for advancement or growth, enjoyment in doing the work itself, earned recognition, and the like. Workers become dissatisfied, we are told, from factors which are mostly peripheral to the job—work rules, environmental things like lighting and smell, coffee breaks, titles, seniority rights, wages, fringe benefits, and so on. You are often unable to do much about these dissatisfiers directly. But the point of the motivation studies seems to be that these individuals don't really bother employees until opportunities for meaningful achievement, enjoyment, and growth are eliminated. Then they become sensitized to their environment and begin to find fault and lack motivation. Therefore, you want to keep challenging this Type II person to grow as a way of keeping him or her from falling prey to the dissatisfaction which might be caused by external factors.

There may also be those individuals about whom you feel are not groomable due to lack of potential rather than lack of desire. Some really would like to move ahead, but you are convinced that they don't have what it takes and never will. If there is any doubt at all, we advise that the person be given a chance to show capability of being groomed, and resolve the doubt by actually proving if further potential exists or not. If, however, you are convinced the individual will be doing well to maintain a position of excellence in the present job, your challenge may be to convince him or her to be satisfied with the positive aspects of being a Type II person.

If the answer to question five is a positive one, you have a person whom you consciously wish to groom for higher level responsibilities. He or she is not yet ready for promotion but shows signs of desire and ability to become ready for promotion. This individual is "upward mobile." The performance at present is satisfactory, but there are needs to be taken care of before we can hope performance in a higher level position would be satisfactory. You will have to identify what those needs are and develop a plan to meet them.

After time, you will want to ask question number six, "Is the person now promotable?" A negative answer here moves you back to question five, where you have to decide once more whether there is reason to believe that with another attempt the person could be prepared for promotion. After two or three times, you may decide the individual is in reality a career person, or you will eventually get an affirmative answer: the individual is now deemed promotable.

Either because of a successful development effort on a Type III person, or because you have determined the person is promotable, you are now ready for step seven: a recommendation for promotion. Even here, the need for development does not stop. Not everyone who can be recommended for promotion is immediately going to get promoted. So it may be a while before your subordinate gets a chance to demonstrate higher level skills. In the interim, the present job is again growing more complex, and so the incumbent must continue to work at staying abreast of developments. Also, he or she can work at growing even further in getting ready for the next assignment, which will also continue to grow even before the person reaches it. The higher position may move out of his or her grasp if there is not continued effort to keep up with it.

There are, then, three basic types of persons in terms of need for development plans. Type I is the person whose performance is *unsatisfactory* and needs *improvement.* The overall strategy will be to make a written plan to improve present performance. This will require that you:

1. Help the person recognize performance deficiencies and the desire to improve.
2. Discuss ways in which improvement can be obtained through appropriate resources and action steps.
3. Mutually select a plan for improvement and write it down with a timetable.

Type II is the person whose performance is *satisfactory* and needs planning to *maintain* that level of performance. The overall strategy will be to make a written plan to maintain a continued high level of performance. This will necessitate that you:

1. Recognize good work and show appreciation for it.
2. Identify areas in which the job may be going to become more difficult, larger in scope, or different in any way so as to identify growth needs.
3. Discuss ways in which development can be achieved (added duties, variations in responsibilities, sharing with others, new challenges)—resources and actions for all.
4. Mutually select a plan for development and write it down with a timetable.

Type III is the person whose performance is fully *satisfactory* and is to be prepared for *promotion*. The overall strategy will be to make a written plan to prepare for greater responsibilities. This means you will:

1. Recognize good work and show the person that he or she has a good future. *Make no promises yet.* Getting ready for promotion does not mean a guarantee of anything.
2. Ask about career goals; help the individual to be ambitious, yet realistic.
3. Explore the knowledge, skills, or attitudes which will be required as conditions for consideration for promotion (based on the nature of the work at the next level).
4. Discuss possible ways in which such needs may be met (resources and actions).
5. Mutually select a plan, accepting some of the responsibility yourself, and write it down with a timetable.

IDENTIFYING DEVELOPMENT NEEDS

Each type of person, then, has certain underdeveloped or underutilized qualities, which, if actualized, could mean greater contributions to what the work group is trying to achieve. Until these needs are developed, the individual will not be operating at his or her maximum potential. The first job of the effective coach is to identify precisely what those needs are, and to gain concurrence from the subordinate.

Growth needs can be arbitrarily divided into three broad areas: (1) one's chosen technical or professional field; (2) the managerial field; and (3) the field of total human growth. You will want to examine your John Doe or Jane Doe in each of these areas to ensure adequate development in all three. In an effort to get into more details on each and to put some "flesh and blood" on our discussion, perhaps you would like to apply these concepts to yourself first, and make notes in the appropriate boxes as they apply to your potential development. If you can do it for yourself, you will then be ready to suggest the same for John or Jane Doe in the next chapter.

Technical or professional growth

Most of us today are specialists of one sort or another. We learn a trade, so to speak, even if that trade is called one of the professions. You're an accountant, an engineer, a systems analyst, a physical therapist, a registrar, a purchasing agent, etc. The world is indeed becoming more and more specialized. There are technical fields today that didn't exist five years ago; there are professions and para-professions today that didn't exist five years ago. And there isn't a single one of these technical or professional areas which isn't constantly growing, if only in the sense of becoming more complex, or becoming more regulated by internal or external forces. Many fields require that practitioners (doctors, nurses, teachers, real estate brokers, etc.) attend continuing education courses periodically in order to have their licences renewed. This is all in recognition that as these fields of human endeavor grow or change, those who work in these areas, especially if they involve any public service, must grow apace.

We probably wouldn't think much of an airline pilot or a physician who boasts of having obtained a license five or ten years ago and hasn't done anything to update himself or herself since; we certainly wouldn't entrust our lives to such a person. So, too, in your field of specialization. Chances are, no matter what your field, a lot has developed since you first entered it. And if you don't apply yourself to keeping up-to-date, you are likely becoming obsolete and ineffective as compared with what you could be contributing to your work unit. Hence, you must periodically find out what is new, exciting, and different in your field and make a commitment to catch up with these recent developments. You will want to measure personal growth to this extent so as to know that you no longer have that particular need.

In order to tell that growth has taken place you will need some way to measure progress, some indicator that development is taking place, that a need no longer exists. Part of the complete identification of needs, then, is a determination of how to monitor growth. There are three ways in which growth occurs in any of the areas we are examining; so before we go on to the other two areas of needs, let us consider the three ways of monitoring growth.

First, there is new knowledge. Maybe what you need is more knowledge about a specific aspect of your technical career. One dimension of growth is simply to know more: new findings, new theories, new laws, new experiences, new inventions, new applications. Have you ever felt sheepish because you were in a discussion with colleagues about something pertaining to your field, and as they started to talk about it, you came to the realization that you hadn't even heard about it, much less understand its ramifications? You very quickly realized you had better fill this lack of knowledge, simply because it might mean the difference between being current and being out-of-date. We all sometimes feel that we have to run just to keep up with the wealth of new information, so we're constantly going to workshops, reading literature, and attending professional and technical meetings. Can you think of something similar in your field of specialization which is a need at the present time—the acquisition of which knowledge would be a mark of development in your career? Be specific.

> Q What specific knowledge would you like to acquire in order to stay abreast of developments in your field?
>
> A

The second way of monitoring growth concerns skills. Maybe what you need is to acquire or improve some technical or professional skill you know to be important in your field of specialization. You know about this area, but you cannot perform to the level of success you desire. You adequately understand something, but your performance lags behind. Every job has some aspect which we find more elusive than others in terms of being able to do what is required of us. Perhaps it's the use of an instrument, machine, or

IDENTIFYING DEVELOPMENT NEEDS

tool. Maybe it's the application of some new procedure or changing some mechanical step in a process. You recognize a weakness of some sort and say to yourself, "If I can improve my ability to do this, I would be more expert in my field." Can you think of something like that in your field of specialization? Be specific.

> **Q** What specific skill would you like to acquire (or improve on) in order to grow in your field of interest?
>
> **A**

The third way to detect and measure growth is in changing attitudes. Maybe your need lies here. You may know what you ought to know about your field, and you may have the skills necessary to perform well in your field, but perhaps there is something about your technical or professional attitude that leaves something to be desired. A physician is sometimes said to be "a great doctor, except for his bedside manner." In many fields there tends to grow a sort of elitism attitude that springs originally from pride in one's profession, but can become a barrier to cooperation with those who are not of the chosen few. "I'm a salesperson; we don't talk to you accounting types who understand only numbers." "I'm an engineer; we don't talk to you marketing people who understand only back-slapping." "I'm in systems design; we don't talk to you production workers who understand only your own machines." So the specific attitude in question could be one of not accepting anyone else's ideas or discounting the contributions of other speciality fields. Can you think of some attitude in yourself that might stand in the way of making an effective contribution to the work organization?

> **Q** What specific attitude would you like to improve or change or acquire to grow in your specialty field?
>
> **A**

Management growth

A second career that you pursue, being a supervisor, is the equally specialized field of management which you share with all other managers. Management is as dynamic as any other field today; it is constantly growing, changing, developing. The individual who says he or she read a book on management or got a degree in management years ago and therefore doesn't need to grow in that field would be as pitiable as the obsolete engineer or doctor. And so, you will wish to keep up with what is new and challenging in the management field and make a commitment to grow by staying abreast of recent developments in management, and measure that this growth has been accomplished to your own satisfaction.

Again, you will need indicators of that growth, and the same three mentioned earlier apply in this field too. You will want to identify some specific piece of knowledge about management, or some specific skill of managing, or some specific managerial attitude. You might, for instance, say, "I'd like to know more about zero-based budgeting," or "I want to improve my skill at interviewing applicants for a job," or "I should change my autocratic attitude toward employees." Can you find something like these for yourself?

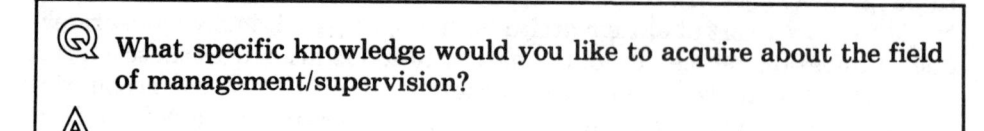

Q What specific knowledge would you like to acquire about the field of management/supervision?

A

Q What specific skill of management would you like to improve?

A

Q What specific attitude as a manager would you like to change?

A

Total human growth

Transcending our field of specialization and our position in the organizational hierarchy is our need to grow as a total human. This refers to those aspects of life which are outside the job, per se, but which can catch up with us on the job. We are, before anything else, human beings with interests in all sorts of areas, who rub shoulders with other humans on the job who also have a wide variety of interest areas which we all use as a platform for communicating with each other. Yet there are some people who seem to have very little interest in anything except the job. They eat, sleep, drink the job, the job, the job. They have no interest in politics, sports, civic affairs, world events, religious activities, hobbies, anything! We call them "workaholics." When it comes to relating to other persons who usually have some of these other natural human interests, they come across as half humans, as stunted in some aspect of their growth as a total human. This in turn renders them something less than effective in dealing with others in and around the job; thus, our interest in this dimension—workaholics will affect organizational results.

This can easily happen to any of us to some degree, so you must periodically pick some outside interest area and make a commitment to develop in this area, if only to be a more well rounded total person. Then you should measure that you have grown in that field, and no longer lack that dimension of personal growth.

As with the other two areas, development can probably be measured by identifying some specific knowledge you would like to acquire, some skill you would like to improve, or some attitude dealing with people in general which you would like to work on. You might think, "I would like to learn more about Russian history, or gourmet cooking, or constitutional law, or . . ."; "I would like to improve my golf game, or learn to play Chopin on the piano, or take up snorkeling, or . . ."; "I would like to become more tolerant of other people's ideas, or become less impatient, or be less chauvinistic, or . . ." Here, as you see, the world is your oyster. Any field of human endeavor, of human interest, of human emotion is open to you. Of particular interest will be attitudes dealing with interpersonal relations, biases and prejudices of all sorts: racial bias, sexual bias, age bias, ethnic bias, cultural bias, religious bias, political bias, and so on. Can you find something like these for yourself?

Q What specific knowledge would you like to acquire just to become a more well rounded total human?

A

> **Q** What specific skill or ability would you like to improve just to be a more well rounded total human?
>
> **A**
>
> **Q** What specific attitude would you like to work on to be able to relate on a more well rounded basis to others?
>
> **A**

ACHIEVING AND MEASURING THE GROWTH

So far we have identified three areas of personal growth (technical or professional career, managerial career, and total human growth) and three ways in which growth is monitored (knowledge, skills, and attitudinal change). The next area is engaging in the appropriate developmental activity to acquire the knowledge, skill, or attitude in question. This is where the effort comes in and where the coach is usually most helpful in assisting, recommending, and arranging for the best means to the desired end. There is a smorgasbord of possible activities which might be pursued to achieve growth—everything from attending courses to reading books to making visits and giving papers.

The important thing to remember is that engaging in a developmental activity is not the same as achieving the desired growth. The activity is simply to be busy, but growth is a result achieved by means of the activity. Some people attend workshops and learn nothing; some people practice a procedure for hours and don't improve their ability one iota; some people try time and time again, yet still have inappropriate attitudes.

So when the developmental activity is concluded, a means must be selected to measure or evaluate whether or not growth took place. The particular method of evaluation will depend on the type of indicator of success chosen earlier. If *knowledge* is what is sought, the appropriate evaluative tool is a *test*. We test that people have intellectually understood what they sought to learn. The test does not have to be of an academic nature; any opportunity for one person to check another's comprehension, any type of feedback of the new information to have been grasped will suffice. It could be a chit-chat over a cup of coffee; it could be an informal report in the boss' office; it could be by use of a company form used to assess meetings attended; it could be an evaluation form used to judge usefulness of workshops attended, etc. Tests are used to evaluate knowledge acquired.

If, on the other hand, it is a *skill* that was to be acquired or improved, a verbal test is not sufficient. You cannot ask a person to tell you whether he or she has a certain skill and expect to be sure of the answer. Skills have to be demonstrated, so the proper evaluative tool to verify abilities is *demonstration* of the hoped-for skill. Most training programs where skills are being taught use some sort of "classroom" demonstration technique to verify that the skill has been learned before allowing or expecting people to put the skill to use.

Finally, if it was *attitudinal* change which was sought, the appropriate evaluative technique once more cannot be a test. You cannot ask people whether or not they still have the same attitudes and be able to rely on the answer. Nor can individuals directly demonstrate attitudes because you cannot see an attitude. We know people have changed their attitudes by noticing that they have changed their *behavior*. It was initially some behavior which first indicated the need for attitudinal change; it will be observation of subsequent behavior which will indicate that the growth has taken place. Behavior is the manifestation of underlying attitudes.

Now it is probably easier to see why emphasis was placed earlier on being specific in identifying the development need. Without being specific, growth cannot be measured. It is too vague to say, "I want to learn more about engineering" or "I want to improve my skills as an accountant" or "I want to be a more dynamic salesperson." These statements do not lend themselves to being measured as time goes by. Notice that nothing is said here as to how anyone will know that you have learned more about engineering or have improved your ability as an accountant or have become a more dynamic salesperson.

Perhaps an illustration will be of help. A member in one of our workshops was a police captain in charge of the weapons section of the police cadet academy. While performing this exercise, he applied this threefold breakdown of knowledge, skills, and attitudes to his work in helping cadets set development objectives depending on where they were in their stages of growth. The technical area under discussion was the specialized field of being a police officer, patrolling the streets, and protecting the lives and property of the citizenry.

The beginning cadets, we were told, come to the weapons section needing all sorts of knowledge about weapons. So, a list of the specific things they should know is compiled: how to tell one type of gun from another, the laws of ballistics, the type of ammunition to use for each type of gun, the names and functions of each piece of each weapon, etc. Instructional activities are then engaged in, and after courses and lectures and demonstrations are completed, each cadet is given a series of tests which are scored to determine whether the knowledge has been sufficiently obtained.

The next category of cadets are those whose growth needs have to do with skills. After they know about weapons and ammunition, they have to begin to use them. Again, a list of specific abilities is prepared. The cadets must be able to assemble and disassemble the weapons, without losing parts. They must be able to load and unload them. They must be able to draw them and holster them without shooting their toes off. They must be able to aim the weapons, fire them, and hit what they are aiming at. Therefore, appropriate activities are engaged in to help the cadets learn these skills. They go through innumerable drills to load-unload, draw-holster, clean-fire, assemble-disassemble all the weapons. They are put on the pistol range where they fire at targets from a variety of positions. Demonstrations are then arranged in which, on their own, the cadets do the cleaning, loading, assembling, firing, etc. Scores are obtained by the use of targets to determine who can and who cannot use the weapons ultimately as intended: to hit what is aimed at.

Then we come to attitudes. Some cadets have passed all the intellectual tests, and they have been awarded marksmanship badges to attest to these skills, but when they are put on the streets to do the patrolling they have been training for, something happens to some of their attitudes. Again, specific attitudinal problems are identified. Some have what might be called a careless attitude with weapons. They patrol the street, pass by a dark alley, hear a noise and automatically fire their weapons in the alley, shooting up all the cats knocking over the barrels. These officers are given lectures and warnings as a means of getting them to change their attitudes. Such attitude changes are measured ultimately by observation of subsequent behavior of not being so careless. At the other extreme are officers who are on the streets to protect life and property even to the extent of using their weapons if necessary, but who somehow freeze when it comes to pointing a gun at another human. They cannot bring themselves to fire for fear of taking a human life, even though that is their sworn job. These individuals must undergo psycho-therapy or other more serious types of activity in order to change such an attitude, until they can show by subsequent behavior that they have overcome their hang-ups.

CHECKLIST OF POSSIBLE DEVELOPMENT NEEDS

As a final aid in helping you identify some development needs in yourself, and to prepare you for the assignment of doing the same for your subordinates, Figure 3-2 is a checklist of common areas needing attention. They are arranged under headings of common job functions, and will include only those to be found in a wide cross-section of workers. To go into the special areas of all technical/professional careers is obviously beyond the scope of any one book, but a catalog of offerings by educational institutions or associations in your field of special interest might be helpful.

Figure 3-2 Checklist of Possible Development Needs

A. The Business Climate

1. Understanding of corporate product lines or services and goals
   Knowledge of marketing plans
   Knowledge of products
2. Knowledge of competition
   Knowledge of competitive organizations
   Knowledge of competitive products
3. Understanding the customer
   Customer requirements
   Customer organization and decision-makers
   Understanding contract requirements, if applicable
   Establishment and proper use of contracts
4. Understanding of market analysis
   Organization's potential versus probable share
   Recognition and exploration of market opportunities
   Understanding and use of market opportunities
   Understanding of methods of conducting market analyses
5. Understanding different types of government contracts, if applicable
   Advantages and disadvantages of each type
   Legal responsibilities of executives
   Incentives and their meaning
6. Sensitivity to social-political-economic trends
   Understanding the current status of public laws and their applicability
   Understanding the effects of the social-political-economic trend on organizations

B. Policies and Decision-Making

1. Knowledge of formally stated corporate policy
   Proper application of policy in decision-making
   Understanding how to enforce specific policy in own area of operation
   Understanding what enforcement of specific policies can do to other functional operations
2. Knowledge of techniques for decision-making
   Extent and limitation of authority
   Limitations of responsibility and accountability
   Use of logic and judgment
   Use of problem analysis
   Selecting alternatives and strategies
   Forcing the decision process to the proper level of the organization
3. Use of policies in management
   What level should make policies
   Difference between good and bad policies
   Policies—general or detailed

Figure 3-2 continued

4. Use of decision evaluation
   Use potential problem analysis
   Understanding effect on existing policies
   Understanding results appraisal and precise measurement
5. Use of available information for policy and decision
   Understanding how to use the organization's resources
   Using different analyses as appropriate
   Using others for advise

C. **Personnel Selection and Development**

1. Understanding selection and staffing
   Determining manpower requirements
   Sources of internal and external personnel
   Interviewing and screening applicants
   Determining proper job classifications and rates
   Proper orientation of the new employee
   Handling the problem of overstaffing
   Attracting candidates by improving the organization's image
2. Understanding upgrading of present staff
   Assessment using psychological tools and techniques
   Handling the low-rated performer
   Challenging the high-potential employee
   Using employee ranking
   Using appraisal system effectively
3. Development of personnel
   Determining the development needs of the organization
   Establishing a total manpower development plan
   Understanding development techniques
   Development of backup
   Preparation for specific jobs
   Planned development for promotion
4. Using techniques for individual motivation
   Manager-subordinate relationships through counseling
   Personal recognition methods
   Profit sharing
   Personal incentives based on individual differences
   Stretching out to achieve mutually set job objectives
   Reassignment for work satisfaction through more responsibility
   Job enrichment through job redesign for personal satisfaction and growth
5. Using techniques for group motivation
   Knowing group motivation techniques and their value
   Use of suggestion system
   Inter- intra-department competitions
   Recreation

D. Interpersonal Relations

1. Understanding balanced relationships with boss, other managers, and subordinates
   Understanding own responsibilities
   Understanding own place in the organization
   Understanding each person's individual differences
2. Understanding the manager's role
   Customers' image awareness
   Suppliers' image awareness
   Public image awareness
3. How to project an image of respect to all that you contact
   Friendliness and cooperativeness
   Helpful attitude
   Stimulating others to positive and creative endeavors
   Personal integrity
   Encouraging subordinate self-development
4. Understanding the importance of being sensitive and alert to reactions of others
   Empathy for others
   Sensitive to others and their needs
5. How to take issue tactfully in a persuasive manner without becoming antagonistic
   Calm attitude
   Sincere in showing positive emotion
   Practicing tactful aggression
6. Personal courage in working with others
   Persuades convincingly
   Adaptable to new group situations
   Presses point in face of strong opposition
   Admits error when proved wrong
7. Disciplines subordinates properly
   Use of constructive criticism
   Disciplines privately
   Recommending changes in behavior
8. Using the chain of command properly—sensitivity to bypassing organizational levels

E. Self-Development

1. Periodically performing self-analysis to establish realistic personal goals and self-confidence
   Logic
   Creativity
   Ingenuity
   Flexibility
   Resourcefulness
   Alertness

Figure 3-2 continued

2. Understanding the importance of physical stamina in crisis situations
   Corrective health measures
   Annual physical checkups
   Establishing physically active recreational pursuits
3. Purposely stretching out for broadening responsibility
   Continuing education in a broadening field
   Establishing a personal reading/study plan
   Using job rotation to gain a breadth of managerial experience
   Using special projects or assignments to learn of other organizational functions
4. Understanding individual social responsibility without jeopardizing corporate responsibilities
   Participating as a member/leader in local or national organizations
   Publishing and/or presenting papers
   Talks to local gatherings
5. Understanding technical disciplines
   Technical aspects of organizations, products, or services
   Technical aspects of present research
6. Management theories
   Management by exception
   Management by objectives
   Theory X vs theory Y
   Managerial grid
   Hygiene vs motivating factors
7. Understanding other department functions
   Manufacturing
   Marketing
   Quality
   Contracts
   Engineering
   Maintenance
   Financial
   Legal
   Material
   Project
   Administration
   Professional and Industrial Relations
   Research & Development
8. Self-Improvement
   Speed reading
   Vocabulary and spelling
   Effective memory
   Effective listening
   Effective writing
   Effective speaking

F. Communication

1. Understanding uninhibited and effective communication—vertically and horizontally
   Communication from peers to subordinates
   Need to keep all concerned fully informed of important and appropriate matters
   How to coach or counsel subordinates
   Using commendation
   Using discipline
   How to motivate through communication
   How to encourage communication from superiors and subordinates
2. Understanding oral and written communication
   What information should be in writing
   When to write procedures
   Understanding how to use interdepartmental communications
   How to use oral communication with individuals and groups
3. Practicing sound communication principles in both composition and presentation
   How to plan and organize communications
   How to sell ideas effectively, either verbally or in writing
4. Using proper organization channels of communication
   Sensitivity to bypassing intermediate management
   When and how to pass information and instructions down through management
   When and how to talk to groups
   When and how to make important announcements

G. Planning and Control Process

1. Understanding the basic techniques of planning and control
   Using the long-range plan in functional planning
   When and how to use Gantt charts
   Input-output charts
   Using PERT time and cost
2. Organizing work and developing a good plan
   Improving proper planning versus reacting
   How to obtain maximum effectiveness and use of personnel, facilities, dollars, and other resources
   How and when to use work breakdown structures
   Proper work statements
   Key items and milestones
   Understanding logical sequence
   Understanding the need for a minimum of details
   Balancing logical tradeoff of time, cost, and schedule
3. Controlling the plan
   How and when to use status reviews
   Understanding exception reporting

Figure 3-2 continued
- How to use early problem determination for implementation of corrective action
- How and when to use reports
- How and when to use charts
- Understanding customer reports
- How to present status information

4. Effectively monitoring work of subordinates and the organization
   - How and when to use early problem identifiers
   - How and when to use key check points
   - Using random sampling as a monitoring technique
   - Using accurate and timely report feedback
   - How to measure results

5. Understanding and using Management by Objectives and results
   - Putting in writing the objectives to be accomplished in terms of results
   - Laying out a program for each objective
   - Securing the understanding and approval of the manager's superior and other managers involved
   - Communicating these objectives to subordinates for detailed programming
   - Defining the limits within which subordinates can operate to include completion dates
   - Defining evaluation devices to determine progress

H. Organization and Delegation

1. Organizing personal work efforts
   - Separating the "forest" from the "trees"
   - Distributing own time to best advantage
   - Placing proper personal emphasis in line with priorities
   - Covering all segments of personal responsibility

2. Establishing effective organization
   - Understanding the dangers of competition and/or conflict between organizational elements
   - Defining responsibility and authority
   - Proper spans of control
   - Effective chain of command
   - Projects, line, and staff coordination
   - Proper balance of skill and classification levels
   - Cost factors

3. Understanding the process of delegation
   - Delegation as a motivational tool
   - Delegation as a developmental tool
   - Analysis of key tasks and priorities
   - How to make clear-cut assignments
   - Expanding decision-making down the line
   - Determining what and how much to delegate
   - Determination to whom to delegate

4. Organizing to achieve organizational objectives
   Developing the organization structure to achieve objectives
   Delegating by functional responsibility
   Establishing organization relationships

SUMMARY

Everyone has personal development needs, if only to keep pace with the changing demands of the present job. Individuals may be classified as a Type I person, whose performance is unsatisfactory and needs improvement; a Type II person, whose performance is satisfactory and needs to maintain that level; or a Type III person, whose performance is fully satisfactory and is to be prepared for promotion.

Each type will wish to identify specific knowledge to be acquired, skills to be improved, or attitudes to be changed in either the technical job, the management job, or in the area of total human growth. Once needs are identified, appropriate activities should be selected to fill the needs. Measurement of improvement will be done by test, demonstration, or by observation of behavior.

Next, you will want a way to record a simplified plan to achieve such needs for each of your people.

4 PERSONAL DEVELOPMENT PLAN

Business managers must do a better job of throwing out challenges that excite people to try harder and grow bigger...
I think we ought to work so hard to build imaginative, continuously learning, demanding people that we will actually increase the risk of losing them.

FREDERICK KAPPEL
AT&T Chairman

We saw in chapter 2 that the first step in the communications process is clarifying the idea we wish to share with others. You wish to share some ideas about personal development with your John or Jane Doe, so the first step is to be sure you have some specific and worthwhile ideas to recommend by way of personal growth. For that reason, it is recommended that you reduce your ideas to a simple format which can be used as the basis for discussion. To emphasize the concept of making a commitment to all that is involved in achieving that personal growth, it is recommended that the plan not only be put in writing but also signed by both you and your subordinate. Figure 4-1 is offered as a simple enough format for accomplishing this. After an explanation of each section of that form you are invited to complete the form, section by section, always with reference to the same individual you have had in mind from the beginning. To help keep that person's identity in mind, you might want to record the individual's name on the line for the employee's signature. (If you adopt this type of form for your use later on, you would have this line actually signed by John or Jane Doe when you have your discussion with that person.) You might also put your name and the date in the spaces alloted.

Sections A and B on the form provide a place for specifying what you think are specific development needs for your subordinate. It will help if you first determine the type of person you think he or she is. Type I is an unsatisfactory performer; Type II is a career person needing to maintain good performance; Type III is one being groomed for promotion. At any point in time, your subordinate will be one of these types, and only one; but over time the individual might, and probably will, move from one type to another. It is highly significant, in gaining commitment from the subordinate, that this judgment be made. A straightforward classification of this sort helps the individual develop the mind set associated with the effort needed to become serious about personal development. This will all be reinforced during the annual performance evaluation. In fact, many will choose that occasion as the best time to discuss the personal growth plan. (See chapter 6.)

Some have found it difficult to make this judgment about their subordinates. But that is one of the responsibilities of managers: to make judgments about the present and possible future performance of the workforce. Hopefully those judgments use inputs from the subordinates, and are subject to discussion with them, but the making of the judgment cannot be avoided. It might help to recall that this is not a once-in-a-career judgment. The individual will move from one type to another. The unsatisfactory performer corrects weaknesses and becomes a career worker. The career person becomes lazy and falls back to being unsatisfactory. The career person has a change occur in his or her personal situation and becomes motivated to seek higher level responsibilities. Someone being groomed for promotion will prove not up to learning new things and may lower his or her sights for the future. As these circumstances warrant, you will have opportunities to update your judgment about the subordinate, so your judgment at this moment is not casting the die forever. Make the judgment now about your John or Jane Doe.

> Ⓠ What type of person is your subordinate: I, II, or III?
>
> Ⓐ

Now you are ready to use either Section A or Section B of Figure 4-1, depending on the judgment you have made. If the subordinate is Type I or II, use Section A and write in the specific knowledge, skills, or attitudes needing improvement or further development to maintain good performance. These can relate to the technical job, to management, or to total human growth as explained in the last chapter and as you did for yourself.

Figure 4-1 Individual Development Plan

(A) Development Needs—Current Position (Specific knowledge, skills, attitudes: Requirements for improvement or to maintain satisfactory performance)	(B) Development Needs—Future Position (0-3 years) (Specific knowledge, skills, attitudes to get ready for the next level of responsibility) Possible job:_____ Needs: _____
(C) Development Objectives (Specific performance to show need has been met)	(D) Development Activities—You and I will work together to implement the following actions:
(E) Actual Results (Date to check _____)	Employee's signature _____ Supervisor's signature _____ Date _____

If the subordinate is a Type III person, use Section B and indicate the specific knowledge, skills, or attitudes which will be necessary to qualify for the next level position. Identifying a possible job, by job title, at the next level in the hierarchy is a good way of keeping your suggestions precise and more meaningful to the one who will be discussing them with you.

Referring to the checklist at the end of chapter 3 might be useful in thinking of specific areas in which growth might be called for. The key is to be as specific as possible. Figure 4-2 is an illustration of how to complete the form and includes examples of specific needs for a hypothetical salesperson.

Figure 4-2 Individual Development Plan

(A) Development Needs—Current Position (Specific knowledge, skills, attitudes: Requirements for improvement or to maintain satisfactory performance) 1. Needs to know more about product features of unloading equipment he sells for our line of agricultural (grain) storage buildings. 2. Needs to improve his ability to close a sale. Current close ratio is 1 out of 17 sales presentations. 3. Needs to become more faithful in the completion of weekly sales reports sent in from the field (50% late).	(B) Development Needs—Future Position (0-3 years) (Specific knowledge, skills, attitudes to get ready for next level of responsibility) Possible job: _____ Needs: _____
(C) Development Objectives (Specific performance to show need has been met) 1. Will be able to make presentation and answer questions at the next quarterly sales meeting in Region, dealing with unloader. 2. Will increase close ratio to 1:10 by July 1st. 3. Will have weekly sales reports in on time 90% of time like everyone else in the Region by year end.	(D) Development Activities—You and I will work together to implement the following actions: 1. Study engineering manual and customers service manual for the unloader and let me ask questions about same for one hour each week on occasion of office visit. 2. Accompany top salesperson in the region and understudy his technique in closing sales. Make at least 2 sales calls this way each week. 3. I will trace for him what happens to sales report when received to impress with importance of being on time. Include on standards of performance for review annually.
(E) Actual Results (Date to check <u>7/10/80</u>)	Employee's signature _____ Supervisor's signature _____ Date _____

Now try to do this as it applies to your John or Jane Doe.

> **Q** What specific development needs do you see facing your subordinate at the present time, either for the current position, or to get ready for a promotion?
>
> **A**

DEVELOPMENT OBJECTIVES

One of the most exasperating things in the world is for a person to want to improve in a certain area, and try very hard to improve in that area, and after time to have someone say, "Well, you still haven't improved in that area." Such a statement is made on the basis of no real objective information, but purely on subjective intuition. If you are going to be effective in helping John or Jane Doe develop, you are going to have to spell out objectives clearly so that you both understand and agree on what it takes to prove it to both of you (and the whole world for that matter) that growth has taken place. For this reason, it is necessary to be *specific* when it comes to stating needs. Knowledge, skills, and attitudes can be used as indicators of progress, as yardsticks for measuring growth as moving from one end of the yardstick to the other (thirty-six inches worth). Or would we be content with one-third that much (twelve inches) in the time frame being considered?

The function of Section C in Figure 4-1 is to afford an opportunity to record, ahead of time, what both of you will accept as a satisfactory amount of growth, whether it be knowledge, skills, or attitudinal change. This is what you both will use to determine that the weakness (deficiency, need) no longer exists. Hence, it is a statement of how you will evaluate success after attempts at growth have been made. For that reason, it will help to recall here that a different method of measuring is called for, depending on whether growth is to take place in knowledge, skills, or attitudes.

If knowledge is the need, then indicate in Section C how the person's newly acquired knowledge will be tested. Will a passing grade on a course be considered the appropriate test? Will a verbal presentation to a group be the way to show mastery of the subject? Will ability to answer questions on a topic be enough to show sufficient knowledge? Will completion of a manual explaining something be the way to show it has been learned?

If the need involves some skill, then show in Section C the type of demonstration that will be required to show adequate level of that skill. It might be the successful completion of some task by a certain date. Or it might be raising the performance standard on some job by a certain degree or percentage. Perhaps it will be reducing errors, saving time, improving accuracy, or some other quality in an assigned area of responsibility. It might be the ability to begin undertaking some duty that was not being done at all by this individual before.

If the development need mentioned in Section A or B concerns some attitude, Section C should list the type of behavior which will be examined in the future. You probably will cite the type of occurrence which made you aware of a need for attitudinal change, an example of a situation the individual encountered, or an incident which occurred in which poor attitude was shown. The objective will then be to have different behavior manifested in similar situations in the future, and you will describe the desired behavior in this section.

What you hope to capture in this section is your view of what the desired situations should be as a way of telling that knowledge, skill, or attitude has been developed. You are preparing all of this material for discussion with John or Jane Doe. And to be convincing as a coach, you must have a clear picture of what it is you are going to challenge your subordinate to accomplish. Hopefully this will be discussed in a way that incorporates his or her ideas about the same. But first you have to have a clear idea in your own mind to communicate to the receiver, as we saw in chapter 2.

Try this now, as it relates to your John or Jane Doe and the needs you have already identified for this person.

> Q What specific development objectives would you like to recommend to your subordinate to show that needs have been met?
>
> A

In order to accomplish the growth you have in mind for your subordinate, he or she will have to engage in some action, with or without help, geared to the specific development desired. This action plan is *how* the growth will be sought. It is not to be confused with *what* is being sought. The action plan is the means—the growth is the end itself. We couldn't talk about the means, however, until we specified the concrete development objective desired; hence, Section C was discussed first. Now that you have a clear picture in your mind as to what you think would be desirable growth for your John or Jane Doe, you can give thought to an appropriate course of action.

Usually it is a matter of selecting from an array of possible actions which typically are considered developmental activities. This list of activities might be called potential resources. Some are often available within the organization; others are external. In listing a recommended action plan, remember again to be *specific;* this means the *precise* publication to be studied, courses to be taken, etc. The following is a list of possible developmental activities:

1. Individual instruction: a one-to-one relationship where one person works with another to learn a new job or to help improve the knowledge or skill needed for the present job; e.g., working with a manager who is successful in settling grievances to find out how to talk to union representatives in the early stage of grievance handling.

2. Attendance at meetings within the company which the person would not ordinarily attend; e.g., attending a monthly budget review meeting in order to prepare for responsibility of having to prepare budgets.

3. Specific visits or trips; e.g., comparison shopping trips in which a department store buyer gains knowledge about competitive pricing.

4. Specific job assignments within the department which helps broaden the individual's job skills to give you back up in an area; e.g., asking a purchasing agent in one line to study the files of another agent's line so as to be available to take the latter's place during vacation.

5. Specific rotation through jobs in other departments to acquire knowledge about how those departments work, to give experience in those areas, and so on; assigning a marketing manager to the job of production control supervisor for a period of time.

6. Specific reading materials: books, magazines, reports, research publications, etc., that deal with the field in question.

7. Specific career program courses at adult education facilities of local public schools, nearby colleges, and the like; e.g., going to the local community college one night a week for twelve weeks to get a certificate in Report Writing.

8. Specific management development seminars/workshops sponsored by universities or trade associations; e.g., going to a seminar on Management by Objectives, as offered by such and such a university with such and such an instructor(s).

9. Specific technical development seminars/workshops sponsored by these same outside agencies; e.g., attending a workshop on Solar Energy Applications, as offered by such and such a university with such and such instructor(s).
10. Specific company training programs on management or technical topics; e.g., signing up for the company course on Introduction to Supervision, to begin on such and such a date.
11. Specific programmed instruction courses (machine or text book courses where individuals work at the time and place of their own choice); e.g., completing a course on Cost Estimating put out by such and such a publisher.
12. Specific correspondence school courses; e.g., completing a course on Market Forecasting offered by such and such a resource.
13. Specific professional association memberships (local chapter or national affiliations); e.g., becoming a Fellow of the American College of Hospital Administrators.
14. Specific civic or fraternal group memberships; e.g., joining the Rotary in connection with a total human growth need.
15. Specific human growth workshops/courses to develop skills not related to the job; e.g., joining the Toastmasters to improve skills of speaking in public.
16. Giving a paper at a professional group meeting; e.g., making a presentation at the annual meeting of the American Society of Training Directors.
17. Having articles or books published by reputable journals or publishers in a field of specialization.
18. Field trips to engage in professional pursuits in other institutions or geographical areas of the world; e.g., studying Gothic architecture by visiting European cathedrals.
19. Visiting professorships, stressing here the developmental aspect of such an honor.
20. Sabbatical activities such as traveling, writing, or consulting, with specific mention of areas, topics, or fields of effort; e.g., spending the next year on leave to assist on a governmental study of the effect of aerosols on the ozone.
21. Committee work; e.g., chairing a task force to study the feasibility of a new product.

22. Coaching or counseling sessions with the individual to review performance and to suggest ways of doing things before mistakes are made or just after phases or projects are completed.

Section E on the form is for recording at a later date the actual results obtained by the individual after pursuing the developmental activities. You should record the results in terms of the objectives stated in Section C, not the activities completed in terms of actions stated in Section D. For now, it would be useful if you simply indicated the appropriate date on which you and the subordinate intend to get back together and discuss how much growth has taken place.

With this, the form has been completed in anticipation of a discussion with your subordinate. You might wish to do it in pencil as a draft, pending finalizing during your face-to-face meeting. Simply having some general ideas in mind ahead of time without specifying them in some sort of disciplined way will lead to a vague and general discussion; hence, an unproductive coaching session.

SUMMARY

The personal growth of your subordinates is so important to both you and them that you want no misunderstanding as to what specific growth is appropriate for each subordinate at the present stage of their development. A written agreement between you and each worker is an attempt to avoid ambiguity and reduce chance of misunderstandings by either of you.

A logical progression has been suggested in the outlining of this written plan for personal growth. After a brief description of the knowledge, skills, or attitudinal change you feel each one needs, you then suggest statements of conditions or results. At a later time these statements will not only evidence meeting these needs, but they may serve as a basis for recommending activities as means to achieve the desired growth.

You have then clarified the idea in your mind and selected wording to deliver your message to each individual. Next you want to complete your preparation for the delivery of the message.

5 PREPARING FOR DEVELOPMENT INTERVIEW

*Do your conversations result in a meeting of the minds—
or only separate monologues?*

JESSE S. NIERENBERG
Getting Through to People

When we reviewed communications as a process, we found you should clarify the ideas you wish to share with another and encode them carefully. Your written development plan for John or Jane Doe is an attempt to do that, as far as the coaching interview is concerned. We also found that selecting the proper time and place for transmitting the information is another important element of successful communicating. Now we turn our attention to the receiver of this information who will be decoding your suggestions. The importance of the message content is probably equal to the importance of considering *ahead of time* what the subordinate's likely reaction will be to the message. So you really are not ready to sit down and have the developmental interview until you have done this kind of preparing.

Who is John Doe or Jane Doe? What do you know about him or her? How much of the person's background or history have you thought of in relation to your proposed message? How is that background likely to influence the reception and implementation of your suggestions? Are you as knowledgeable about the total person as you want to be before genuinely recommending activities geared at impacting his or her entire future? Is there the possibility that what you have in mind for your subordinate is quite logical based on a superficial review of outward appearances, but might not be valid in the context of the individual's total situation in life? How much of that total picture do you know?

In order to determine how well you know your people, ask yourself a series of questions about the subordinate you are preparing to interview. The questions are under five major headings, each having to do with one facet of the person's background. They will include: (1) physical background, (2) intellectual/cultural background, (3) emotional needs, (4) work experience, and (5) personal goals. As you read the questions, record the answers as they pertain to your John or Jane Doe in the space provided following each set of questions. It is not necessary to answer each question, just those you think relevant. The questions are really thought-starters. Try to indicate also how the information you record might have a bearing on what you will be recommending, how you will state it, or what the likely response from the individual might be. After the five questions, we will share some examples from others and how they thought recognition of these items made for a better-prepared interview.

PHYSICAL BACKGROUND OF YOUR SUBORDINATE

What do you know about the physical condition of this person? Is he or she in good health or bad health? Has the employee had a physical check up recently? Is the person strong as an ox or a little weaker than he or she should be in terms of physical exertion? Is he or she just getting over an operation or a serious illness? Maybe there is a chronic illness or disease to be thought of, for example, a history of high blood pressure or a weak heart. Does the person have any physical impairments or bodily abnormalities? Is the person hard-of-hearing or suffering from poor eyesight in any way? Does he or she wear contact lenses, walk with a limp, talk with a stutter, have one arm longer than the other, tend to cock the head to one side or the other to make up for some physical impairment? What about general appearance? Is the individual neat and tidy and well groomed? Or is this person sloppy, untidy, dirty, or disheveled? Is the person good looking (and perhaps vain, conceited, or arrogant) or rather plain (and perhaps jealous, insecure or defeatist?) What about stature? Is he or she tall or short, straight or stooped, erect or slouched, self-assured or always running away? Are there any habits—like smoking—which are very important? What do any of these characteristics have to do with the way you will have to approach the individual? Are there ways you must compensate for these conditions? Should they be considered when choosing development activities for this person? Note the emphasis here is not so much to change any of these physical facts (some you might be able to, others you couldn't), but to recognize them ahead of time so as to consider how to work around or through them during your interview.

> **Q** What do you know about the physical background of John or Jane Doe?
>
> **A**

Here are some examples of how some of these items might be important for you to consider as you prepare for the developmental interview:

1. If your subordinate has temporary or permanent physical disabilities, this may make a difference in selecting work assignments, in recommending strenuous studies, in judging time periods for competition of tasks, or in scheduling physically demanding trips, visits, etc.

2. If there are impairments of sight, hearing, or speech, you should remind yourself about these so as not to be surprised when they show up again during the interview. Not to be mindful of such impairments might cause you to show by your conduct that you are uncaring or thoughtless; whereas being mindful of them, you will speak more loudly and distinctly, or will favor a poor eye, or will keep away from glare on contact lenses. All this, of course, will improve the transmission of information.

One individual told of a case where the manager was convinced the subordinate was inattentive and unable to concentrate, and therefore thought to be uncaring about getting ahead. In reality the individual was very ambitious, but he had one glass eye and it tended to "float" out of focus, leading to the thought that he was not paying attention!

3. The physically untidy, disorganized person will tend to be the same way with regard to planning work and personal development. You will probably wish to take extra pains that the plans are carefully recorded, arranged logically, itemized clearly, and scheduled unmistakably so as not to get lost in the individual's usual confusion. Some people tend to lose things—an extra copy of the written plan will be a good tactic.

4. The person who places an exaggerated importance on looks may be too self-conscious and require the right kind of stroking to compensate for this. In turn, you may need to overlook some vanity in order to see objectively the work worth of the individual.

5. Where stature and personal bearing is a factor, you will want to arrange the furniture in the room to offset this. Try to sit where there will be eye to eye contact; have chairs that force a more erect posture.

6. If you smoke and the other person does not, are you willing to jeopardize the meeting by bothering the individual's concentration with smoke? If the other way around, will you be able to tolerate a little smoke in order to make him or her more comfortable?

INTELLECTUAL/CULTURAL BACKGROUND OF YOUR SUBORDINATE

What do you know about the overall mental abilities of this individual? Do you know the IQ level? How would you typify the person's general acuity: very sharp, quick on the upbeat, fast to catch on, maybe even ahead of you in speed of comprehension? Or is this a plodder, one who takes things calmly and slowly, who considers one unit of information at a time, who is deliberate about everything said and done? What do you know about the formal education of your John or Jane Doe? Do you know the school he or she attended? Did the person earn a high school diploma, college degree, or perform post-graduate work? What was the major field of interest? Is the person working in one field whereas the studies were in another area of specialization? Is the person working in your field as though just passing through on the way to his or her heart's desire? Does the level of education bother the person? What about the individual's command of language? Does he or she have a large or small vocabulary, good or poor grammar? Is he or she an English scholar or a second generation American who is still grappling with English because it is not his or her native language? Then there's jargonese—is the person trained in your field and knowledgeable of the special acronymns? Does the person tend to befuddle others by throwing around esoteric terms? And what about the individual's cultural heritage? Anything in the racial, ethnic, or geographic origin of your subordinate which gives rise to habits, values, outlooks, mannerisms, or speech patterns which might antagonize, amuse, befuddle, or disconcert you to the point where the communication process might be jeopardized? In particular, are you aware of how any of these cultural heritages might differ from your own? And what difference might this make in being a good coach?

> Q What do you know about the intellectual/cultural background of your subordinate?
>
> A

Here are some points highlighted by others who have performed this exercise concerning the mental characteristics of subordinates:

1. Depending on the person's general sharpness or lack thereof, you may have to speed up your delivery, cover only the important points and leave the details to be filled in by the other individual, and expect to cover a lot of ground in one sitting. Or, you may have to slow down the pace, say everything very deliberately, maybe repeat things to be sure of comprehension, and expect to have several follow-up sessions to be sure everything is covered.

2. The education preparation for the present assignment and for any possible future job will suggest the aptness of supplemental instructional activities. The success in previous scholastic endeavors might shed light on reticence or desire for more of the same.

3. The person's command of the language has an obvious bearing on your choice of words in discussing developmental activities, and might also determine preparedness for options requiring language skills. Here, of course, you must be careful not to talk down to a person, nor to talk over the individual's head. The difficulty with English might itself be a factor in explaining success or failure on certain work assignments, if you are aware it exists.

4. If we are smart enough to inquire about one's culture, it can explain many things about a person's behavior. Are you ready to make allowances for such differences, to capitalize on whatever values or customs a person's cultural inheritance brings? One executive told of firing a subordinate for what was considered to be a look of dishonesty. The subordinate in question had a habit of coming to the superior and never looking him in the eye when asking a question. "You just knew the man was hiding things, probably robbing us blind," said the manager. "Such shifty-eyed conduct is always a sure sign of petty thievery. I can spot them a mile away!" Upon reviewing of the case, it turned out the subordinate in question was a Mexican-American by birth with highly developed instincts of humility. He was trained from childhood that you never confronted a person above your position by staring him in the eye; you were supposed to cast your eyes at the ground out of respect. The man was docile, not deceitful.

EMOTIONAL NEEDS OF YOUR SUBORDINATE

What do you know about the current emotional equilibrium of John or Jane Doe? Here we consider all the nonphysical aspects apart from the intellect. All the emotions can be important. Take, for example, anger. Is this individual quick to fly off the handle or liable to respond to criticism by swinging at you, yelling back, or storming out in a rage? Does this person sulk? Will he or she crawl into a shell if the discussion does not go the direction desired? Does this person have a distorted sense of humor, for example, he or she can't take anything seriously? When you are talking about an important development for the future, does this individual crack up laughing as if it's a joke? Or perhaps the opposite extreme—in the face of serious discussion, is this subordinate likely to burst into tears? All of these are emotions of the moment. There are also the more lasting emotional strains. Is there some great stress on the person right now because of things outside work? Pressure from home, getting over the loss of a close relative, going through a divorce, or a financial setback of major consequence can all affect the employee. Has there been a series of trying events which have been building up within the individual so that signs of a nervous breakdown are present?

Q What can you note about the emotional needs of your subordinate?

A

Here are some comments from others regarding this series of questions about emotional needs.

1. The person prone to anger must be prepared for words likely to infuriate; it really doesn't take away from the manager's position of authority if he or she couches words in a way that their possible antagonistic flavor is mollified. The person likely to guffaw when you are being serious must be constantly reminded of the seriousness of the discussion and helped to correct that penchant which undoubtedly gets in the way of other communications. The person you expect to shed tears must be encouraged to take hold, to look at the picture impersonally, to take your words as a help not as a blame, etc. None of these tactics is new, of course. The point is that if you prepare yourself for such an encounter in the interview because of the past history of the individual, you will not be caught off guard when these things occur and you thereby gradually reduce their frequency and impact on discussions.

2. A stressful period is hardly the time for taking on major new challenges. Even people who thrive on a dare need to have their strength in hand before they embark on fearless forays. You might delay bringing up the part of your plan which might accentuate present pressures until they have had

a chance to subside. Alternatively, you might show sympathy for the source of the challenge of the developmental plan as a way of diverting attention away from the self to the work. Then, of course, there is the human relationship you are building just to show recognition of outside factors which might be having this emotional strain on your subordinate.

3. Deep psychotic-neurotic imbalances should be referred to professional therapy. Additional comments on these and related types of reactions to your development plan are discussed in the next section on rare birds.

WORK EXPERIENCE OF YOUR SUBORDINATE

What do you know about the work history of this person? Is he or she the chronic failure—every job undertaken needs an undertaker? Does the worker never produce as high as originally aimed? Does he or she tend to hide performance results under the rug because when they see the light of day they're deplorable? Or do you have a person with a Midas touch—everything he or she touches turns to gold; the shining star in your firmament? Does this individual have a proven record of success on job results and personal growth challenges too? And in either case, what is the resultant impact on the individual's outlook—defeatism? lack of any concern? refusal to admit? egotism? unrealism? shooting at the moon? honest appraisal of what brought about results? Because most people have a history of winning some and losing some, do you know in which areas your individual tends to be a winner and in which a loser? What are the strong and weak points, jobwise, of the person's career? Which parts of the job tend to be overemphasized? Which parts of the job tend to be ignored? What does the person find important beyond the priority of the job (occupational hobbies, for example)? Are there things generally swept under the carpet? How long has the person had the present job? What about jobs before that? How long has he or she been with the company? How long in (or out) of the individual's speciality field? What career path did the person follow to get where he or she now is? What kind of evaluations did the person receive from other superiors? Were they objectives-based? Has the work history been consistent, sporadic, or spotty? Just what is his or her track record?

Ⓠ How much information can you answer about the work experience of your subordinate?

Ⓐ

Here are some thoughts from others about the meaningfulness of your subordinate's previous work history in regard to your developmental interview:

1. The previous successes or failures of your John or Jane Doe set up a pattern which tends to repeat itself. If you have a fast mover, competent, realistic, and hard-working, chances are you can safely project a trend line into the future to encourage similar objectives in terms of both work and personal growth. If you have an erratic, sometimes unrealistic and/or repeated failure on your hands, you are likely to be much more cautious in planning the future, even in the face of a recently concluded successful operation.

2. Almost everyone has parts of the job which are liked more than others and parts which tend to be (deliberately) forgotten. Noting these will be an important part of readying a realistic growth plan. Not to take them into account runs the risk of having the other individual once more set the priorities for the future and perhaps hide certain things from your attention.

3. Being aware of the person's career movements in the past, especially those before he or she became under your supervision, is the only way to get the full picture of the person you are helping develop. Noting persistency versus straying off course is a help in delineating future plans. Knowing how realistic the person's ambitions of the past have been is an aid in judging the realism of new plans. Here, as in so many other things, history tends to repeat itself.

PERSONAL GOALS OF YOUR SUBORDINATE

What are you aware of regarding the personal goals and ambitions of this individual? Does the person have any personal goals, work goals, or goals in life? Does he or she have hopes of moving up in the organization? Does this individual have any financial goals that provide incentive or any professional growth goals to work toward? Does he or she plan to stay in your work unit continuing working in the same field? Or does he or she plan to change directions in terms of professional or technical interests? Does this individual have designs on your job? Is he or she desirous of changing geographical location? Is he or she applying to join your country club? What kind of family plans does the person have—more children, college education for the children, a new car, a new spouse? How will all this influence your developmental interview?

> **Q** What are the personal goals of your John or Jane Doe?
>
> **A**

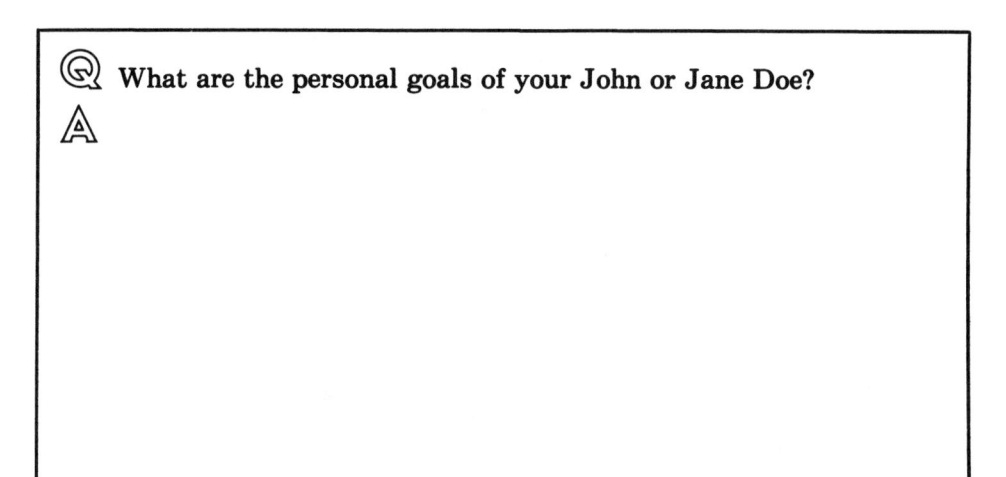

Goals are what stimulate people to action. The more you know about your subordinate's goals in life, the more you have to work with in order to motivate him or her to put forth the energy it will take to engage in the developmental activities you have in mind. You may need an incentive to prompt the person to make a commitment to your plan—what you know about personal ambitions provides that incentive.

Personal goals which are clearly inconsistent with the assumed goals or direction of the plan you have developed are of obvious importance in reconciling the views of the two of you. It will do little good to encourage growth in one technical area, when the individual already has his or her mind set on changing careers to another area. So too, planning growth that will require continued help from you as a supervisor won't get much support if the person has already decided to ask for a transfer away from you.

The person without goals, or who never verbalizes those goals (even to self) is in need of some coaching about the importance of having goals in life. You have prepared a plan of development and now you realize that plan assumed something which doesn't exist: goals. You must therefore devote most of the time in the upcoming interview to help delineate some goals and delay the growth plan to a later time.

There is a story about Mrs. Franklin Delano Roosevelt when she was a student at Bennington College. She was required to get a job in the communications industry in order to earn certain credits. Her father got her an interview with his friend, General David Sarnoff, then chairman of RCA. "The General asked me what kind of job I wanted," Mrs. Roosevelt recalled. "I told him I'd take anything. But the General told me he didn't have a job classification called 'Anything.' He looked me straight in the eye and reminded me that the route to success is paved in goals."

As you look back over the list of answers to our series of five questions, you must be honest with yourself. If you have actually attempted to write down the answers as we went along, you probably feel (as do 80 percent of workshop participants,) that you do not really know your subordinate as well as you might like to. We always seem to take so much for granted, even about those very close to us.

If you find this to be the case, you may wish to develop within yourself the ability to be more observant and remembering of the important characteristics of your workers. You do this by practicing writing such descriptions as we have just tried. It's much like a painter who seeks to improve the skill of capturing on canvas the details of what the painting depicts. In order to fix more of these details on the mind so as to be more descriptive of the real world, the painter simply paints. It is by painting that the painter increases the skill of capturing details.

So here you can improve your skill in describing the important characteristics of your people by practicing. Repeat the exercise we have just done on several of your employees. Get the facial characteristics, the mannerisms, the work habits, the relationships, the things outside the job that pressure them, as well as the more familiar job situations. Begin to look for things and recall these things when you are planning to communicate with them. As you practice, it is not the length of your answers that counts; it is the accuracy.

Finally, as you gain practice, try coming up with a description of your "best" subordinate and then of your "worst." Which one is a more detailed and accurate picture? Chances are you have done a more exhaustive job on the "poorer" performer because this person is more often in your mind and in your way. And while this individual deserves your attention, so does the good performer. All need to grow, and if you ignore the good performer for being good, that's a strange kind of reward.

SOME NOT TOO RARE BIRDS

To be a good coach and succeed in the kind of developmental interview we are preparing for, the manager has to be a bit of an ornithologist. There are some not too rare birds which you will want to be able to identify as the interview develops, so as to use appropriate strategies which will enhance the communications process. If you can anticipate that John or Jane Doe, based on what you know about their background characteristics, is likely to turn into one of these common birds, you can be prepared to take effective measures. What follows is a description of seven birds based on typical reactions on the part of people you are trying to develop. About each you will be asked what tactics you might want to suggest. You can then compare your suggestions with the advice given in the text based on discussions with practicing workshop participants.

The Angry Person

This is the person who "flies off the handle" whenever you suggest there might be some area of improvement. Some people get quite angry when you use a tactful approach.

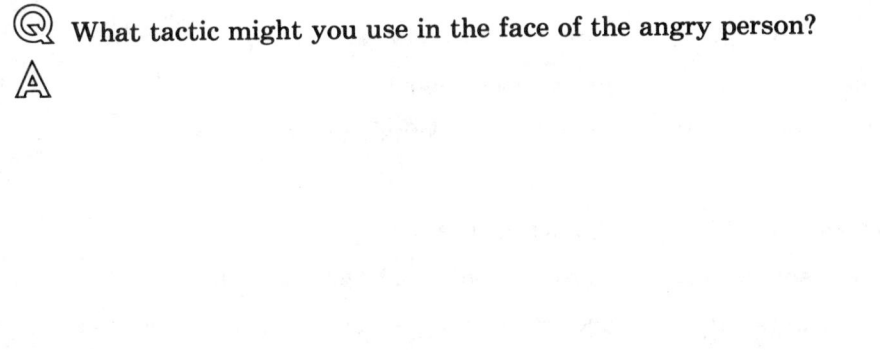

Q What tactic might you use in the face of the angry person?

A

Suggestions: Don't add fuel to the fire. Let this person get the anger off his or her chest. If you argue, or show your authority, or become angry yourself, you may come out of the discussion a victor in your own eyes, but it's not likely to change the other person's attitude or bring about improvement. Be a good listener. Beneath this individual's words may lie feelings of insecurity, disappointment, or resentment. If you remain calm you might understand those feelings and help overcome them by being more realistic.

Don't expect to accomplish too much in one sitting. Try to set up a follow-up meeting to nail down the development plan. Hopefully, this person will be more prepared for it and not lose his or her temper then. To help the person calm down, remember the technique called *reflection* or *mirror*. For example:

Supervisor: John, I'm especially concerned about the complaints we've been getting from the production department. Now, they're probably unfounded in some instances, you know, due to pressure being put to them and so forth; but what do you think we can do about the complaints that you don't provide any help?

Subordinate: Don't provide any help? Me? (Rising and now starting to bang fist on the desk.) Why, that's the pot calling the kettle black! I'm having trouble with every single production supervisor out there in explaining what it is they want from me. I'm not a mind reader! It's those supervisors who are uncooperative! Not a single one of them answers my questions!

Supervisor: Everyone of them is uncooperative?

Subordinate: Yeah, they're not helping one single bit.

Supervisor: Not a single one helps you?

Subordinate: Well, most of them anyway.

Supervisor: Most of them refuse to help?

Subordinate: Well, they don't really refuse; but they're all dumb.

Supervisor: They're all dumb?

Subordinate: Like I said, most of them are.

Supervisor: Most of our production supervisors are dumb?

Subordinate: (By now talking much more slowly and beginning to return to his chair.) Well, not most of them, but enough.

Supervisor: All right, just how many is enough?

Subordinate: Well, most of my contact is with John Brown, and that guy really doesn't understand what I'm looking for. If we could talk to someone else down there we might give them the help they're looking for. . . .

Notice what has happened. The simple repetition of the unverifiable shoutings, the opportunity to hear how wildly generalized they were is all it takes to help the outraged individual calm down. Hearing how unsubstantiated his own words are, the angry individual is pacified.

The Person Who Agrees Too Quickly

Some people agree almost instantly in order to avoid emphasis on the need for improvement. Some do it to avoid criticism. Some agree because they don't understand what you are driving at or to cover up their disagreement with you.

Q What suggestions do you have to handle the person who agrees too quickly?

A

Suggestions: There are two main species of this rare bird—the one who agrees very quickly, and then acts accordingly, making no inputs; and the one who agrees and then does the exact opposite. For the first variety, it's a matter of opening up the individual. You will want to use open-ended questions or statements. You will provide on-the-spot training in coming up with creative suggestions. Review everything about the atmosphere, your tone of voice, and so on, to do away with anything threatening which may be holding the person back. Again, you must practice listening skills, especially the pause, so as to encourage talk by the other party. Perhaps emphasizing the team or participative approach to searching for a development plan will encourage him or her to voice an opinion. For this individual, it is especially important to get solid feedback. A ready assent may not be assumed to mean a ready comprehension. Get the commitment voiced back in the person's own words. Be extremely wary of over-committing this individual because he or she is apparently so willing to go along with you.

For the second variety, use all the previously mentioned strategies with particular emphasis on the details of feed-forward. Get a specific statement of exactly what is to happen next to ensure the subordinate does not go off and do something other than that to which assent is being given. The more personal involvement you can get out of the other party, the more likely this bird will fly a true course. Your ability to ask good open questions will help. It might be a matter of his or her feeling intimidated or anxious to get the meeting over; consequently, he or she promises anything, with no intention of living up to it. Establishing good rapport (even to the point of going back to square one and almost starting the interview over by reestablishing rapport) is essential.

The Older Person

The person who happens to be your elder deserves special, considerate treatment. Do not assume there is no need for development just because he or she has been around for several years. Such a person may not be enthusiastic about promotion, but may be very concerned about holding his or her present status. Ambitions may be more modest than in the younger person, but worries may be greater.

Q What tactics would you advise for the older person?

A

Suggestions: Team spirit, explained in such a way that age is immaterial, is especially important for the older person. In any team, the ability of the individual to fulfill his or her role is what counts. You should establish good feelings by showing empathy for the individual who might have added family responsibilities. Such persons need clearly defined goals to know they are carrying out their assigned responsibilities in a satisfactory manner. They usually accept responsibility and need to know they have the authority that goes with their position—that they have earned this authority and that you (younger person) are not going to deny them that. Let the older person realize you are not going to show any special favoritism because of age but, by the same token, you are going to expect them to follow the same procedures as anyone else, even to the point of personal growth.

You will have to expect more resistance to change from the entrenched individual, and therefore must be careful to show reasons for changes you might be introducing. Remain objective when you respond to the "good old days" routine which the older person likes to throw up to you; don't descend into similar subjectivity. Above all, be ready to learn from the older person, calling upon him or her to help develop others through a buddy system, for example. Stress the contribution the older person has already made and can continue to make, with more and more emphasis on teaching others.

Be sensitive to role expectations. Older persons can make life miserable for a younger superior by statements like, "OK, young fella, what new tricks have you got? I've been through twenty other supervisors in your shoes. How long will you last?" On one such occasion, I was asked to counsel with the older person to find out the reason for this behavior. The older person said, quite candidly, "Oh, that's just a game we're expected to play. Everyone knows I treat them all that way. I assumed he'd been warned and I wouldn't want to disappoint him."

The Person Who Won't Talk

Sometimes you find someone who just won't open up. He or she answers direct questions in a few words, but does not enter into the conversation freely, even when encouraged to do so. Why is this person unresponsive? Is it nervousness? Is it just the person's nature?

Q What advice do you have for the person who won't talk?

A

Suggestions: This is probably the individual who is most insecure. Above all, you need a relaxed environment; the self-appraisal and invitation to prepare his or her own development plan is paramount. You will thereby not only show this is not to be a scolding session, but a positive one and hopefully establish rapport, but you will also be priming the pump, so to speak. Let the person know that when you meet, you will be expecting him or her to be the first one to come up with items to discuss. Perhaps all that is needed is for the individual to hear the sound of his or her own voice. Then you will need to give a considerable amount of positive reinforcement at first. That insecurity will forever be a wall between the two of you if you do not breech it by supportive encouragement and showing a personal interest that comes across as sincere and genuine. Remember, too, all we said about the person who agrees too quickly: show good listening skills, good questioning techniques, and constantly ask for feedback.

The Person Who Wants Too Much

Some subordinates may expect commendation to result in an immediate reward (raise or promotion), or may otherwise overemphasize quick appreciation by you for a job well done.

Q What tactics would you use with the person who wants too much too soon?

A

Suggestions: This individual needs to see the difference between the long range and the short range. While every job well done deserves to be appreciated, it takes a series of short run successes to qualify for consideration of a permanent reward like pay raise and/or promotion. And even then, it would only be a consideration. This type person is the one who must not fall into the trap of the Peter Principle, as explained in chapter 6. Competence on the present job does not guarantee success on the next job. This thought ought to open the door to a consideration of how you are going to get the subordinate ready for the next step up the ladder, which will be your developmental plan for him or her. By demonstrating a series of short-range achievements, this good worker will qualify ultimately for the reward being asked for now. Each success is one more milestone on the road to qualifying, but one must traverse the whole road, not a single piece of it.

Parenthetically, it should be mentioned here that earlier "promises" (such as those made by a recruiter) may be what has brought about the unrealistic expectations on the part of the subordinate. "They told me I could make Department Head within six months when I took this job." Such avowals are always impossible to verify, and even when taken at face value must be explained as a kind of recruiter's hyperbole. The individual who made such a statement should not be encouraged to continue doing so, for such wild phrases made in the heat of trying to fill vacancies with up-and-coming performers come home to roost when you, the manager, have to face the impossibility of living up to them. You may literally have to "eat a little crow" because of someone else making such rash statements. Usually there are company policies regarding promotion, average length of time in grade, prerequisites for consideration of moving ahead, qualifications for pay adjustments, and the like. These could be helpful to show the person what it takes on the part of anyone in the organization to enjoy the kind of rewards he or she desires. Of course there are always exceptions to any policy regarding qualifications, otherwise the really outstanding performer would be held back. But now you have a chance to objectively examine whether the person in hand has, in fact, performed steadily enough at exceptional levels to deserve special consideration.

A final mental block such individuals often have regarding not being moved up as quickly as they might like is their lack of appreciation for the experience to be gained in the same or other job of the same level before being promoted. Your developmental plan may include suggestions by way of job rotation, for example, which would provide useful rounding out. The subordinate must be made to see the knowledge and skills gained from those assignments as prerequisites for the next position. It is up to you to clarify the nature of those assignments and show how they enter into judgments and decisions to be made at a higher level.

The Quitter

Sometimes during a development discussion, you discover that the subordinate wants to quit. You had intentions of helping the person improve his or her position (even without promotion), and now you find that you have a shorttimer on your hands.

Q What tactics might be used with the quitter?

A

Suggestions: In many instances this revelation brings about an immediate stop to the conversation, when it actually ought to open up a whole new discussion. Using good listening and questioning skills, you must probe to find out the real reason for the decision or threat to quit. Is there some factual reason, such as the transfer of a spouse to another geographic location? Is it a matter of another job opportunity, perhaps with the promise of more money? Is it because of boredom, or perception of no opportunity for advancement, or displeasing assignments, or a personality clash on the present job, or your own style of supervision, or something similar which falls within your power to examine and possibly change? If the reasons are completely outside the pale of your influence, you probably will not try to get the individual to change his or her mind, but you should argue for giving a whole-hearted performance on the job as long as the person is still with you. If the reasons have to do with something within your purview, you now have a golden opportunity to strike a bargain with the person. We have stressed that development, provision of opportunities for growth, is a mutual thing; so if your subordinate will expend the energy needed on the development plan, you will offer to work on the aspect found to be unacceptable.

This does not mean you are going to let yourself be blackmailed. There are those who quit every other Thursday like clockwork. Of course they never mean it, but simply use this as a ploy to get management to yield on some point. If you sense this ploy, you will probably accept the resignation. Even then, however, the individual must continue to earn a paycheck until the resignation becomes effective, so growth is still a topic for discussion.

The Individual With Repeated Needs

About some subordinates you may ask yourself, "What can I say month after month, year after year, to the same person when nothing I've said in ages has helped bring about any significant change?" You talk about development and you realize you've been over this ground before, and you wonder if it's any use.

Q What can be done with the individual with repeated needs?

A

Suggestions: Apparently you have an unsatisfactory performer on your hands, someone who has repeatedly not been making progress as desired in the past. Going back to the three types of workers we identified in chapter 3, you will recall that after two or three attempts to help someone grow, repeated failure to raise performance to an acceptable level may eventually bring you to the realization that this person will never be able to make the grade. Sometimes you just have to face the fact that dismissal may very well be the appropriate action step. An interim step, as a first stage before the final blow, could be some formal warning or other provision of the disciplinary procedure for unsatisfactory performance.

But these steps should not be taken until you have made absolutely sure the fault might not lie with you. It could be that the repeated needs you have identified are really not worth the individual's effort. Go back to the first step of the communications process and challenge the idea in your own head: is it really worth communicating, deserving of the energy you're spending on it? Then go to the second step of the process—your attempts to get the idea across to the other individual. Could it be you are not as skilled in presenting the issue to your subordinate as you should be? Perhaps you could get the assistance from someone else in explaining the need, or in working out successful ways to overcome the need. In other words, you are challenging your own ability as a coach before you give up on the potential of the other person.

SUMMARY

Preparing for an interview is extremely important. Having something important to say and figuring out how you will say it is a large part of that preparation. Of equal importance is sizing up the individual whose performance and development you will be discussing. If you take the time to review what you know about the background characteristics of the particular person, you will minimize poor communications. The two of you will be more on the same wavelength because you will be aware of a lot of things important to that person. Then if you can recognize characteristics on the part of the subordinate which sound like one of our not so rare birds, you will be preparing yourself not to get caught unexpectantly. You will have some possible strategies to draw upon as needed and will more than likely have a better interview than if you go in cold, feeling, "Well of course I can have the interview—it's only talking to so and so...."

Peter Drucker, in the opening essay of his *Technology, Management and Society,* maintains that we know more about communications than we have been able to apply. We know, for example, that the communicator does not communicate—he only utters. Whether or not the communicator gets through depends less on his or her eloquence and logic and more on the frame of reference available to the perceiver by virtue of experience. The communicator's success depends largely upon how well he or she understands the perceiver, *but managers rarely make the required effort.*

6 THE ANNUAL PERFORMANCE PREVIEW

Those who cannot remember the past are condemned to repeat it.

GEORGE SANTAYANA

Now that you have clarified your ideas as to what you wish to recommend to your subordinate by way of personal growth or development, and considered the likely reaction on the part of the receiver (decoder) of that message, you will set up a meeting to discuss these ideas. We suggest that the most appropriate vehicle for this sort of discussion is the annual performance evaluation meeting. It should provide the optimum environment for personal growth communicating.

Much has been written and said about this annual exercise concerning whether it wastes the time of a lot of people or if it accomplishes any good. Every so often someone will do a survey to find out what practicing managers think of the advantages or disadvantages of formal performance appraisal programs. Over the years, the same basic pros and cons are mentioned.

Reasons *for* a performance appraisal program include: (1) it provides an orderly system for salary reviews; (2) it summarizes the day-to-day observations of a supervisor about his or her team; (3) it gives top management a formal review of the strengths and weaknesses of its human assets; (4) it helps in selecting people for higher-level responsibilities; (5) it provides a system to eliminate "dead wood"; (6) it offers a means to improve management of the business; (7) it uncovers talents and provides a basis for people-power inventory; (8) it shows if operating plans have been implemented; (9) it assists in placing the right person on the right job; (10) it encourages and facilitates the development of managers; (11) it gives managers insight on how they are doing in their job; (12) it insures continuation of good management and promotion-from-within; (13) it shows in what areas additional training is necessary; and (14) it provides a basis for establishing goals for improvement of performance.

Some reasons *against* a performance appraisal program include: (1) top management is close enough to other supervisors to measure results; (2) a competent manager continually appraises and discusses performance with subordinates; (3) it does nothing for the incompetent manager and saddles the competent one with more paper work; and (4) it usually becomes only a paper exercise which offers too few results for the effort and time expended.

Despite all this, it has been estimated that about 80 percent of this country's business firms and somewhat less of the other organizations (government, health care, educational, etc.) have some form of formal annual performance appraisal system. Such a percentage therefore includes a number of organizations with people who feel very strongly about some of the reasons against having formal appraisals. One such executive's comments might serve as the jumping-off point of the approach we would like to offer with regard to this often misused tool:

> Some form of management appraisal is necessary to do as good a job of development of people as business does in the development of its technology and operations. The difficulty in devising and administering an effective one can be divided into two areas: (1) the program has to be designed for a specific purpose—it cannot do all things for all people; and (2) the people who administer the program must be in sympathy with the objective, understand and accept the program's limitations and work hard at achieving objectivity in administering it. If managerial appraisal can help managers help themselves it is good idea. Since it is not an exact method of measurement it can be misleading if given too much weight....

For those who believe in a results-oriented approach to management, which must include both determination of desired results and evaluation of actual results against what was desired, the concepts of annual performance appraisal can be vastly improved if essential caveats are heeded.

First, the annual formal review can never take the place of the manager's ongoing responsibility to evaluate performance. Performance ought to be examined, applauded, or corrected as soon as possible after it occurs. Hence, evaluation is a daily chore, not something done once a year when the personnel office sends a form asking for a written report of an individual's behavior to justify some payroll action. As a matter of fact, if the evaluating is not done on a day-to-day basis, there can be little objectivity in the annual evaluation, due to lack of data upon which to base an impartial judgment.

Second, the focus of the annual discussion must be changed from salary administration to people development. This might be accomplished if managers were more cognizant of the total rationale behind the annual ritual. To become more aware of this total rationale, let's back up and ask the question holistically:

> **Q** Why should you, as a busy manager, take the time each year to sit down with each subordinate and conduct an annual performance evaluation interview?
>
> **A**

I have some pretty definite thoughts on a useful way of answering the previous question. You might wish to check off your reasons against mine. I believe there are five basic reasons why you should devote your valuable time to this exercise. They in turn suggest certain things that take place during the performance interview. You might wish to ask yourself about each of these as we go along: "When I conduct a performance interview, do I accomplish this item?"

PERFORMANCE IMPROVEMENT

Without a doubt, the first and foremost reason why you want to review performance with your subordinate is to try to bring about improved performance in the unit which you manage. After all, that is the focal point of all your supervisory functions from planning to motivating to controlling. Hence, you should periodically examine and compare the actual results with the desired results in order to maximize the latter. This suggests that discussion ought not to stop with an examination of the past but should move on to the preparation of some plan for action based on what has been learned from the past. If performance has been good, what can we learn from that successful experience in order to get more of the same in the future? What can we point to in the record of John or Jane that helped make the good results? Can these results be shared with others so they can emulate John or Jane? If performance has been poor, what can we learn from that unsatisfactory performance in order to prevent the same from occurring the next time around? How can we prevent the same mistakes from happening? In order to better ourselves we should look at the past as though it were a mirror reflecting the future. The reason we study history in any context is to learn from the experience of the past.

This exercise is probably misnamed; Performance *Pre*view is a lot more meaningful than Performance *Re*view. What we wish to do during this interview is not reach into the closet and drag out all the skeletons, reminding John or Jane of all the mistakes made during the past year, or pat them on the back for the things done well—they should have heard about those things when they happened. What we really wish to do is learn from those events and ask their cooperation in building upon those experiences for the future. And because recollecting past events usually takes less time than planning future ones, perhaps at least as much time should be spent looking to the future during these interviews as looking to the past. Can *you* honestly say that when you conduct performance evaluation interviews you spend at least as much time talking about the future as about the past? (If you can, you're in the minority.)

DEVELOPING PEOPLE

A second important reason to take the time to conduct annual performance interviews is the desire to develop people. As a manager you have a responsibility to the firm to constantly work towards the best organizing of resources possible. People organizing is part of this ongoing concern, and hopefully not always in a crisis mode; that is, scurrying around trying to find someone qualified to fill a position after it opens up. Rather, you hope to get to the point where you have *organizational surplus,* an abundance of people qualified for bigger and better things, so that when an opening does occur, there will be someone there to fill it.

You also have a responsibility to motivate your people to help the individuals who wish to acquire the knowledge, skills, or attitudes needed to be eligible for one of these bigger and better jobs when the opening occurs. The hope is that you practice a promotion policy which combines some promoting from within and some hiring from without. Too much hiring from without hurts morale because people think their jobs are dead-end. Too much promoting from within sometimes leads to management feeding on its own ideas and perhaps stagnating. You will be able to stimulate your people to grow because they know some individuals do get to move ahead when the nice plum jobs come along.

For both these reasons, then, you will want to spend a good deal of time talking to your subordinate during the annual performance interview about getting ready to handle performance in bigger and better jobs. This is what the personal development plan you have worked up is all about; hence, this interview is the appropriate time to discuss it. Have you? Can you say that when you conduct performance evaluations you spend a reasonable time talking about personal growth?

THE PRESENT AND FUTURE

Closely related, and maybe only another way of saying the same thing, is a third specific reason for conducting the annual performance appraisal interview. You wish to answer the three questions which seem to be the recurrent concern of almost every member of the organization, and which can be answered with finality only by the manager: "How am I doing? Where might I go from here? What are we going to do to help me get there?"

This is an attempt to put yourself in the other person's shoes. He or she comes into the interview expecting to get straight answers to these questions. The individual already has a personal opinion (sometimes based on objective facts) as to the answers, but needs them confirmed by the authority figure. This has happened all through our life. From the time we are children, we look to the authority figures in our life to confirm or deny our behavior patterns. The child learning to ride a bike or adding a column of numbers says, "Hey, Dad, is this right?" or "Hey, Mom, tell me how I'm doing." When the child becomes a student in school, he or she needs the authority figure to confirm performance in the classroom. The student knows when a test has been passed or failed, but sometimes hopes against hope that the teacher grades on the curve, and so once again an authority figure is needed—this time the teacher—to confirm the best or worst. Now in adult life, the subordinates, all the way up to officers of the corporation, ought to have a good idea of how well they've done, but still need the reality of the authority figure as proof positive that what they anticipated is for real. And so, as a manager you will give direct answers to these questions in the mind of the individual you are interviewing.

Notice it is not only a matter of judging present performance, "How am I doing?" but also two questions which are future oriented: "Where do I go from here?" and "What are we going to do to help me get there?" These last two are clearly developmental questions which are the reason for the development plan we've been preparing so far. Yet, these are the questions which are all too often neglected in the evaluation interviews.

This is when we become a statistic to prove the Peter Principle. You'll recall the work of Professor Lawrence Peter and others indicating that there is a tendency in many large organizations for people to rise to their level of incompetence. This happens, we are told, because all too often the promotion decision is made after considering only one question: "Is the individual performing well?" A positive response seems to get the conclusion, "Therefore this person deserves a promotion!" when in reality, that is a faulty syllogism. A second premise must be established before we can conclude anything about promotion. We must be assured that the individual shows signs of being able to perform well at the next level before we can be safe in recommending promotion. Or we get a negative answer, "This person does not perform well." Immediately it is concluded, "Oh well, then he or she does not deserve a promotion." End of discussion! That should be the beginning of quite a long new discussion. What are we going to do about such a person? Fire him, train him, transfer him (Peter's lateral arabesque), ask him to step back a level to where performance would be satisfactory, or what? Something must be done besides just leaving the person there.

Our study of client organizations shows there is a 50-50 chance that any given subordinate will not get a straight answer on these three questions. The reasons for this lack of candor between managers and their people are varied. Try your hand here at guessing what they are. First take your strong right arm, the trusted assistant who is the backbone of your unit, the person who undoubtedly has accomplished all his or her assignments well. Chances are 50-50 you will not tell this individual straight between the eyes how good performance has been.

> **Q** Why is it that half the time you are likely not to confirm for such a good performer that results are so good?
>
> **A**

Perhaps you gave any one of the following answers:

1. You really don't know performance is good, but just assumed it and don't want to put something in writing you cannot prove.

2. You fear the individual will accept the praise and then ask for a pay raise, and you have no way of increasing pay right now.

3. You're afraid the individual will get big-headed if performance is so good, and will ask for a promotion; worse, ask for your job.

4. You fear that your strong right arm, knowing how good a performer he or she is and that you cannot give money or promotion, may get designs on a better job somewhere else, leaving you holding the bag.

5. You fear that too much praise will lead the person to become overconfident or careless in the future, leading to poor work.

These are the most common reasons we have encountered in discussions with practicing managers. If you go back and look at the list you will find the common denominator in each one is the manager's fear of something that will hurt him or her. There is no concern for the good of the subordinate or the organization, but only of the manager—good old number one! Fear of not knowing how to cope with a request for money or promotion; fear of losing a valued person because that means picking up the load; fear of being caught without substantiating information for a laudatory judgment; fear of work slackening and hurting the subsequent reputation of one's own leadership abilities.

Now consider another situation. Think of the weakest individual in your group, the person who has not met performance standards, the one who may be dragging the whole unit down. Chances are 50-50 you will not tell this individual either exactly how poor performance is.

Q Why is it that half the time you are likely not to confirm for such a poor performer that results are bad?

A

You could have thought of any one of the following reasons:

1. You really don't have any proof of poor performance beyond a lot of crises and subjective judgments you cannot document.

2. If you tell the individual the frank truth, the reaction will be to punch you in the nose.

3. You fear that if you level with the individual, your name around the organization will be mud from then on due to back-stabbing.

4. You fear that such an honest judgment will cause the individual to quit trying altogether, being convinced there is no way to please you.

5. You fear that, faced with the facts of an unpleasant future with you, the individual will ask for a transfer or will quit outright.

6. You feel your judgment might be appealed.

Notice again in this list the common denominator is still your fear for yourself. Fear of physical or verbal attack; fear of not being able to prove your point; fear of even worse performance to hurt your reputation; even fear of losing the individual, because if that happens, you might have to do some of the work yourself, or train a replacement, or worry about whom you're going to get next, when you're already scraping the bottom of the barrel!

It must also be pointed out here that if the subordinate comes to the interview with these questions in his or her mind, and does not get an answer, perhaps this individual has some responsibility to verbalize the questions outright in order to help the manager overcome some of these fears and answer the questions. But, respect for authority or fear of the boss being what they are, it often takes quite a lot before a subordinate will be that aggressive.

An illustration of how bad things can get might help. One manager related this story about his own experience:

> I never got straight answers to these questions, and that didn't really bother me until last year when my personal situation made the answers imperative. You see, my wife and I had one child and a second was on the way, and so we were looking for a new home since we were outgrowing the old one. And we'd been saving, so we had enough money for the down payment on the home we wanted, but the realtor told us we wouldn't get the mortgage approved unless we could point to expectations of further pay raises in the near future. Well, I waited until my annual performance review, hoping to find out then. But do you know I talked to my boss for four hours in the interview and the so-and-so never told me anything concrete! So I was forced to tell him almost with tears in my eyes and clenched fist that if he didn't have anything more specific to tell me, I'd miss this chance on the house and maybe face increasing prices and never get caught up. . . ."

First, this case borders on injustice. The manager has the well being and future of that subordinate and his whole family in the palm of his hand; yet he won't speak openly and straightforward. Second, the individual must at times ask for the straight answers when they are not forthcoming on their own. The same comments are relevant for the employee who has never had a performance review of any sort at all by the boss.

TEAM BUILDING

A fourth reason for conducting the annual interview after considering performance improvement and personal development is to bring home the point that both of these are being encouraged on the part of the individual as a member of a larger work group. This means that the discussion affords a golden opportunity to reinforce the need for coordinating the company, division, department, and individual goals and performance. This is team building. You want the subordinate to know that when results on his or her part were favorable, the entire organization benefitted.

You also want to stress that when results were below satisfactory the entire organization suffered. This is what the football coach does week after week in reviewing the films of the previous game. He will tell an individual player to watch how a block missed here or a cut made there was responsible for a play being broken apart. It's hard enough in the midst of day-to-day pressures to keep the overall mission in mind. The interview provides a time of reflection in which this important realization can be reviewed.

Do you, when conducting performance reviews, take advantage of this opportunity? Of all places, this is where our major theme—that individual achievements are a contribution to organizational results—can be helpful.

DOCUMENTATION

The fifth and least important reason, in my judgment, for performance interviews is to provide necessary documentation for appropriate personnel actions. The form to be completed during this discussion is often called Personnel Action Form, which has all too often stressed this aspect of the discussion much more than it deserves, and has been the basis for much of the abhorrence of evaluations. While it is true that in a complex organization we need some mechanism for documenting performance records, appraisals, and recommendations, the documentation is only the tail and should not wag the dog.

You will recognize the syndrome if you find yourself grabbing a subordinate five minutes before quitting time and saying, "John, before you go, I wish you'd sign this appraisal form. They've been after me in Personnel for over a week now, and if we don't get this sent in to them, they won't have your pay adjustment ready for the next paycheck.... Thanks.... Have a nice week-end."

Doing all or any of this just to send in a form to some staff office is clearly putting the cart before the horse. You want the face-to-face meeting first, and only as a logical conclusion do you wish to notify others who need to have this information in order to be of assistance on filling their proper role. Perhaps one way of improving the appraisal process is by changing the very title of the paper work used. We have already recommended use of a form labelled Personal Development Plan. This should be part of the paper work and thereby force attention to this aspect of the discussion.

An anterior document might also be helpful, one which calls for a written judgment about the present performance of the individual and which then leads to the determination of development needs. This is often done in many organizations by the use of what is most often called a Performance

Appraisal (Review, Evaluation) form. Typically the form looks like Figure 6-1. It is called a *Performance Evaluation* form, but the items listed for evaluation are basically *personality* traits, characteristics which it is hoped are found in all useful employees. The difficulty is that even when there is an attempt to define these terms, the only way to rank a person exhibiting them is through subjective judgment. Another subjective judgment is involved when the form itself uses the column approach which asks for a check in an appropriate box. Could you clearly define the difference between someone whose initiative is "very good" versus someone whose initiative is only "good"? Nor does it get any easier when those who push quantification convince you to remove the adjectives from the columns and replace them with numbers. What's the difference between a 7 and a 6 on initiative?

These subjective judgments are what have led most employees to resent the whole appraisal idea. They go before a supervisor who presumes to play God with their future by making evaluations on the basis of some sort of assumed superior knowledge, rather than on the basis of any demonstrable facts. The employee under such a system really has little chance of receiving any help. Either he or she has pleased the manager who simply marks the person's performance satisfactory and is happy the whole thing can be dispensed within a matter of minutes, or he or she is not "in favor" with the manager who proceeds to scold or demand unrealistic changes in personality without ever constructively showing the connection between these demands and the actual job performance.

Because it is so difficult to justify any rating using the approach shown in Figure 6-1, most managers fail to make a convincing explanation, and most subordinates don't listen to the poor one that is given. Result? Little communication takes place. The upshot of the whole encounter is an exposure of raw nerves, with little attempt at conversation. A piece of paper is signed and sent to "document" the subordinate's worth to the organization.

What has happened is that a means has become an end in itself. What should be discussed as tools or obstacles to a job (attitudes, skills, and the other traits) have been made the end-all and be-all of the evaluation because they are the items listed on the form. The subordinate does not understand why these highly personal characteristics are of any concern to the manager and usually resists discussing them. The individual is not convinced it is any of the manager's business and would prefer to choose his or her own analyst, if indeed one is needed!

Tracing the origin of these trait-oriented forms is interesting. As industrial, health care, educational, and other types of organizations became more complex it seemed appropriate to "measure" the performance of all employees by some standard set of criteria which could then be used for comparative purposes when it came to salary considerations, promotions, and the like. At a loss as to how to start such a system, these organizations went to sources who had been doing something like that for a long time—the

Figure 6-1 Traditional Evaluation Form

Performance Evaluation

Name of Employee _____   Department _____

Name of Supervisor _____   Title _____

Period Covered _____   Date _____

Instructions: Rate your subordinate on each of the items listed. Remember this evaluation will determine the salary progress of the individual. Above all, be fair.

	Superior	Excellent	Very Good	Good	Fair	Poor	Unsat
Intelligence							
Loyalty							
Initiative							
Smiling							
....							
....							

military and the civil service people in government. The upshot of it all was borrowing the process and, in some instances, the very forms which were used by others, with the same problems entailed therewith. Of course what might have made sense in an army where discipline and rules and the forming of a million copies of the same type of performer *might* have been appropriate, was not appropriate for other organizations. Possibly such a form might serve a valid purpose during the probationary period. This is the time to find out if employees have certain basic working habits. We do want them to be intelligent, to show initiative, to be cooperative, to have loyalty, to be neat and clean, to come to work on time, and so on. But after they demonstrate they have these characteristics, maybe we really shouldn't be checking twenty-nine years later to see if they still have the same qualities.

Furthermore, with the trait system, it is too easy to "beat the system." There is a delightful story of a little old lady who was the head bookkeeper

108   THE ANNUAL PERFORMANCE PREVIEW

Figure 6-2 Employee Performance Review

Name _____ Date of Birth _____

Department _____ Classification _____

Location _____ Date Employed in System _____

Education: High School _____ Years College _____ Years

Special Training _____

Other _____

Date Assigned
to Present
Classification _____

――――――――――― RATING ―――――――――――

Factors	Marginal	Acceptable	Good	Excellent	Score
	1 2	3 4	5 6	7 8	
1. Knowledge of Work	Inadequate. Relies on others.	Knows job fairly well. Requires normal instruction and supervision.	Has mastered most details. Requires little supervision.	Thoroughly informed. Requires minimum supervision and guidance.	
2. Quality of Work	Occasionally careless; makes numerous errors.	Acceptable performance. Has normal accuracy.	Work is usually organized, orderly and accurate.	Work is consistently well organized, orderly and accurate.	
3. Quantity of Work	Makes poor use of time. Frequently completes less than expected.	Performs the work assigned.	Usually produces more than expected.	Works hard. Accepts and completes more assignments.	
4. Cooperation	Occasionally causes friction or slow to follow instructions.	Business-like manner; gets along with others. Follows instructions without complaint.	Generally gets along well with supervisors and co-workers. Adapts quickly and willingly to change.	Goes out of his way to cooperate with supervisors and co-workers. Exercises self discipline.	

Figure 6-2 continued

5. Dependability

Needs to be checked on frequently.	Dependable if given normal supervision.	Dependable. Needs only occasional supervision.	Deserves confidence. Work completed on time. Willingly makes personal sacrifices.

6. Initiative

Seldom takes action alone.	Handles normal situations well, but wants help if at all out of ordinary.	Suggests improvements. Attempts to learn all related jobs.	Constantly developing work methods. Seeks knowledge of complete Company operations.

7. Judgment

Jumps to conclusions. Fails to consider facts and foresee results.	Considers facts but fails to foresee the results of decisions.	Considers facts and most decisions are acceptable.	Makes sound decisions based on thorough analysis.

8. Leadership

Does not have the respect and confidence of employees. Has difficulty communicating.	Maintains fair relations with employees, but has occasional misunderstandings.	Has respect and confidence of practically all employees and seldom has misunderstandings. Communicates well.	Outstanding in ability to plan well, assign work to best advantage, and maintain constant control of work. Makes excellent use of manpower.

9. Supervisory Ability

Lacks planning and work-control ability. Must improve appreciably.	Planning and assignment skills are limited. Needs help from superior frequently.	Shows good ability to plan and control work. Assigns work satisfactorily; makes good use of manpower.	Outstanding in ability to plan well, assign work to best advantage, and maintain constant control of work. Makes excellent use of manpower.

of a bank in a one-horse town for about twenty-nine years. And at the end of that time, they caught her embezzling—and not penny-ante stuff, either. She embezzled over one and one-half million dollars over that time (even though the bank only had assets of one million). Well, according to the story, when the auditors first suspected her of this, they inquired about her performance evaluations. And sure enough, there in the personnel files were these forms, carefully filled out for twenty-nine years. Intelligence: superior (of course she was—look at what she managed to accomplish without being detected for so long). Loyalty: superior (with a footnote averring that she never even took a vacation—guess why!). Initiative: superior (sometimes this is called "quantity of work," and this lady kept two sets of books instead of one, so . . .). Smiling: superior (as you would be if you had one and one-half million dollars belonging to the bank).

The same kind of fallacious copying of others occurs when it comes to evaluating various managers in our organizations. They are the last group to come under such scrutiny, and again we find firms turning to the approach represented by Figure 6-1, probably out of desperation. The form for hourly people was available, so it was turned into a form for supervisors' evaluation.

In recent years the weaknesses of the personality trait approach have been seen in their true light. Some have reacted by a campaign to do away with performance evaluation completely. That is like throwing out the baby with the bathwater. Because a poor approach was taken to do the job doesn't mean the job doesn't need doing. There is very good reason to take stock of one's performance on a periodic basis and document what we learn. But perhaps it ought to be self-evaluation first, done in an objective fashion; that is, a judgment based on predetermined and previously agreed upon and accepted objectives to be achieved. Managers as well as nonsupervisory personnel with discretion on the use of organizational sources can commit themselves to work toward a set of objectives. An evaluation of their accomplishments could be based on these goals, not on some other less meaningful set of criteria. (Any good text on Management by Objectives, including those by this author, will be useful to explain the principles and mechanics of setting this kind of goals.)

Some have recognized the advantages of a results-oriented approach to evaluation and have been experimenting with objective-based appraisals. Some have seen the value of appraisal and have attempted to improve the forms being used. At times this is done by providing a better definition of the scale to be used, as exemplified in Figure 6-2. At times the improvement is in better definitions of the traits being rated, as seen in Figure 6-3. Other attempts require use of an incident to justify ratings given, such as one of the latest versions of the military officer review form, partially shown in Figure 6-4.

DOCUMENTATION 111

Figure 6-3 Employee Performance Rating

Name _____	Position Title _____
Division _____	Department _____
Supervisor _____	Date _____

Instructions: Select appropriate rating from those listed for each performance criterion as explained.

Performance Criteria	*Exceptional*	*Above Norm*	*Normal*	*Below Norm*	*Poor*
Skills and Ability (personal qualifications including the skills, knowledge, and judgment to meet job requirements)					
Quality of Work (thoroughness and accuracy of work; resourcefulness and initiative; reliability)					
Dependability (ability to follow through on assignments, work without direct supervision; accountability)					
Attitude and Conduct (attitude toward work; cooperativeness; skill in dealing with others)					
Attendance (frequency of absenteeism, sickness, tardiness; length of relief time and lunch periods)					
Managerial Effectiveness (ability to direct work of others; effectiveness in training subordinates; effectiveness of communications with supervisors and subordinates)					

Figure 6-4 Dept Army Form 67-7 (partial)

Part IV - Professional Attributes	Yes	*Needs Improvement		*No
		Some	Much	
1. Has this officer demonstrated moral and character strength?				
2. Did this officer demonstrate technical competence appropriate to his grade and branch?				
3. Did this officer state, as appropriate, his honest opinions and convictions? (Not a "yes" man)				
4. Did this officer seek responsibility?				
5. Did this officer willingly accept full accountability for his actions and the actions of his subordinates?				
6. Is this officer emotionally stable under stress?				
7. Is this officer's judgment reliable?				
8. Did this officer maintain effective two-way communications with juniors, seniors and peers?				
9. Did this officer demonstrate concern for the best interests of his subordinates?				
10. Did this officer contribute to the personal and professional development of his subordinates?				
11. Did this officer subordinate his personal interests and welfare to those of his organization and subordinates?				
*You are required to cite *specific* examples or illustrations in Part VII to support this rating.				

These forms probably make it easier for the superior to make a judgment. In fact, they often put words in the mouth of the manager in trying to capture what a subordinate does or does not do. But they ignore the issue of getting pre-agreement from the subordinate that these descriptions are, in fact, the kind of performance to which he or she feels committed. Only an approach where objectives are agreed upon mutually in advance provides the criteria which will be acceptable to both as a means of measurement. When this is done on an individual basis, as we have been stressing throughout this book, then the real message can come through—the person is being appraised not to find out if he or she conforms to some hypothetical ideal, but to find out if he or she is keeping the commitments made. The interest is not in who the person is, but in what he or she accomplishes. The competition is not against other employees to get a promotion or pay raise, but against the challenge which was set by that same individual as a description of satisfactory performance. This applies to job related objectives and to personal development objectives. Examples of attempts to do this are found in Figures 6-5 and 6-6.

STEP-BY-STEP PROCEDURE

If the five previously mentioned purposes of the appraisal interview are to be accomplished, there should be a step-by-step procedure instituted in the organization to ensure the right kind of evaluations. You might wish to consider the following, making modifications to fit different classifications of personnel. For example, those with less discretion about the use of their

Figure 6-5 Review of Objectives, Performance, and Development (for supervisors)

Name_____	Date _____
Department_____	Time in Position_____
Title _____	Last Review Date_____
Immediate Supervisor _____	Type of Review: 6 mo, 1 yr, Prob.

I. Objectives: These are the four most important objectives   Target Dates

  1. _____ _____

  2. _____ _____

  3. _____ _____

  4. _____ _____

In order to meet these objectives, I would like to get the following kinds of knowledge, skill, or understanding:

I feel this additional knowledge, skill, or understanding can most economically be obtained by:

II. Results of past twelve months:

Strong areas of performance:

Areas where performance should be strengthened:

Probable causes for poor performance:

Way employee displayed potential for increased responsibility in present position or at higher level:

Figure 6-6 Performance Evaluation and Activity Report

This information may be used in decisions concerning advancement, reassignment, future training needs, performance related salary adjustments, and as evidence in contested disciplinary actions. The employee may legally refuse to provide the information, but failure to do so may hinder any of the above decisions. Activity managers are required to report on program budget objectives via this form, however, the Program Budget review *will not* enter into individual performance evaluations.	
Employee _____	Position Control No._____
Position Title _____	Department/Division_____
Classification _____	Appraisal Period _____ to _____
Supervisor _____	Date Performance Measures Est. _____
Employee's signature _____	Date _____
Supervisor's signature _____	Date _____
Description of Current Operation: (Activity managers should complete this item; others need not)	
Responsibility Number from Position Description / Results to be Accomplished (State objectives and task steps; these should contain specific performance indicators for quantity, quality, time, and resources used.)	Results Achieved / Remarks: Is performance outstanding, above average, satisfactory, marginal, or unsatisfactory? If necessary, explain.

time (nonmanagers, nonexempt blue collar or office workers, especially if unionized) will be less able to play the role described below.

Step one: Employee self-appraisal

Just prior to the scheduled time for an appraisal interview, you should ask the subordinate to prepare a memo to you summarizing his or her self-evaluation. The memo should include:

1. The objectives agreed upon at the last appraisal.
2. The results achieved for each objective.
3. Any extenuating circumstances involved where objectives were not met.
4. Any accomplishments that go beyond the previously agreed upon goals.
5. A list of areas for personal growth as seen by the individual for improvement on the job and by way of preparation for future assignments.
6. A list of development plans agreed upon at the last appraisal with a report of progress in carrying out these plans.

An added word about this self-appraisal recommendation. Self-appraisal is a vital part of participative management. When the individual shares the burden of appraisal with a superior, he or she approaches the performance review situation with a significantly different attitude. When invited, urged, and assisted by the procedure to appraise his or her own performance, the appraisal is colored by the knowledge that one plays a vital role in shaping his or her own destiny. The feelings of futility, frustration, and antagonism toward the superior and entire organization experienced in other appraisal systems is not apt to exist under the practice of self-appraisal. Here, the individual sees that no longer is the subordinate to be called in, allowed to read a completed and signed review, and informed of his or her status, no questions asked or tolerated.

Another aspect of self-appraisal shall be recognized: we grow and learn through experience on the job. It is easy, however, to become so involved in the day-to-day process of getting the work out that we have little time or inclination to study and analyze what we have been doing. The self-appraisal elements of the performance review forces us to study, analyze, and give self-critical attention to the activity of the past year. We gain new insights and we continue to grow.

The connotation, possibly through usage related to the labor movement, of the word *negotiation* has become tainted and has been avoided in our discussion of these interviews. Yet, active managerial participation must take place. A dictionary definition of *negotiation* reads "mutual discussion and arrangement of the terms of a transaction or an agreement." It is the discussion, arrangement, and agreement, plus mutuality that we desire. We can negotiate with each other without animosity, militant aggressiveness, or other forms of strife often associated with the word. We *must* negotiate, not only from the strength of our conviction and confidence in our capacity, but from our participative involvement in the breadth and depth of our business. We need great objectivity and realistic study of our problems and opportunities. We cannot confuse objectivity and realism, however, with obedience and compliance with the rules of the game. We are management. We must manage and negotiation is a management process. But no one can negotiate unless there is a point of departure. Hence, the self-appraisal is helping the subordinate to take a position on this very important topic, and the discussion will thereby be much more meaningful.

Your subordinate will not do the self-appraisal unless invited by you to do so. You might advise the person of this task by saying something like the following:

> John (Jane), I've set aside about an hour beginning at 9:00 A.M. a week from Tuesday for the two of us to sit down and have a thorough discussion of last year's accomplishments. This is as much your meeting as it is mine. Before we meet I ask that you prepare a memo to me which is, in effect, your self-appraisal. By that I mean I want you to study the entire year (not just your written objectives areas) and come in with a well-formulated idea of how well you've done. Bring any supporting data you want with you. You should also be prepared to discuss your personal growth as a member of our organization. If we find we need more time either to prepare or to hold our discussion, just say so. I don't want our meeting to be limited in any fashion.

Step two: Your tentative evaluation of the other person

At about the same time you should make an independent summary judgment about the past performance of the individual. You may have a company preprinted form. Hopefully it does not stress personality traits, but covers:

1. Major responsibilities. This is a list of the person's principal duties and responsibilities. You both agreed to them as high priority when you set objectives last year. They were taken principally from the approved job description, and cover rather broad areas, not likely to change too much from one year to the next.

2. Performance goals. This is a corresponding list of results the individual has been trying to achieve all year. Again, you both agreed to these a year ago, as the statements of performance showing the job was being handled well. They were measurable, realistic, and listed in some order of priority.

3. Actual results achieved. This is a list of the actual level of accomplishment which can be substantiated by objective information, to be compared with the desired results.

4. Review comments. This is an opportunity to record any extenuating circumstances to explain goals not met; additional accomplishments beyond agreed-upon objectives; personal development needs related to any work objective; and reminders about changes in objectives which had been agreed upon during the year. For example, "Accomplished 70 percent of what we planned to do—I believe this was due to the goal being too ambitious for present conditions within the plant" or "Loss of three people in this department during the year caused reduction of the department's productivity for several months."

5. Summary judgment about overall worth of the individual to the organization. This is the final "rating" which will be communicated via the official personnel record form to others in the organization. This is your best judgment concerning the person's contributions to the total results and future potential. (We will return to this in Step Five.)

Step three: Results oriented performance interview

This is the face-to-face discussion in which you wish to compare notes with the individual about performance and future potential. In addition to the practices already recommended for interviewing in chapter 2, suggestions for this particular interview include:

1. Establish an open atmosphere by selecting the right time and place for the interview. Be sure the interview will be free from interruptions.

2. Plan the interview carefully, selecting two or three key points which you want to be sure to get across before the discussion is over. Don't make the interview sound as though these topics are the only thing on your mind, however.

3. Let the other person talk first, discussing the summary memo prepared earlier. (You may or may not have asked for that memo in advance.) Be alert in this discussion for opportunities that may help you inject the two or three main points you have on your mind.

4. Concentrate on the positive aspects of performance and offer constructive criticism that points the way to future development. Rehashing past errors and failure should be done only to illustrate possible development needs. Remember you've probably had quarterly opportunities to discuss these points, so make this year-end summary exactly that—a summary, not a rehash.

5. Encourage the individual to analyze his or her own performance to determine areas of weakness and areas of strength. Ask questions like, "What do you believe may have caused that project to fail/succeed?" "Why do you feel this way?"

6. At times, you have to take the initiative and, like a good coach, point out why performance failed or succeeded from your vantage point. This may lead to a discussion of the personal development plan you have prepared as preparation for this meeting.

7. Make sure the discussion stays on specifics, on measurable results. But don't get bogged down in arguments about minutiae. Be willing to modify your preliminary judgments about performance based on new information and insights brought to your attention by the individual. This is why Step Two was considered a tentative evaluation.

Step four: Set objectives for next year

Build upon last year's performance to set objectives for the coming year. For example:

1. Your people's objectives should flow from yours; therefore, they must know your objectives before they can set theirs.

2. The individual should bear the major role in determining his or her objectives. This can now be done in full recognition of what last year's accomplishments were and thus be more realistic than otherwise.

3. As much as possible the objectives should be written out specifically as to level of achievement desired. The more specific and detailed the objective, the easier it will be to measure the level of accomplishment next year. The discussion you have just had in measuring last year's work should go far in reinforcing this need for specificity.

4. The individual employee, even more than the job, ought to be the strongest factor in establishing objectives. This does not mean to shape jobs to fit individuals; but in determining what is a realistic level of accomplishment to aim at, the individual's strong and weak points are paramount in getting any kind of commitment. Objectives should therefore take into careful consideration the knowledge, skill, and attitudes of the individual who will try to achieve them. This again opens the door to recommitment on personal growth objectives.

5. Define results sought, not activities which are the means to those results. For example, "a 10 percent reduction in operating expenses" is certainly more explicit than "install a cost reduction program."

6. Realism will depend a lot on available resources, so be willing to discuss people, money, space, information, and the like to show you realize your part of the objectives is putting up the means to the ends you desire.

7. Objectives must be within the scope of the individual's responsibility and authority. It often happens that several persons or departments have overlapping objectives or the same basic targets. Be sure the individual checks out such shared objectives with the others involved to avoid working at cross purposes.

Step five: Post-interview overall evaluation

After completing the discussion of past performance and objectives for the next year, it will be good to render an overall evaluation *before* the person leaves the meeting. This frequently includes one or more of the following four items (illustrated in Figure 6-7):

1. Overall performance rating. This is usually a check mark in a box or column to indicate whether you think the worker's overall performance is low, satisfactory, above average, outstanding, or whatever. The words or numbers used here should be defined somewhere in the instructions for both of you to understand. Note that performance rated below standard can be because a person is relatively new on the job, or because of a culpable weakness. This section approaches the old guessing game on personality traits, typical of review techniques used in the past. However, you can avoid "crystal ball gazing" if you remember:

   - You are not rating the individual's personality.
   - It will be difficult to score well in this section if results were poor in the objectives section.
   - Even if objective results were good, they might have been better if sound management practices were followed.
   - This rating is a combination rating, taking into account all the person's work, including the objectives on the form and other work not specifically covered by goals.
   - The "halo" or "horns" effect can trap you. Be wary of allowing a single (especially recent) occurrence to sway your overall judgment.

2. Summary performance comments. This should be your overall impression now that you have had a chance to meet with the individual. These comments should reflect that person's self-appraisal as well as your judgment. You might write, "I feel that you underrate your accomplishment on this appraisal. Much of the work you have done will pay off in the next few months." "You feel you have done a better job with stock control than I do. You have made some progress but compared to performance in similar departments, you still have a long way to go." If there is a serious gap

Figure 6-7 Concluding Sections of Appraisal Form

Summary Performance Comments

Overall Performance

Consider whether or not the goals were challenging; whether the goals expected of the position were below average, average, or above average; and the degree to which the performance goals were met. Then check the appropriate space below.

1	2	3	4	5
☐ Performance low due to newness in the position (in training). -or- ☐ Performance low due to definite weaknesses. Improvement expected in 3–6 months or further action will result.	☐ Making satisfactory progress toward standard. -or- ☐ Showing need for progress toward satisfactory performance.	☐ Performance satisfactory; meets overall requirements. No longer in training.	☐ Performance above standard, exceeds overall requirements.	☐ Performance exceptional; consistently high level.

Recommendations

Check appropriate actions:
___ Recommend for step increase
___ Recommend for merit increase
___ Recommend for promotion
___ Recommend for further training at present level
___ Recommend for termination of probation
___ Recommend for transfer or reassignment

_____   _____   _____
Supervisor reviewing   Date   Individual reviewed

between your appraisal and the individual's, the problem may be an outgrowth of faulty establishment of objectives in the first place. Should this be the case, the error is a shared one, and you must be prepared to accept your share of the responsibility and take commensurate action.

3. Recommendations. This area concerns personnel action. Recommendations will pertain to salary, promotions, transfers, probations, and the like, and are of obvious importance to the individual. Try not to discuss specific amounts of money, dates for promotion, or other such actions. As a rule, these items will be subject to approval or processing through other managers or offices. As a matter of fact, you will note no mention of discussion of salary matters in this interview. We strongly recommend the separation of the discussion of performance and the discussion of money. They should be *logically* connected so the person must know when a salary adjustment occurs it is because of the performance you have been discussing; but they should be *chronologically* separated so that the individual will not come to the meeting principally to hear about dollars. Furthermore, in many organizations, while it is desirable to have all evaluations performed near the end of an operating year (so everyone is setting objectives at about the same time), it is also desirable to spread out the impact of salary adjustments over the year, so as not to have too big a jump in the salary outlay all at once.

4. Signatures. At the end of the interview, both of you ought to sign whatever document is being used. Explain, if necessary, that the signature does not imply total agreement by the individual with your judgment, but is a confirmation that the appraisal interview has taken place, that the person understands your position, and that a chance has been provided for his or her opinions to be recorded if they differ from yours.

Step six: Discussion with your superior

In some organizations the appraisal you make is subject to a review by your immediate superior before becoming a permanent part of the employee's record. At times this is said to be for the protection of your subordinate; that is, to correct any unfounded bias on your part. At times it is recommended for your benefit; for example, if you are recommending some very stringent action (discipline, discharge), keeping your superior advised along the way prevents these strong measures from being a surprise to anyone. In general, the review by the next higher level is intended to get one more point of view on the record.

The value of this step very much depends on the ongoing contact you may or may not have had with your superior. You have probably been communicating with your superior throughout the year in a number of ways. He or she has been influenced through informal conversations as well as more formal scheduled discussions and by a study of performance on a day-to-day basis. In addition, in the ordinary course of work, your superior has probably communicated directly with the subordinate whom you are now reviewing. On the other hand, you have a close working relationship with the individual being reviewed and have an important stake in the success or failure of that person's work performance. Your task in this step is simply to make certain that you and your superior are in complete agreement as to the quality of the results of this year's job and the individual's potential for growth.

If you think back to the linear responsibility chart you prepared in chapter 1 (Figure 1-2), you will recall that your superior's column was marked several times as sharing with you some of the developmental activities for your John Doe or Jane Doe. If you checked that your superior oversees/approves such things as identifying developmental needs, preparing developmental plan, giving instructions and/or corrections, reviewing progress periodically, or identifying promotion potential, then you need to carefully go through this Step Six with your superior. This person brings greater perspective to the discussion than you could normally be expected to have. If you both prudently discuss the person being reviewed, you may both alter your value structure slightly. Judgmental standards based on no facts will be adjusted. Too stringent or too liberal ratings will be modified. Wiser interpretation of factors affecting results and plans will be possible. Strategies you may have overlooked may be thought of.

But if you find that you did not honestly see your superior being involved in more than one or two of these activities on your responsibility chart, then there is little to be gained from this step, and you might question its presence in the procedure of your organization. This would indicate that your superior is far removed (physically or workwise) from your people and his or her countersignature to what you plan and evaluate would be only superficial. You and John or Jane Doe apparently work things out pretty much between the two of you. Both of you make the contract regarding objectives, and so the two of you ought to have the only say in judging the completion of that contract.

Finally, it should be mentioned that some organizations still cling to an archaic procedure requiring that evaluations be signed, countersigned, triple signed, and at least initialed all the way up to the desk of the chief operating officer. The only justification offered for putting so much paper work on the senior people's desks is that they want to be kept advised of the best and worst talent in the company. In a situation where nothing is delegated from the top down and all decisions are still made in one office, this might be a consistent policy. But where attempts are made to force the decision-making process down through the organization, there is no longer need for all this initialing and countersigning. Until it gets to the point of recommending a promotion (when it might have to be passed on to whatever level can make that decision), there is no reason to go beyond your immediate superior.

Step seven: Maintain a file on the employee during the year

To assist in making a meaningful appraisal at the end of next year, you might wish to maintain a file on each worker. Keep a record of memos, reports, revised objectives, and so on, that occur during the year and would be useful in next year's appraisal. You should be reminded that recent rulings by governmental agencies charged with protecting equality of opportunity, have found keeping private "auxiliary" personnel files apart from the official company personnel file to be discriminatory. This has caused some to wonder about the advisability of keeping this kind of record. We are not talking about your own personal "enemies list" to blackball undesirables. What we are referring to is a list of work-related and personal development objectives negotiated with your subordinate at the start of the year, in writing, signed by both of you. It is simply suggested you keep information with the original "contract" to help both of you refresh your memory when the year ends. You might take note of:

1. successful completion of an objective,
2. initiation or completion of a phase of personal development,
3. notice of an unforeseen problem encountered that may affect completion of performance or development objectives,
4. notice of developing conditions or factors that may affect performance activities (new equipment, organizational changes, etc.),
5. periodic budget and expense reports,
6. outstanding or unusual achievements in performance,
7. constructive criticism or discipline interviews,
8. outstanding or unusual failures in performance,
9. coaching/counseling interviews,
10. revision of objectives,
11. complaints lodged against the worker and/or his or her work,
12. deficiencies you had to answer to because of neglect on the part of this person,

13. commendations received from your superior/customer due to proper performance on the part of this person.

SUMMARY

Important as the formal annual performance preview discussion is, it is only a chance to tie together all the loose ends that have come up during the course of the year. This once-a-year meeting can never replace an ongoing day-to-day mutually supportive coaching relationship. Without the mutual trust that comes from repeated informal checking, guiding, suggesting, and revising by which you learn to respect each others' judgments, you will never be able to conduct the kind of annual preview we have outlined, which has as its focal point both the work to be done and the development of the individual.

Such frequent feedback on a day-to-day basis must also be made in a systematic fashion. A detailed description of how to set up such a system of constant feedback is outside the scope of this book. It could be a computerized MIS (management information system), a formal program of MBO (management by objectives), periodic written reports of performance results, a publicly displayed bulletin board, or any way to provide automatic, regular, and objective feedback on progress towards desired results. Any text on performance standards or goal-setting will be helpful in this regard.

Where there is good day-to-day evaluating, there is still need for the formal *written* preview. This enables both you and the subordinate to take time out, collect thoughts, and organize your judgments for a new assault on the job to be done. Without this, there is always the chance that something discussed informally may fall through the cracks and be forgotten. The faintest ink lasts longer than the fondest memory.

7 PROFILE OF AN EFFECTIVE PEOPLE DEVELOPER

He's a guy who got t'ings did!
                    Chicago cabbie describing Mayor Richard Daley

There are literally dozens of books purporting to describe the optimum background traits and behavior characteristics of effective coaches/counselors/people developers. Instead of quoting from them, let's come up with our own list based on personal experiences. Using the worksheet shown in Figure 7-1, draw upon your previous experience and describe someone who comes to mind as a successful coach, one who deserves to be imitated by others. The desire to emulate must be the only reason for looking for such a profile to start with. Certainly we cannot become any of these people in our background. But we can study their personalities and behavior patterns; we can take note of the many occasions they encountered in which they manifested these desirable traits; and we can attempt to follow their example in similar situations.

So far, we have stressed your role as a coach in the context of the written formal development plan as part of the annual appraisal of the performance and potential capabilities of each subordinate. But people development is a constant challenge. The formal written plan is always subject to change in the course of the operating year, and should be supplemented by whatever opportunities for growth that may occur.

Some coaches are so alert for these opportunities that they quickly develop a reputation for being more skillful in people developing than others. What are the traits and behavior characteristics of such a recognized people developer? Call to mind someone from your past experience whom

Figure 7-1 Profile of an Effective People-Developer

> Instructions: Call to mind a manager you have personally known who seems to you to possess the characteristics of an effective people developer (coach) worthy of imitation by you and others.
>
> 1. Why did this person come to mind as your choice?
>
> 2. What behavior on his or her part is worthy of imitation in improving your own ability to coach?
>
> 3. Recount an incident involving this person which identifies a specific skill, trait, habit, or attitude which ought to be included in a profile of an effective people developer.

you have always thought of as effective in developing people. It need not be someone you worked for in your employment background. The individual could be someone you knew while you were in school, some personal friend, a leader in the religious field, an athletic coach, a social acquaintance, and so on. As an example, here is how one person responded to Figure 7-1:

1. Why did this person come to mind as your choice?
   This person was first my teacher in graduate school, then later became my boss in a job I had as I went on for graduate degrees. As a matter of fact, it was he who encouraged me to further my education, which I would otherwise never have done. He convinced me I had it in me, and I know of at least six other persons he challenged the same way—to realize their full potential—and then assisted in one way or another to make it happen.

2. What behavior on his or her part is worthy of imitation in improving your own ability to coach?
   - He was always on the look-out for high talent people.
   - He was affable, with a constant open-door policy.
   - He treated each individual as a unique person, taking that personal interest that showed he really cared for you personally.
   - He had a way of inspiring self-confidence.
3. Recount an incident involving this person which identifies a specific skill, trait, habit, or attitude which ought to be included in a profile of an effective people developer.

   I recall one work assignment he gave me—a study to solve a problem dealing with overcrowded conditions on this service area I managed. I knew it was a chronic problem not only for us but for all other similar organizations, and I was at my wits end, ready to just accept the inevitable as everyone else had. This person helped talk me through the situation, gave some suggestions, drew out the best solution from my own thinking, made me think I had worked it out by myself, supported me in my recommendations, and gave me the authority to implement my solution. I distinctly recall walking out of his office feeling ten feet tall, when I had gone in there ready to throw in the sponge. Ever since, I have always tried to work with my people to give them that feeling of being able to conquer the world and showing that I wanted to help them do it.

A list of the most important traits and characteristics of a good people developer has been compiled from the answers given in seminar workshops using Figure 7-1. The following are the most often cited characteristics:

- is affable
- shows personal interest in people
- shows trust and confidence in people
- stands behind subordinates (backs them up)
- practices good listening techniques
- is sympathetic and understanding
- always gets all the facts before jumping to conclusions
- is patient and forebearing
- is objective (as opposed to subjective) in weighing matters
- is firm but fair
- shows you are always welcome if you don't take advantage
- requires high standards of performance

- lets people make their own decisions
- delegates authority to go with responsibilities
- expects people to be able to explain failings
- holds people accountable
- insists on practice before trying things where they count
- gives guidance and direction, especially while learning things
- makes you work out most of your own tough situations
- refuses to be made a scape goat
- goes to bat for you
- explains the reasons for any instructions given
- is friendly, courteous, and shows good manners
- asks for my opinion before giving his own
- makes corrections in private
- lets bygones be bygones
- is even-tempered even when things are pretty bad
- makes me feel comfortable when I go in to see him
- doesn't always make me come to him, but often comes to my place of work
- lets me learn by making mistakes (about little things)
- doesn't hide information from me
- is available without wasting time when nothing important to say
- doesn't let me bite off more than I can chew
- knows how to make and keep peace in a group
- doesn't impose ideas on others
- shows leadership qualities of initiative, direction, and control
- inspires confidence so that others rally around
- is value oriented
- sense of values is one I can identify with
- does not take advantage of his position
- does not flaunt title or authority
- somehow I know he's the boss without him reminding me of it
- sincerely desires my ideas on topics up for discussion
- knows how to bring discussion to closure
- isn't afraid of being disliked when principles are at stake
- doesn't put words in my mouth

- tries to demonstrate what it is he's teaching me
- never divulges a confidence
- lets me set my own deadlines, within reason
- won't let me quit
- knows how to make me see goal ahead all the time
- points with pride to those he's developed, even outside the organization
- gives credit where credit is due
- works as hard as anyone else
- does not seek the limelight
- helps me refine my thoughts before presenting to others
- establishes a sense of personal worth
- let's you know where you stand
- is humble
- is straightforward at all times
- is open and honest
- refuses to discuss one person with another individual
- gives at least a second chance
- uses easy to understand language
- concludes discussions with a time and action plan
- likes to put things in writing
- doesn't pull surprises on me
- gives me adequate time to prepare for discussions
- lives up to promises or doesn't make them to start with
- hates to say "I told you so"

Reading over this list very rapidly, you will find very little new and enlightening information in terms of how any manager would like to behave vis-a-vis members of the work team no matter what level in the organization. There is probably very little originality when it comes to human beings relating with each other. The worth of the list, and pondering it, lies not in its originality then, but in its banality. It doesn't take a genius to figure out how a good coach should behave. What it takes is the time to remind oneself of these characteristics, the self determination to imitate them, and then super human effort in living up to the challenge.

Participants in workshops using Figure 7-1 have compiled a list of occasions during which admired coaches evidenced their effective people developing traits. The following are the most often cited occasions:

- when making corrections
- when giving assignments
- when delegating authority
- when giving direct orders/instructions
- when answering questions
- when giving advice
- when setting objectives
- when encouraging personal development
- when evaluating performance results
- when discussing career plans
- when solving problems
- when seeking suggestions
- when solving conflicts
- when making schedules
- during salary discussions
- when resolving complaints/grievances
- when explaining/enforcing policies
- during budget meetings
- when reviewing periodic progress reports
- during committee meetings
- during staff meetings
- in the introduction of change
- when analyzing one's potential
- in casual conversation

As we continue to examine the mannerisms of an effective coach, keep these sets of important characteristics and occasions in mind. Following is a series of more general situations for examination, which transcend some of the day-to-day examples of the next chapter. For each situation chosen, there are some suggestions for effective behavior. The treatment of these situations is not intended to be exhaustive. The idea is to remind ourselves of what we already know about handling people in these situations and relate it to the role of a coach.

TEAM BUILDING

When engaging in team building, you are, as the manager, ultimately evaluated by the success or failure of your total team. In fact, it is impossible for you to advance if your team does not perform satisfactorily. That's probably why, when any team starts losing consistently, it's usually the manager/coach who is the first to go. The real measure of an effective coach is his or her ability to take whatever raw material there is to work with and draw out the full potential therein. How often have we seen an athletic team which has been failing miserably do a complete about face after a new coach arrives? Where a previous coach working with the same material was unable to produce a winning team, the new one has the synergism to make all the individuals come together as one. Suggestions for producing a winning team include:

1. Begin by reviewing your own methods, abilities, structures, assumptions, and the like when an excessive number of problems or failures present themselves. Before replacing people, blaming outsiders, or abandoning ship, consider that maybe you are not properly organized yet. If too many unsatisfactory performances occur, the fault might lie in your leadership qualities rather than the fault of your people. Be sure your own skirts are clean first, so to speak.

2. Always conform to the rules of the organization yourself. An effective coach is a good example to the rest of the team. The best way to get others to show allegiance to the team goals, policies, rules, and regulations is to show loyalty to them yourself. The old saying, "What you do speaks louder than what you say" greatly applies here. The coach who places himself or herself "above the rules" shows that there are first-class members of the team and second-class members. Rank usually has its privileges, but those should be spelled out in the rules of the organization, so that the team members do not perceive you as being "too good to follow the rules."

3. Never permit anyone to violate the rules of the organization. Every team must have rules of behavior, either explicitly or implicitly agreed to by all joining the team. Taken together, they make up role expectations on the part of each member. If you, as the coach, allow anyone special privileges which go counter to those expectations of the others, you have planted the

seeds of dissension and low morale. While there may always be extenuating circumstances which call for a rule to be broken or waived, those reasons had better be seen and appreciated by the others on the team, or the exception still comes across as favoritism on your part. When a rule has been violated, the expected disciplinary action should be meted out, or again, the others in the team will think you are playing favorites.

4. Develop a technique of questioning for discovering the weaknesses of your organization. Just as individual members will be questioning themselves and will be examined by you periodically to find out where weaknesses might exist, you will likewise want to examine the collective effort periodically in order to find weaknesses and prevent damage before it occurs, if possible. What you want here is a collaborative effort with the members of the organization which will periodically call to everyone's attention those areas in need of support, improvement, or outright change. One such technique employed by those who use participative objective setting is known as *needs analysis*. All members of the team are invited to discuss as a group the overall mission of the unit and then provide answers to the following questions as a group: What are our strengths in meeting that mission? What are our weaknesses in meeting the mission? What obstacles do we face in meeting that mission? What opportunities can we discover to assist in meeting that mission? The group analysis encourages all the others to begin to see things from your perspective, and thereby appreciate the efforts of the coach. It also prevents any individual from venting pet peeves which cannot stand the challenge of the rest of the team members.

5. Never criticize your manager or higher superiors in the presence of your people. First of all, you are management to your team, so any criticism of management belongs on your doorstep first. Then, of course, if your team hears you criticize publicly your superior, they can infer that it will be alright for them to criticize you publicly. Wouldn't you really rather have them come to you privately with any disagreements? Again, showing by example is the safest way to instill the kind of behavior you wish to develop in others.

6. Say *we* instead of *I* wherever possible. This does have its limitations, however, as all things do. You are an individual and are well expected to have your own views, express your own opinions, make your own decisions, and so on. But from the team building vantage point, you want to get used to speaking and thinking in terms of *our* challenge, *our* effort, *our* reward, *our* success, *our* failure, *our* ideas. The coach who accepts all the credit for work done well, and never accepts any of the blame for mistakes soon finds the team loses all respect for his or her leadership.

WORKING WITH EQUALS AND SUBORDINATES

Many of the occasions cited previously for acting as a coach involve interactions with equals and juniors/subordinates. The way you come across to them will in great part determine the degree to which you will be effective as a coach. The image you build among them collectively and with each of them individually may very well spell the difference between being a figurehead and being a dynamic force in the group. The following are suggestions for effective interaction:

1. Acquire the reputation for being cooperative for the good of the overall organization. You and your team are probably part of a larger organization. How you see your team integrating into the overall effort along with other work units is a measure of recognition of the common good. Even though you may be in competition somewhat with other work units by seeking to excel in your assignments, you do not want to put success of your work unit ahead of the overall company's achievements. Hence, you may very well wish to find ways of assisting other teams besides your own to be successful, not at the expense of your own people, but in addition to their success. By showing this kind of cooperation for others, the same will come back to you in time of need.

2. Recognize the ability of your peers. There is a tendency for some to let personal competition for the few openings available at a higher level lead them to seeing all things in the light of what effect they will have on their own career, instead of taking pride in the abilities and achievements of colleagues aspiring to the same next promotion. If you can be fair and unstinting in praise for your associates when they deserve it, you will have a reputation for objectivity that will put you in good standing on those occasions when someone might otherwise question a judgment you have to make.

3. Give praise only when praise is due. This is a caution against being phoney. Some managers adopt the routine procedure of starting every discussion with words of praise because they heard somewhere that you always start off on a positive note. When a situation or an individual does not deserve praise, then don't invent things. Being objective never hurt anyone. Allow the facts to dictate whether your message is a laudatory or fault-finding one. To falsely raise hopes by giving undeserved praise only serves to confuse the mind of the individual who is probably very surprised at words of praise which are out of place.

4. Be available to your people. Instill a feeling that when people need you they will find you a sympathetic listener and/or advisor. This means you will have to show your people that you place their needs ahead of your own

schedule of activities. It means you have to really put your money where your mouth is when it comes to recognizing team effort. It must be understood, however, that being available does not mean you are on call twenty-four hours a day. It does not mean encouraging others to come in and "shoot the breeze." It does not mean being taken advantage of by the unproductive who bother you about everything they have to do. In other words, it calls for some common sense.

5. Encourage your people to prepare for advancement. This is the major thrust of the entire text. But it has special meaning here regarding building the reputation you desire among your peers and juniors. You want to be known as a leader in the movement to prepare people for bigger and better things. You want to develop the reputation for seeking people with potential and encouraging them to the fullest possible development of that potential. You want to be a real champion of people development.

6. Make yourself the first person to whom an individual might turn in case of trouble. There are several persons whom someone might think of when needing advice. When you are the one your subordinate goes to first, it shows a relationship based on trust and respect which no title earned for you. It shows you have succeeded in becoming the rallying point for this person, not in the sense of a security blanket, but in the sense of a source of strength, advice, and inspiration. When you have this kind of relationship, there is no doubt you will be an influence for growth and development.

7. Have respect for the feelings of workers of all ranks. Objectivity and being results oriented does not mean you become devoid of human feeling or that you must treat others as though they have no feelings. We are all human, with all the emotional components that make up our race. While focusing on the work to be done and the development to be sought, you must show that you recognize that people have feelings which at times make it hard to be completely practical or matter-of-fact. You won't want to start giving therapy, but you might very well wish to modify your stand, or couch your words, or time your messages in a way that takes people's feelings into consideration.

8. Express sympathy and interest in a person's views even though you might disagree with them. A good coach wants to look at things from every side, and one important side is the point of view of the person you are coaching. You may see things differently, but you cannot begin to share your views on matters very clearly until you understand where the other person is coming from. The better you are able to see the picture from that person's perspective, the better you will be able to get your own concept appreciated. You might even change your initial point of view after honestly trying to understand another's position.

9. Study your people. The more you know about each one of them the more help you are going to be to them in developing and, therefore, in making a greater contribution to what the team is trying to achieve. Professional sports teams have made a highly complicated science out of keeping track of players and potential players. When the annual drafts come around, computers whir away, analyzing the strengths, weaknesses, claims, hopes, and dreams of each player in order that what the team can benefit from the most is kept in mind in making selections. You want to be nonetheless adept at integrating the potential of your people into the planning you are doing for your work unit. The only way you can hope to continuously develop your subordinates is by using what you know about them and what you know about the job they are called upon to do.

MAKING ASSIGNMENTS

When making assignments to your people, maximizing the talents of your workers means trying to utilize them where they can make the best contribution to the bottom line. You will seek to build upon the strong points of each individual while assisting each one in overcoming deficiencies that might be present in fulfilling the assigned role. Consider the following suggestions:

1. Make sure your people have clear, direct, and meaningful responsibilities. When making assignments, avoid talking or writing in generalities. Each duty should be explained in understandable language, preferably in terms which indicate how you both will judge that the particular responsibility is being handled in a satisfactory manner. This means that duties should be stated in measurable terms. Your people will always perform some task so that some specific results can be achieved. Try to state those results in the accountability statement. Make these assignments face-to-face or they will not be direct. If you have to use the written word to require something accomplished, try to follow up as soon as possible with direct discussion. Be sure each duty is meaningful, calling for the person to really make use of his or her talents in an area which he or she finds important. To work on insignificant things quickly erodes a person's self-concept.

2. Tell *what* is desired as an achievement, not how to do it. If you spell out all the minutiae to the individual, you are not showing much confidence in that person's ability, knowledge, or competence. When you come right down to it, you probably don't care exactly how it is done as long as it is done within the overall bounds of how the business operates (legally, ethically, professionally, with respect for other people's rights and responsibilities, etc.). Telling an individual that you have confidence he or she will

decipher how to accomplish the result without a lot of detailed instructions inspires confidence in your trust.

3. Never talk down to your people. In giving assignments, there is a tendency to at least leave the impression of looking down on people, if only because they tend to look up to receive directions. You may have to compensate for this tendency. Perhaps you give the impression that the duty is beneath you; or perhaps you discount the difficulty of the assignment in the way you explain it; or perhaps you state it as though it is "filler" work. Any of these can be quite unintentional but just as damaging as if planned deliberately. Take sufficient time to explain all that needs explaining with ample opportunity for questions or other feedback to be sure the assignment is understood the way you understand it.

4. Follow the chain of command. You want to give assignments directly to your own subordinates. Anything you might wish done by their subordinates should be transmitted through the immediate supervisor, with the option of challenging your selection of personnel. If you repeatedly give out responsibilities to those people two or three levels below you in the organizational hierarchy, you will undercut their authority and get the reputation for "wanting to run the whole show."

5. Do not club or coax. When making assignments, you don't want to come across as punishing people by extra work, nor do you want to inveigle people into doing what needs doing. It's the team needs that are being served by the assignments you are making and people want to hear from you straight out what the needs of the group are and how you think each one can best make a contribution. This means you won't have to "pull rank" to get a job done because your demonstration of the need for it will be more cogent than your positional authority. Nor will you have to appeal to them on the basis of personal friendship or out of "blind faith" because, again, the factual presentation will be cogent enough.

6. Avoid an overbearing attitude. Try to achieve a feeling of "let's go" instead of "get going" when you give an assignment. In your explanation of a chore, show the worker how it ties in with what others are doing at the same time, including yourself. The person will sense being one player on a whole team, seeing that everyone is getting some assignment on each play.

7. Act as if you expect your people to do a good job. You don't want them to become complacent, nor do you want them to be overconfident. But you do wish to instill a sense of counting on them because you know they will perform well, and successful performance is the normal and expected thing. Tell your workers that you do not have people on your team who do not per-

form well. Explain that this is not meant to be a scare tactic, but simply that success has become a way of life, and they can accomplish new assignments just as well as previous ones.

8. Never make a promise which you are not sure you can keep. Avoid the temptation to sweeten the assignment by tacking on a promise of some sort of reward as a means of providing incentive. First of all, the only incentive people should need if you are coaching well is self-satisfaction from succeeding in a job, plus the social well-being from being recognized by others as carrying a fair share of the load. But more important, mentioning a reward for accepting the assignment is building the expectation that the coach cannot ask anybody to do anything without "paying" for it, when really the coach's job is to pass out assignments continually in response to changing conditions. The subordinate's job is to carry out the assignment because it has to be done, and because he or she takes pride in the team's well-being, not because of a promise.

DISCIPLINE

Here we are thinking not so much of the narrow definition of discipline as "punishment intended to correct or train," but the wider sense of "a state of order based upon submission to rules and authority." As the coach, you are responsible for setting up and maintaining such a state of order, not in the militaristic model where fear might prevail, but after the example of a team where everyone has assigned roles to perform out of a desire to be mutually supportive. The following are suggestions for maintaining good discipline:

1. Inspire enthusiasm for discipline rather than fear. Just as you recognize the value of good order as a means of jointly arriving at a destination, so you wish to engender the same kind of respect and enthusiasm for keeping order, balance, perspective, and structure in the way work is done in your unit. You may have the authority to keep such order by means of punitive measures, but you would prefer compliance out of a sense of desire for the common good. Any team building achieved in discussing how your people do or do not follow prescribed procedures will be helpful.

2. Be impersonal in keeping good order. The right thing in the right place at the right time is not a matter of personalities, favoritism, or shooting in the dark. An impersonal matching of the needs of the organization with the potential of the various members of the team and the best known way of proceeding can provide not only the most sensible assignments but also the most efficient ways of acting. Rules of behavior will follow and compliance with those rules can be seen as well as violations thereof. As you speak to

your people about staying within the rules, let objective fact be your guide rather than suspicions, rumors, or dislikes.

3. Always give people the benefit of a doubt. At times it might be necessary to consider the punitive measures set up in the discipline procedure. If there is a doubt that an action deserves even a simple reprimand, proceed cautiously. More is gained by mutually examining whether there really was an infraction than by wielding the big stick.

4. Take into account whether the infraction was intentional. If the purpose of the punitive side of discipline is to correct behavior, then meting out punishment for accidental behavior is not going to change anything. You are not really a judge being called upon to levy what some law ordains as just desserts for a violation. You are a coach trying to be sure everyone knows what behavior is expected of him or her. Intentional thwarting of good order needs the corrective measures of punishment; but where unintentional actions resulted in only a factual violation, and not a willful one, there is nothing to be gained by punishment.

5. Avoid mass disciplining. Again, penalties are to correct behavior. If there is need of mass correcting of behavior, try training programs, brainstorming, review of organizational structure and procedures, or examination of your own ability to set up and/or maintain good order. Giving out punishments to the whole team (or a major portion of it) is bound to have the effect of peer pressure building up mass dissatisfaction with you and your leadership. Then what kind of a coach will you be?

6. Consider a person's past records in meting out discipline. If you are trying to bring about cooperative behavior and not just "uphold the letter of the law," someone with a good history of following correct procedure and obeying all the rules ought to be considered more malleable than a chronic violator of expected norms. Such a person, therefore, is less in need of serious measures; a lighter penalty could be just as conducive to changing behavior than a stronger one.

7. Never take an infraction of discipline as a personal matter. When an individual does defy good order it is best seen as exactly that, a momentary violation of the rules and not a vote of lack of confidence in the coach. Captain Queeg of *Caine Mutiny* is undoubtedly an exaggerated case, but he shows what can happen when a leader begins to see disruptions of good order as a challenge to his authority. Unless you want to wind up rolling steel balls in your hand as a way of calming your nerves, deal with the outward facts of the behavior and don't impugn ulterior motives to those in need of discipline.

8. Avoid multiple punishments for the same offense. If the individual is going to learn from the imposition of some form of penalty, let one form of punishment do it rather than a string of consequences for the unsatisfactory behavior. A policeman was explaining one of the theories for the malcontent of many young people today. He alluded to the typical course of events for a juvenile who has a serious traffic offense. First there is a citation (ticket) which costs whatever the fine is, so that is a monetary punishment. Then there is often a court appearance (and costs) which interrupts the work (or other) schedule of the offender, a time punishment. And usually the result is a record which causes the insurance rate to go up, another punishment. No wonder, said the police officer, that young people sometimes say that our system is a little heavy handed.

TRAINING

One of the frequent postures of the coach is that of a trainer. To develop the potential that exists in people you will spend a lot of time working with them in an effort to impart some of the knowledge, skills, and attitudes you personally possess or understand. Teachers, drill sergeants, athletic coaches, dance instructors, golf pros, and so on are all involved in training. You, as a manager, are also a trainer, sometimes in a more formal setting (classroom, conference hall, workbench) and sometimes in more casual situations of the work environment. Suggestions for becoming an effective trainer include:

1. Know exactly what your lesson objective is and consider growth stages as you try to achieve it. It is not by accident that good teachers always begin with a statement of the learning objective. This should be a concise statement of precisely what it is you wish to bring about in the learner: the acquisition of certain knowledge, the development of some skill, the adoption of some behavior pattern, the change of some attitude, and so on. Since success on the part of the coach is measured only by success on the part of the learner to master the lesson, you want to be especially careful to have a well-stated objective. Most of the time when you train it will be a matter of moving someone from a current level of knowledge or expertise to some new level. So, if you always state your lesson objective in terms of movement from one stage to another, you might find it easier to measure success for both of you. (A review of our practice in chapter 4 where we developed John or Jane Doe's personal development plan will be helpful in this regard.)

2. Prepare in advance. Plan how you will do the training—be sure you can do it or get the resources who can. The simple desire to train someone is not enough; nor does the demonstrated fact that you have the knowledge or the

skill qualify you to start training others. Some of the great professional athletes failed miserably as coaches or managers, not for lack of charisma, but for lack of hard work or ability in developing the same prowess in others. You have to be able to break down the learning process into stages. You have to organize your material (words, readings, diagrams, other visual-aids, etc.) in some logical sequence. You might arrange them by order of difficulty. You might go from the known to the unknown. You might take them in chronological order. Every story, every demonstration, every game, every process has a beginning, a middle, and an end. So should your training lessons, even if they are no more than a chance for you and the subordinate to sit down in the office and review last month's operating statement. Even those who pick up the lesson almost by osmosis or intuition can stand to have the polishing effect of your well-prepared and delivered coaching.

3. Show as well as tell. Without falling into the trap of saying every training effort ought to have some kind of an audio-visual aid (because that's what all the text books say), it is a fact that the more cognitive senses we apply to the learning process the easier it is to comprehend and the faster we get our message across. Remembering the basic communication process discussed in chapter 2, we realize that each medium of transmission is suited for certain things and each has its good and bad features. By using demonstrations, mock-ups, films, etc., we make the most of using all five senses to grasp the idea in your mind as sender.

4. Solicit feedback and self-correct. Practice makes perfect in most training endeavors. Practice is also the best way to make everyone confident the individual is ready to put to use what has been learned. It is an opportunity for the individual to check on his or her own ability to use what has been learned, and it will also afford the person a chance to begin telling whether performance is satisfactory or not and start down the road to self-correction. The coach watching from the sidelines is upset enough when a player misses an assignment on a play; but when the player can't even tell when the assignment was not carried out or how to do it right the next time, that's when the coach takes the player out of the game.

5. Reinforce the lesson. The drill from repeated practice is one way to reinforce something. What you are trying to do is impress the correct procedure indelibly in the other person's mind. Recognition for doing an assignment well is another method of reinforcement, so any kind of reward system available can help. A certificate, plaque, medal, write-up in the paper, posting on a graph/chart/report, letter of achievement—are all ways of calling attention to the right way of completing the lesson objective. Repetition by way of summary is still another way of reinforcement. Recalling what was said in chapter 2 about the listener's ability to grasp about 25 percent of what is

said because of all the bad habits listeners have, you can usually run the risk of boring people with a little repetition to make up for what doesn't get through the screening mechanisms. I have had participants in the same workshop for the third or fourth time because as they put it, "I still hear different things each time I attend."

DEVELOPING YOUR ASSISTANT

Because of your ongoing concern for the growth and development of the organization, you always have an eye on the future. In particular, you want to devote considerable effort to developing a dependable assistant who might, in a pinch, have to provide for some continuity in the case of your sudden departure from the scene. This is not to designate an individual as your heir apparent, for such crown prince designates have been proven in the past to very often be a disruptive influence. So, without making any promises, but only as a means to furthering that good order in the team which you work toward all the time, you want to groom a reliable assistant, recognized as such and no more. Suggestions for such grooming include:

1. Use the person to assist you. There are many good reasons why you might need an assistant in fulfilling your own duties. First of all, you probably have to give your personal attention to almost every item that arises, unless you have someone to whom you can refer certain routine issues. Second, when you are away (extended vacation or just in a meeting) your unit's efficiency can be kept from being impaired if there is someone recognized as your stand-in, with a carefully delineated and agreed upon range of authority to exercise. Finally, until you develop a competent replacement, you can hardly be considered for your next career move. So this assistant, as a potential fill-in at least on an interim basis, becomes an aid in allowing you to turn your attention to the knowledge, skills, and attitudes you will have to develop in yourself for the next job.

2. Keep your assistant thoroughly posted on your plans and the progress of these plans. You cannot expect this individual to make intelligent decisions in your absence unless you keep him or her current on your thinking about the future.

3. Teach your assistant to get into the habit of giving you frequent progress reports. Insist on being kept informed of the progress being made on the various assignments you have delegated—the difficulties encountered and the methods used to solve problems, make decisions, and otherwise act in your behalf. A review of these reports is the most practical procedure you can use to prepare the individual to assume your duties on a permanent

basis. These are the types of items that will make up the whole job after the assistant's promotion comes through.

4. Give the assistant practice in thinking things through alone. Ask for an opinion on problems that arise, even if not within the purview of those items now delegated to him or her. When a problem is presented to you for a decision, insist that the assistant think it through specifically before bringing it to you. You get much more help from a person who brings you not only questions but well-thought through alternatives and/or recommendations. And you will be bringing home the point that problems are not solved by the first solution that pops into one's mind.

5. Place responsibility on the assistant gradually. Remember that the "feel" of the job which you have comes only with time. Add one new responsibility at a time, allowing time for it to be absorbed before another is added. Let the individual be completely responsible for certain parts of the work. Keep out of these things yourself, except for supervision. If the assistant devises other methods of handling those jobs, as good as your own, let the other way be used to build up the feeling of responsibility for the job.

6. Hold the assistant accountable for what you have delegated. Check up that what you have placed on that person's shoulders is being carried out well. This is not only because you are still the one who has ultimate responsibility for those jobs, but also because the assistant must become used to feeling "the buck stops here." Part of the person's preparation to wield authority is getting ready to put his or her neck on the block. If you find progress too slow in measuring up to responsibilities, it could be due to your lack of constructive check-ups.

7. Make the assistant feel free to ask for new responsibilities as fast as he or she can carry them. Don't give the feeling that you are holding back, that you resent progress, or that you don't want your assistant to become as good as you are. Make the person feel you are as anxious to see development as anyone, and have a lot more to teach and pass on, but only when asked. Have a long range development plan as well as a series of short range duties to be shared one by one, so that the individual can get some feel for the overall length of time it takes to prepare for the next job.

8. Back up your assistant. Consider orders given as important as your own. Give your support in disputes when criticism might arise. Correct and counsel with the assistant in private, not in front of others over whom he or she has some authority. If it is necessary to reverse some decision made by the assistant, talk to this individual about it, and let him or her reverse it to others. Give praise and commendation when deserved.

9. Teach the assistant to admit mistakes promptly. Let it be known that you are fair enough to overlook a reasonable number of mistakes. Point out that you would rather have the person bring up mistakes to you directly than to have someone else in the organization report errors, for then they become complaints and a challenge to the assistant's competence. This includes being responsible for the acts of whomever might be direct subordinates of your assistant—you expect him or her to be big enough not to pass the buck.

SUMMARY

We cannot let this chapter conclude without some attempt to challenge your grasp of what we have been discussing, and to allow you to test your own instincts especially in working with an assistant. What follows is a multiple choice test in which you are to select for each situation one of three alternatives you find yourself doing most often. The question, then, is not what would you like to do or prefer to do, but what do you usually do?

How I Work With My Assistant
(Being groomed to take my place)

1. When "rough waters" are encountered in the managerial job, I:

| let the person ride it out: sink or swim. ( ) | promptly try to give the individual a hand with the problem. ( ) | break in only when asked for advice or help. ( ) |

2. When the reports submitted are less than satisfactory, I:

| kick it back with a memo "You can do better than this." ( ) | try to edit/improve it myself, rather than interrupt the job of the the assistant. ( ) | call the person in, identify the weak spots, listen to rebuttal, and suggest a new try. ( ) |

3. When his or her attitudes toward people seem to irritate them, I:

| chalk it up to personalities and let nature take its course: improvement will come with experience. ( ) | try to act as peacemaker and assure people no offense was intended. ( ) | report the incident to the assistant, discuss it, and let him or her do what should be done. ( ) |

4. When things get stalled on a problem needing a solution, I:

| don't worry about it; the delay is his or her risk; I know who's accountable. ( ) | urge a decision before things get out of hand. ( ) | think it through with the assistant in a confab at my request but let the decision come at his or her own pace. ( ) |

5. When giving a trouble-shooting assignment for me, I:

| get the word around to those concerned and leave it up to the assistant from then on. ( ) | wait until the trouble-shooting job is over, and pass judgment on how it was done. ( ) | confer with him or her from time to time to check progress being made, and offer advice on problems. ( ) |

6. When the assistant appears to be bungling a job, I:

| withdraw the delegation before things get any worse. ( ) | let the person see it through to learn from mistakes. ( ) | try to see if the task is clearly understood and if it can be put back on the right track. ( ) |

7. When I see managerial time not being used wisely, I:

| wait until a deadline is missed on an important item and then criticize. ( ) | break in to remind of the difference between priority items and and routine ones. ( ) | point out my observations and try to teach how to budget time more effectively as a manager. ( ) |

8. When he or she comes up with an idea about which I differ, I:

| brush it off and say, "Don't rock the boat." ( ) | go through the motions of reviewing it/passing it higher with no endorsement on my part. ( ) | discuss it candidly, ask that it be thought through thoroughly; encourage another try, without squelching creativity. ( ) |

9. When he or she is working away at a reorganization of the department, I:

| wait until the whole plan is finished so it can be presented as a complete package. ( ) | keep my superiors advised to let them know what's in the works. ( ) | advise that the assistant work closely with subordinates for their their participation/suggestions. ( ) |

10. When a "one-man show" appears to be developing in the way the work unit is being handled, I:

| wait and see whether it comes off all right or a revolution ensues. ( ) | alert the assistant to the morale consequences among subordinates resulting from this situation. ( ) | discuss ways to get the job done with his or her people through better utilization of their talents, saving the assistant's time for management. ( ) |

After you have completed the test, go back and see where you placed most of your check marks. If most of the items checked are in the first column, you're not doing very well in coaching or developing your assistant, but rather expecting the flower to bloom by itself. If most of the items checked are in the middle column, you're doing fairly well but tend to be hot and cold in your coaching responsibility. If most of the items checked are in the third column, you are doing a very good job in bringing along your replacement.

8 DAY-TO-DAY COACHING OPPORTUNITIES

Nora Watson may have said it most succinctly, "I think most of us are looking for a calling, not a job. Most of us, like the assembly line worker, have jobs that are too small for our spirits. Jobs are not big enough for people."

STUDS TERKEL
Working

We saw in the last chapter how many different situations arise on a day-to-day basis for you to exercise your coaching responsibilities. It is in this sense that your role as coach is almost synonymous or at least coextensive with your position as manager. Whenever you are functioning as a manager, you might wish to keep the coach model in mind as the most effective way of getting things done through other people.

There are four very important and frequent opportunities which will be singled out for detailed examination here: (1) the occasion of giving someone an order; (2) the times you have to correct an individual; (3) the process of delegating; and (4) the group discussions that occur in a variety of contexts. There are some do's and don't's about each of these which can be viewed as ways of becoming more effective in coaching others by changing or improving your own behavior—which is always easier to change than someone else's.

As in the previous chapter, the treatment of each of these topics is not exhaustive. The assumption is that you are somewhat cognizant of each or can refer to indepth texts on each. The intent here is to build upon what you know about each of these by relating them to your role as a coach, that is, recognizing them as opportunities to develop people.

HOW TO GIVE AN ORDER LIKE A COACH

Giving orders is one of the most severe tests of your ability to coach. The seemingly simple process of telling somebody to do something is a straightforward instance of engaging in the basic communication process we studied in chapter 2. You have an idea that you wish John or Jane Doe to perform a certain task; except that it really isn't as easy as it sounds, or we wouldn't be besieged in all organizations with the numerous occasions when orders are not carried out as desired. Here are some of the reasons why we fail in order-giving and some of the things we can do to improve in this skill.

Errors

Some common mistakes in giving orders include:

1. Using ambiguous or vague words in framing your request, such as, "Give me your opinion on this report when you get a chance," instead of, "I'd like your opinion on this report sometime within the next two days."

2. Assuming that the instruction is understood the way you intended it, without getting confirmation that you have made yourself clear; that is, neglecting to get useful feedback.

3. Failing to motivate the individual by explaining *why* the request is being made. The more onerous the assignment or the more it might be seen as an imposition on an already busy schedule, the more necessary it will be to give reasons. It is not because you need to justify that you have the authority to give the order; rather it is a matter of helping get the other person intimately involved in wanting to carry out the order because it deserves to be done on its own merits.

4. Not tailoring the extent of details given to fit the needs of the particular individual. When you give too many details to an experienced person, he or she will have a tendency to feel bored or resentful. Giving too few details to an inexperienced person will result in floundering attempts to comply.

5. Neglecting to couch the instruction in words and tone which fit the situation. In some cases a direct order, brief and straightforward, is called for; in others, more of a request would be appropriate.

6. Mistiming the order. We discussed in chapter 2 the importance of having the individual's attention for any communication. Quitting time, rushing down the corridor, in the middle of a crisis—these and other times when the distractions are likely to cloud your message would be incorrect times to give that order.

7. "Throwing your weight around." The manager who relies principally on *positional* authority expects that people will carry out instructions simply because someone with a title issues an order (as in the army). A better way is to use *inner* authority, which is based on competence, insight, and understanding of the requirements of the situation. Sometimes you get outward compliance with the bare minimum of your order by depending entirely on your position; but the job is usually done more effectively when people are motivated to cooperate willingly because they want what you want done.

8. Giving too many orders at once. By covering too much at one time you run the risk of confusing either priorities or details of the work itself. There is a tendency to do this in order to save time, *your* time; but you often contribute to much wasted time on the part of others who are befuddled by the amount you dump on them at once. Often you wind up spending more time on the projects later yourself anyway because things were not made clear in the first place.

9. Mumbling, talking too fast, or giving orders over your shoulder, so to speak, as you rush off somewhere. The manager who is in a rush, or who perhaps is a little shy about giving orders to someone else, may just blurt out an instruction on the run, leaving confused subordinates behind.

10. Giving an order before you have had time to think it through yourself. The very first step in the communication process, we learned in chapter 2, is to clarify your own idea before attempting to convey it to another. Sometimes you might find yourself asking for a job to be done only to come back later and change the instructions because you had time to consider it more thoroughly yourself. When you do this there is not only a delay, but an erosion of confidence in you. "I wish he'd make up his mind" is the first reaction you get.

Alternatives

When giving orders, try some of these approaches:

1. Develop a desire to *cooperate* with the intent of the order. Only when people really cooperate is there a team approach to carrying out instructions. Some people have a strange definition of cooperation, however. "By that I mean," said one manager, "do as I say and be damn quick about it." A much more developmental approach to giving orders would be to explain the reason for the request so that the person not only does what is required but grows in the process. Such a procedure raises the individual a level above where he or she was before. The next time a similar situation occurs,

you probably won't have to give an order; the other person will be able to sense the need for action. A developed sense of wishing the common good of the team will move the individual to action; that's motivation, teamwork.

2. Vary the tone of your order to fit different situations, even with the same subordinate. You can *request* that things be done, for example. Your people will know that you are giving an order even though it sounds more like you're asking. The task will usually be completed more willingly because people feel their cooperation is being asked for rather than demanded. Then there is the *suggestion*, which is even a less formal tone for your order. "I wonder if we could get a revised proposal ready so our final bid can be ready by the end of the week." Here you are implying what you want done, but your staff understands your meaning and responds positively because you are kind of letting them decide. The *direct order* really can be used sparingly, primarily in dealing with individuals who do not respond to any other type of order. After a lot of discussion where there is no consensus the leader has to take the helm.

3. Set up *procedures* to reduce the need for a lot of personal order giving. A classic study of interpersonal relations in the restaurant business found this was the best way to get orders carried out among persons where there is a history of animosity. It seems there was a lot of friction between waitresses and male cooks who hated to take orders from women, resulting in feuding, bickering, and incorrect order filling. One of the waitresses came up with the idea of putting orders on a spindle, so the cooks received the orders without thinking the women were actually *giving* them. Schedules, logs, daily instructions posted on a board are all attempts to minimize the need for a lot of person-to-person order giving.

4. Where there is a very close relationship and mutual respect between you and the subordinate, you can use the *situational hint*. Orders are getting behind, so you place a stack of them right in the middle of the other person's desk. Reports have not been turned in yet, so you wave a blank copy of the report form around. The point is that you have developed such a rapport that people don't look to you in a decision-making way for these orders. You are only a spokesperson for the situation which sometimes can speak for itself if you simply arrange the necessary physical reminders of work which cries out to be done.

5. Lead others to frame the order with your concurrence. For example, one supervisor of six design engineers had been working very hard with the group in preparing designs for a big project. They put in all kinds of overtime, working day and night to meet the Friday afternoon deadline. At the last minute, they were advised they would have to revise the whole job over the week-end and chop out some $25,000 costs or the firm would be really

hurt. The supervisor called a meeting of the six engineers and began by praising them and their families for their dedication to the job over the previous few weeks. "But," he went on, "the boss says the job has to be cut $25,000. He says he thinks we can do it. What do you say?" At first the reactions were loud and vehement: "What? First they want our sweat—now they want our blood too." "My family doesn't even know me." "Why didn't they say that in the first place?" Through this the supervisor remained silent. Finally one of the six said, "Well, I agree with your complaints, but if we don't do something we may all wind up out on the street. After putting this much into the job, why should we quit now? How much did you say we have to shave off?" "Twenty-five thousand. Any ideas?" A little more silence, and someone ventured, "Well, what if we did . . . ?" Now they were into it and giving each other orders without the supervisor having to use his authority.

6. Time the order correctly. Unless it's urgent, it is best not to give an order to someone who is harassed, rushed, or preoccupied. The assumption is that people are always busy, so we can't wait until they have nothing to do and are looking for orders. But you must be sure you have the full attention of the individual or you will miss the mark in aiming your message at the receiver.

7. Pretest all orders before giving them. The way to avoid having to change instructions or find out too late that they were not clear and concise is to check it out in your own mind first against the following questions: Does the subordinate I have in mind really have the background, training, and skill needed to carry out the order? Is giving this order the right way to accomplish the objective, or is there another way that might be better? Am I prepared to explain to the subordinate the reason for the order? Are all the details of the order complete in my mind so that I will be able to tell the other person what is needed to know how to do the job? Have I thought through the best way to give this order so the individual will be fully motivated to carry it out? Have I picked the best time to give the order?

HOW TO MAKE CORRECTIONS LIKE A COACH

Anyone who accepts the responsibility for a work unit must expect to correct the actions of the people in that unit from time to time. One of the best ways people learn is to rely on someone to point out errors in the way things are done. Coaches are expected to know the most effective way to do a task and are given the prerogative of pointing out deviations from the most acceptable way of doing things. How the correction is made goes far beyond the single incident at hand. When you correct someone, you influence that person's attitude toward his or her own self concept. Correct the wrong way and people will resent it and you; correct properly, and they will appreciate it and you. Here are some important reminders about the correct way of correcting:

1. Try to give correction, not criticism. What you say and how you say it are both important. Most people see criticism as a personal attack, a put down, a lowering of esteem in the eyes of others and one's self. On the other hand, nearly everyone wants to improve, to know an easier, better, faster way to do the job. If your remarks are to be constructive, be sure they include suggestions on how to improve. If you must draw attention to anything, attack the job, the facts, the results of the incorrect action, not the individual.

2. Correct for the right reason. The purpose of correction is not to inflict punishment, embarrassment, or more work on the individual, but to guard against a repetition or to undo damage done by unacceptable behavior. Behind all behavior is a cause. The corrective effort must remedy the cause, not the person. Find out why the individual saw fit to do what was done and straighten out the reasoning if there was any. In the absence of any reasoning, provide positive probative reasons for the behavior you prefer.

3. Correct at the right time. The right time is as soon as possible after the error is discovered. As soon as you have all the facts, share your views with the offending person so everything will still be fresh in everyone's mind. But you must also remember the other communications caveats we have seen several times, such as, don't expect to have a mature and sober discussion of an error if either party is under emotional strain.

4. Correct in the right place. The right place is a private setting, not within the hearing range of others. The feelings of the other person are bound to be affected by the correction, no matter how circumspect you are. So, out of consideration for his or her desire to be held in esteem by others, you want to do your dressing down in private. Since the corrected individual will doubtless feel bad enough about the error, you don't want to compound things by calling it to everyone's attention.

5. Correct in the right manner. Treat the person as an individual, remaining "friends" while talking about the facts. Avoid disputing things. Make sure you obtain any facts he or she can add to your understanding of what happened. Point out the correct part of what was done as well as the incorrect. Then point out the effect on the work and on the organization, due to the mistake that was made. Be fair in placing the responsibility, which means accepting some of the blame yourself, if such is the case. Assist in determining not only the cause of the error, but in determining a way to eliminate the cause so there will be no repetition of the mistake. Explain

how you think the individual can improve. Ask for a commitment to a course of action which will mean better performance in the future. Express confidence in the individual and his or her ability to do the job correctly. Be sure to follow-up and check the results of the renewed attempt to perform according to the help you have provided. Make sure at the conclusion of the conversation the corrected party leaves with renewed enthusiasm, not deflated as though it had been a "bawling out" session.

HOW TO DELEGATE LIKE A COACH

The process of delegation is probably one of the most useful techniques available to a manager in the effort to help other people grow, but only when *real* delegation is being practiced. A lot of managers think they are delegating, when, for instance, they appoint a subordinate to be in charge of a given sub-unit. This is not delegation if this new duty is to become part of the subordinate's routine activities. Delegation involves releasing to another person part of your regular job, over and above the other person's regular job. In this act, you are narrowing your area of day-to-day work (though you remain responsible for the results of that work) and expanding the responsibilities of the other party. This expansion beyond the normal confines of a person's duties is a golden opportunity to draw out some of the latent potential existing in that individual for the purpose of testing its strength, practicing a skill still in need of further development, or opening up new vistas beyond the horizon of everyday work. The following are some suggestions for ensuring that the delegating you do is developmental and not oppressive:

1. Be sure there is a true need for you to be untied from some of the day-to-day work you do before passing it on to someone else. If there isn't you will probably find yourself overly concerned with how things are being done with a tendency to want to stop the growing process of the other person.

2. Pick a likely candidate for the work to be delegated. Select someone who has demonstrated an ability to handle the normal work assigned to him or her with potential for still more. Also, be sure to select the appropriate person for the particular chore you have in mind. The new duty should be one which will contribute to the overall development plan you have in mind for the individual. The trick is be cognizant of long range plans when considering someone to whom you are going to delegate a job, instead of passing it on to the nearest walking body.

3. Delegate the what, not the how. What you want to be passing on is the responsibility for producing some results that need producing. How the individual achieves those results is something he or she will want to think

about and choose in accordance with personal tastes and abilities. If you start spelling out all the details of exactly what steps ought to be taken, the individual will be likely to say, "Do you want to do this job?" And of course when all the minutiae are dictated to the individual, there is little room for growth to take place, and that defeats one of the big reasons you are doing the delegating.

4. Give the authority needed to carry out the new assignment. What you are literally surrendering from your own storehouse is your authority over a certain area. You want to transfer that power to the person and thereby convey part of the tools which will be necessary to do this job. Again, this means really transferring that authority to the individual, not keeping it yourself, not half keeping it, and not repossessing it when the job gets bogged down a little.

5. Be sure the delegated duty is a meaningful one. If all you delegate to others are the "stinkers" you don't want to bother with yourself, you will soon create a reputation for passing on all the dirty work and keeping the more interesting and exciting things for yourself. This clearly defeats the developing process you seek, for while undesirable parts of the job must be taken along with the more interesting parts, it is usually the exciting ones which stimulate the developmental process.

6. Don't delegate to someone else a task which has specifically been delegated to you by your own superior. To do so would be to miss a chance at developing yourself through this assignment. And you might find yourself not as helpful as you might want to be in coaching your subordinate through the assignment, which is still not part of your own regular job. Further, your superior will probably look askance at your passing on something which he or she expected you to handle personally.

7. Follow-up on how well the delegated task is being carried out. Because it is an unusual chore for the subordinate, because it is something you retain accountability for yourself, and because it is a learning situation for the other individual, you will want to set up intermediate checkpoints with the person so that you both can touch base with each other about progress. Any questions that need asking, any advice that needs giving, any explanations that need to be given to found out the growth process can then be provided for. The good coach will discuss progress not only in terms of the completion of the task, but in terms of the learning taking place.

8. Stress accountability for the satisfactory completion of the delegated duty. When you delegate, you pass on the work to be done, you give up authority over the task, you retain accountability for the results, and you create a new accountability with the subordinate, making him or her answerable to you for the results. Without this, the other person is not

growing into a bigger job, for being accountable is what he or she will be when delegated tasks become part of the individual's regular job. You want the person to *feel* that accountability and only when he or she feels comfortable with it will you judge if the developmental need has been taken care of. You also wish to stress accountability so that each of you will measure success or failure in the expanded area of responsibility and thus determine whether or not the other person shows the ability to handle tasks at the next higher level job.

9. Don't let the delegatee put the monkey on your back. During the course of completing the assignment, the individual may run into some difficulty. He or she may:

   a. ignore the problem, hoping it will resolve itself;
   b. bring the difficulty to you saying, "What do I do now?";
   c. advise you of the difficulty, present several alternatives, and ask you which one you prefer;
   d. make you aware of the difficulty, present several alternatives and the pros and cons of each, plus recommend a solution for you to approve;
   e. think it through, resolve the issue, and report it all to you.

If you allow (a), no one is managing the work and you are both likely to face a failing operation, with no growth taking place. Nobody learns by ignoring things. If you allow (b), you are accepting the responsibility and work of making the decisions in this job and have not been relieved of any burdens. Nor is the other person learning anything except that you can handle the situation, which you both knew before. If you allow (c), the other party is at least helping you do some of the thinking that should be done. So, some help is being given to you and some learning ought to be taking place for the other person, but you still have the ball back in your lap. The same is true if you allow (d), though still more work is being done before it gets tossed back to you. The only time this would be desired is if the recommended solution exceeds the delegated authority you vested in the individual. The most desirable behavior on the part of the subordinate would be (e), assuming he or she had the authority called for in the solution. Here you have not had to resume control of the duty and the person has grown by the process of figuring a way out of the difficulty. Some people would question how you, as the coach, have been of any help when following the (e) approach. This last approach still allows for discussing alternatives with you prior to putting the solution into effect. You want the subordinate touching base with you on scheduled progress report days and whenever a problem arises; but discussing with you to get assistance of the direction being pursued is different from dumping it back on your desk for decisions.

HOW TO WORK WITH A GROUP LIKE A COACH

You are not only the coach of each individual on your team, you are the coach of the group as a whole unit. Sometimes you will have occasion, therefore, to work with the people as a group and will want to use these occasions for the continual development of the team. Just as when you delegate, you wish the individual to make his or her own decision under your umbrella in which participative decision-making is fostered. This enables growth to take place instead of everyone looking to you to make all the decisions.

Participative decision-making is not everyone's cup of tea. "I just know I cannot adjust to the new role I am expected to play since this organization decided to foster shared decision-making—mostly because of my many years of running things and making the final decisions." The manager who made this statement took the only logical step he saw open to him—he resigned his position and asked for an early retirement rather than face what he considered a new era. He honestly believed he could not reconcile what he considered two incompatible values: the need for "one man to make final decisions" and the desire of others to share this responsibility as a way for them to grow. Many other managers are wrestling with the same problem in a variety of organizations today. A few have formally resigned. A greater number have, for all practical purposes, "retired on the job," awaiting retirement age. The majority still seek "a way out of the dilemma."

Before continuing the explanation which follows, take a short test of your reactions to two typical life situations. Questions I and II each have five possible answers, a through e. Read each question and rank your reactions to the answers, by marking numbers 1 through 5 in order of your agreement. The answer you mark 1 would be the one you most strongly agree with, and the answer you mark 5 would be the one you least strongly agree with. Be sure to mark some number beside each of the alternative answers.

The participative decision-making problem admits of more than an either/or solution. It all depends on one's basic assumption regarding the two values at issue. One value is a concern for the best possible decision; the second is concern for the commitment of the group so the members will help implement it and grow for having had this involvement. Given these two concerns, the manager may have one of three assumptions regarding them:

1. You may believe they are mutually exclusive. That is, you may believe it is impossible to protect the quality of the decision to be made and also open the process to many heads at the same time. "Too many cooks spoil the broth."

Q I. When someone you respect disagrees with you in front of others on a matter of importance, what are you likely to do?

A ____ a. I bite my tongue and try to keep my feelings to myself hoping he will discover his mistakes without my having to confront him.

____ b. I lay it on the line and tell him openly how I feel and why he's wrong.

____ c. I call attention of the fact that we are at odds. I try to explain what I know about his position and tell him my position so we can find something mutually acceptable for a trial run.

____ d. I try to play it casual, letting him know in subtle ways that I am displeased. I may try to use humor or the experiences of common acquaintances, but I avoid a direct face-off.

____ e. I let my actions speak for me. I will very likely convey my feelings by silence or lack of further interest in the matter.

Q II. When you disagree with the proposal of a group or a delegation from the group, and it is an important matter, how do you act?

A ____ a. I forthrightly stand by my convictions and explain my position, actively trying to get it accepted by the group.

____ b. I try to avoid being put on the spot. I may let them have their way, but I don't feel bound to support their decision publicly.

____ c. I appeal to their logic, seeking a middle ground in the hope of convincing at least a majority that I am right, though I would be willing to yield on some points.

____ d. I explore where we agree first, then I discuss where we disagree and how they feel about it and why. I press for alternatives that take everyone's views into account.

____ e. I usually wind up going along with them to avoid being an obstacle to progress or risking hard feelings just because I thought differently.

2. You may believe these two values (quality of decision and commitment of people) are basically incompatible but capable of compromise. That is, you may believe the group decision-making process is at best a negotiation. The person finally responsible gives in a little from his or her personal position on a matter in order to win some acceptance from others in the group and thus arrive at a mutually agreeable decision.

3. You may believe the two (quality of decision and commitment of others) are not only compatible but necessarily complementary. That is, you believe the only way to get a high-quality decision is precisely by the involvement and commitment of others.

Depending on which of the three assumptions the leader of a group has, he or she will be likely to favor one of five possible patterns of behavior regarding the group decision-making process. We say *favor* one because research in this area indicates an individual is likely to use all five approaches in differing situations, but generally one is your predominant style, with also a favorite "back-up" style. These five behavioral patterns regarding group decision-making are:

1. The *ramrod* decision-maker. If this is your style, you believe in the incompatibility of making a good decision and involving the group, so you react by making all decisions yourself. You consider the group as the wrong context for decision-making. You're afraid discussion will lose sight of the most important issues. You trust basically only your own assessment of the facts (and often will keep all pertinent facts to yourself). You think the coach is supposed to know best. When you must work with a group, you push strongly for your own solution for any problem as the best. You are so conscious of your final responsibility that you are compelled to force or impose your will on others—only then are you comfortable with the final outcome. Your open or subtle use of power or authority will determine success in getting your ideas accepted. Your understanding of a "good meeting" is one in which you are able to get everyone to go along with your views.

If you are a ramrod decision-maker you understand only a win/lose situation. And of course you always want to win. You cannot stand indecisiveness. You have no use for committees, which, in your judgment, are necessarily slow and inefficient. The ticklish part about your position is that often you feel this way for all the best reasons. "I must uphold the policy of the organization . . ." I have been put in charge here and cannot abdicate my responsibility by avoiding making the decision . . ."

2. The *contented-cow* decision-maker. If this is your style, you believe also in the incompatibility of a good decision with the involvement of a group, but you opt for "keeping the troops happy" as being the value to be pre-

ferred. You believe it is more important to keep harmony in the group than to come up with necessarily the best possible solution. As a result, you seek agreement at all costs. Your goal in the group process is to reduce conflict in favor of cooperation. (The cost is the loss of good that might come from conflict.) After all, contented cows produce more milk; so above all, protect against anyone being unhappy or walking out of a meeting!

At times this approach seems to be based on a strong desire for fairplay, trust, and peace; when often it is really a fear of one's own views or one's ability to deal constructively with conflict in the group. As a result, it often leads to conformity with the loss of openness to innovation because a person mistrusts his or her own ideas, or fears discord. One's own judgment is distorted due to social pressures of "keeping peace" in the group. Such a manager becomes a human relations devotee in the syrupy sense of going overboard for "warm and sensitive" relationships among the members of the group. If this is you, you really win appeasement at the expense of getting an improved decision. In meetings where conflict threatens to erupt, you find yourself interjecting humor, calling for a coffee break, or otherwise diverting attention from what you consider a failure: disagreement in the group. You are convinced all conflict is personal (motivated by personalities or bound to lead to someone getting hurt), so it is to be avoided at all costs.

3. The *cop-out* decision-maker. If this is your style, you also believe in the incompatibility of a high-quality decision and the satisfaction of the group, but your way of reacting to such a choice is to stop being a leader. You abdicate your responsibility for either the completion of the job or the satisfaction of others. In a word, you give up the struggle to reconcile the two. You may formally resign, or you may just lose interest and let your leadership sour gradually without even realizing it.

Studies indicate this is not a "natural" style of behavior. It is almost always a reaction to something. It is a common "back-up" pattern of behavior. For example, if the ramrod manager feels power thwarted—that he or she is unable to come off a winner—this person will often pull out entirely. "All right, I gave you my ideas. You won't accept them? Then do whatever you want to do. But don't blame me if things don't work out." This is the small child who can't have his way, so he picks up his marbles and goes home.

Or again, the contented-cow manager might disagree personally with what the group wishes to do, and mistrusting his or her ability to put across a differing point of view, might acquiesce passively, which is giving up any leadership role. This is moving to conformity, not so much to avoid hurting someone (the real contented-cow approach) as to avoid seeming different, or because others are seen as a threat and there is fear of being shown up in front of the group. Such a person has probably been promoted to a level of incompetence.

In a meeting, the cop-out sits passively observing, growing more uncomfortable as time progresses because discussion is painful. "After all, what's the use? Life is full of differences of opinion, and you'll never get everyone to agree, so why bother?" Any recommendation from the cop-out is usually to get an "impartial" outside arbitrator, showing once again abdication of any active role for the supposed coach.

4. The *compromise* decision-maker. If this is your style, you are not convinced of the complete incompatibility of decision and cooperation. You think they can be reconciled by negotiation. You believe virtue is somewhere in the middle of these two values and so you play one against the other. You basically want a quality decision and want to get the job done, but you trade a little off the top to get enough commitment from the group so they will accept your views. You are the home-grown garden-variety American leader who puts great trust in the so-called democratic way of life where the majority rules.

Being this type decision-maker might have a strong appeal to you because of the adherence to majority rule. You are convinced that if a majority can be brought to accept your position, even if you have to modify it a little, this will insure success because the group must accept the democratic way—doesn't everyone? And so you spend a lot of your energy gaining support for your point, rather than facing valid issues and differences.

You seem willing to confer and share with others, and modify your position to reflect some of their views. The trouble is, you do so in order to gain their agreement, with tongue in cheek, not because of a belief in a greater result. This at times leads to manipulation because of a view of the decision-making process as a vacuum seeking to be filled by someone smart enough to win a compromise between opposing factions.

Managers of this type frequently think all they need for handling the group process is *Robert's Rules of Order*. Their role is to be parliamentarian. They reduce all discussion to a process to get a motion carried—no matter that four out of nine voted no; as long as five voted yes, there was a successful discussion because a majority agreed with something. They stop the idea-getting stage too soon. A little more discussion might have innovatively come up with another alternative position with which all nine could have agreed.

Compromisers are very skillful as a rule. They prepare for discussions by knowing how much to ask for and also what they will settle for. They figure out in advance the areas for bargaining. They indulge in power-plays between spokespersons for differing points of view. They are the great mediators. Often the time wasted in compromising is at the expense of the good which would be accomplished by moving to the next style.

5. The *creative* decision-maker. If this is your style, you espouse the third assumption previously described regarding quality of decision and commit-

ment of the group. You believe the way to get the highest quality is through the group process and the conflict it sometimes engenders. You believe involvement of the group members not only leads to a greater level of commitment on their part, but also means the use of more resources in tackling the problem and thus enhances the likelihood of a more creative solution. You believe involving everyone will stretch each individual to maximize the potential locked up within. It is a belief in the creative potential of the group as opposed to the need for the pacification of its members which is paramount for you.

If this is you, you are aware of your own responsibilities and intelligence, but you are also aware of your limitations and honestly seek to round out your views by adding (not substituting) those of others. You do not fear differences of opinion or shun them; you welcome conflict as the breeding ground of new ideas. You seek to combine the disciplined knowledge of interpersonal relations with a frank and constructive approach to opposing points of view. So you seek to expand your horizons by actively soliciting points of view, reasons, arguments, and contributions of others.

As stated previously, no one person has only one of the five patterns of behavior. You use them all from time to time. But one predominates with a favorite "back-up" as a rule. As a coach, desiring to help others develop through whatever process is going on, you will prefer one to another. There is a hierarchy of these approaches in terms of which is likely to aid you in helping others to grow more:

1. the creative (integrated)
2. the compromise (negotiator)
3. the contented-cow (people are involved)
4. the ramrod (something gets done)
5. the cop-out (no help to anyone).

You might agree theoretically with the analysis of five approaches to the group process, yet not be sure how they manifest themselves in typical situations. Behavioral scientists have developed self-scoring instruments which permit an individual to test his or her ability to recognize these differing styles. The two questions and answers you ranked earlier in this chapter are based on some of these. Let's examine the answers more closely, trying to read between the lines and see how each answer shows an individual typical to one or another of these five styles.

I.a: The key words here are "bite my tongue" and "without having to confront." These are sentiments of the contented-cow style, placing a higher value on feelings than conflict resolution.

I.b: "Lay it on the line," "man to man," and the insistence in advance that the other party is "wrong" are all indicative of the ramrod who has to be right all the time.

I.c: All phrases here describe a procedure geared at getting more information and exploring new positions based on values of both parties which describes the creative approach.

I.d: Here we find sublety, humor, third-party mediators as an argument, and avoidance of direct face-off. All are familiar ploys of the compromise style.

I.e: This answer describes the cop-out as can be seen from the silence and lack of interest.

II.a: Here we see an appeal to convictions, to forthrightness, and a steady purpose of getting other people to accept views, without any mention of anything else. This is the ramrod in action.

II.b: This answer describes the person who chooses not to be put on the spot, and begs off from responsibility for their actions, with no attempt to do anything constructive—which is no role at all. This is the cop-out.

II.c: The appeal to majority vote, the willingness to buy some votes by compromise, the mention of logic as though to say human feelings are expendable are all characteristic of the compromiser.

II.d: Again we see a whole process: points of agreement, points of disagreement, a concern for feelings as well as reasons, and a search for creative alternatives.

II.e: Concern for feelings comes through as the dominant reason for stepping aside, which exemplifies the contented-cow philosophy.

Obviously, it would take many more such life-like situations and possible responses to enable you with any certainty to find your own definite pattern of behavior. Our purpose here is to be illustrative rather than definitive. You cannot develop any kind of profile for yourself from two questions. But instruments and programs are available and are being used successfully to learn how to cope with the problem of learning new roles with groups. The group decision-making situation is only one facet of the total newer approach to being a coach, which is really a search for skills in being creative and open to a multitude of views, interests, and areas of expertise, and assisting in the development of all that potential as it is applied to the work of your particular organization.

Since you undoubtedly will continue to participate in group encounters regularly, you will wish to do so more in the creative, integrated, developmental style. But how does one do this in order to derive maximum benefits? Are there some specific techniques of handling group discussion which you can learn and practice to become more adept at this part of your coaching responsibility?

As with most things, there are advantages and disadvantages to the group process. Learning techniques should include how to maximize the good features and how to minimize the undesirable ones. Perhaps you should also review these assets and dangers with the group with whom you relate.

ASSETS TO MAXIMIZE

1. Many heads are better than one. This is not to say that sheer numbers of people involved will guarantee a mathematically greater sum of knowledge or skill, especially if the question is one requiring specific training or one in which the coach has had the best or longest experience and success. But it does mean that a group of people with diverse backgrounds, interests, intelligence, and abilities will more than likely fill in any gap of knowledge or communicative skill on the part of the coach, no matter how gifted.

2. Different perspectives for viewing the same problem is the second advantage of group discussion which would be maximized. One person mulling over a problem for any length of time seems to get into a rut. (And, as someone put it, "The only difference between a rut and a grave is a casket.") What is needed is a fresh new look at the problem by others. That is what a group can provide.

One writer refers to this as the "zig-zag" approach to problem solving, as opposed to digging in the same (vertical) rut constantly. Those highly trained in logic tend to need the zig-zag approach more than others. We need to approach problems at times from unconventional points of view, what Robert Townsend in *Up the Organization* would call "the man from Mars" approach. This refers to approaching problems without the constraints of thought that come from being trained to think logically or from relying so much on tradition. For example, pretending as though you had just arrived from Mars and were blissfully unaware of earthbound constraints. In a group, there is more likely to be at least one thinker who may want to approach the subject with little regard for previous "givens" and who just may open the door to a new or faster solution. To illustrate, try this problem:

164 DAY-TO-DAY COACHING OPPORTUNITIES

> **Q** You are in charge of a tennis tournament and have to arrange for a total of 135 people to play sufficient matches so that one winner will emerge. The rules are that one lost match eliminates a player from competition. How many matches in total must you plan for in your schedule?
>
> **A**

The typical person will immediately begin to work out pairings on a chart, noting that the first round (135 players) would require 67 matches with one player receiving a bye; the second round (68 players) would mean 34 matches; the third round (34 players) would take 17 matches; the fourth round (17 players) requires 8 matches and a bye; the fifth round (9 players) needs 4 matches and a bye; the sixth round (5 players) would be 2 matches with a bye; the seventh round (for only 3 players now) would be one match and a bye; and the eighth round for the last two players would be the last match. Add up all the matches in each round and you get a total of 134 matches. The zig-zag or man-from-Mars thinker would come at it through the back door and say, "Well with 135 players and one loss to disqualify, there must be enough matches to disqualify 134 people, or a total of 134 matches." Simple!

3. Group participation enhances acceptance of any decision. As a rule, it is the members of any group who are going to have to carry out decisions made for that group. This means the coach, after making a decision, must often "sell" the solution to the group in order to gain its commitment to doing what is necessary to implement the plan. At times this is impossible, or at least of uncertain duration. But if the members of the group share in the discussion and feel they are making the decision, a greater number feel some responsibility for carrying out the decision, and do not need to be "sold." So, even if the decision arrived at by the group is identical to the one the coach would have made alone, you are ahead of the game in getting it carried out.

4. Group participation also enhances understanding the decision and what it takes to carry it out, making success in implementation more likely. This goes a step beyond the acceptance of the decision. It suggests there is also need of knowing what to do about it after one does accept it. If the group has some chance to discuss alternatives, to weigh pros and cons of each, to help select the final choice, there is greater likelihood that individuals will be more prepared to carry out this part of any action program, and less need

for the one decision-maker to do a lot of extra training or explaining. Growth in understanding has taken place because of the involvement in discussion.

The recommendations of efficiency experts and the trouble we often encounter getting them implemented are a prime example of forgetting this principle. All too often it is these consultants who work out all the minutiae of new procedures, new layouts, new methodologies which promise all kinds of savings on paper. Then in one fell swoop these changes are laid on the work force, and there is great surprise that the people don't understand what it is all about. It is often not a matter of accepting the change; it is lack of appreciating what the fuss is all about. They had not been a part of any discussion because the technical aspects were thought to be a matter for the analytical engineers. Maybe so, but greater involvement in the matter at an earlier stage might often expedite awareness of what would be taking place after the changes had been implemented.

Dangers to protect against

1. Social pressure and desire to be agreeable in a group at times inhibits honest discussion. There is a danger that not all ideas will be surfaced, that differing points of view (critical to the creative process and the developmental process of each individual) will not be voiced due to a desire to reach a consensus. This is to be guarded against. Yes, it is preferable to arrive at a consensus in a group process (rather than simply a majority vote). But no, this should not be arrived at before there has been a search for alternatives.

It could very well be that a minority view has more merit than what the majority hold. In the desire to arrive at consensus, the individual must not allow social pressure to silence any disagreement which deserves at least a fair hearing.

2. The bandwagon effect is a second danger which must be guarded against. It too often happens that the first one or two speakers in a discussion, especially if they are articulate, start a snowball rolling which picks up more and more support—to the point where even someone who came to the meeting with the opposite opinion now hesitates to voice it and decides to join the bandwagon. This is quite similar to the social pressure just mentioned, but in this case it sometimes is deliberately done. A smart operator can plant a supporter or two who will immediately second any motion made by their ventriloquist, and before you know it, someone is calling for a vote, and the whole group has passed something without any real discussion.

A helpful technique here for you as the coach is to deliberately ask for a differing point of view after two or three people seem to be stating rather similar views. It may turn out there are no dissenters, but at least any potential ones will not get steamrolled into silence.

3. Then there is the danger of the loudmouth, the person who dominates a discussion if you let it happen. This means one person gets more than a fair share of influence on the discussion, and is therefore defeating the very purpose of group discussions. Where it is a matter of someone monopolizing the conversation, group pressure frequently can result in the individual giving someone else a chance.

At times, however, it turns out to be the appointed leader of the discussion, you, who dominates the conversation. This has led some to emphasize the role of the discussion leader as being primarily that of a moderator—one who keeps the discussion going, is sure that no one's feelings are hurt, and who definitely does not interject his or her own ideas into the conversation. The advice is that at meetings the major function of the moderator is to perhaps throw as few ideas into the ring for discussion as everyone else, to make sure the procedures are being followed, to keep to the time and subject limit for the meetings, and to keep the discussion on the main point. The facilitator may want to take into consideration opposing viewpoints, but in general, the job is to give a clear picture of just what the meeting is trying to resolve.

While this advice is well-intentioned and aimed at keeping the coach from being a one-person decision-maker, it might go a little too far. It might reduce you to a parliamentarian. It does not identify the role you can take in seeking the creative output of the entire group by *including* your own contributions. After all, you were made the coach because you had some qualifications for directing the efforts of the group. Perhaps, therefore, a better piece of advice for you as discussion leader is to be found in the following distinction between the leader who is trying to persuade or sell others predetermined ideas, and the leader who actively seeks cooperative creativity.

Persuasion activity includes trying to sell predetermined ideas, defending a position held, talking so much there is no time to listen, listening only for a chance to give rebuttal, talking dominated by a few, not allowing disagreement to be voiced, limited involvement of some members, quickly moving to a formal vote, being intolerant of those who challenge a presentation, and so on. Discussions that do take place seem to be more a series of interpersonal debates between one individual and another, with each person retaining his or her own identity and clinging to his or her own ideas. Several solutions exist and discussion is really a conflict due to commitment being made by individuals too soon to their own solution.

Cooperative creativity includes searching, trying out ideas on one another, listening to understand or to be able to ask intelligent questions (rather than to refute), making relatively short speeches, seeking differences of opinion as stimulating, offering both pros and cons on all positions, objectively assessing the potential outcome of each alternative. The general pattern is one of rather complete participation, involvement, and interest.

Interaction occurs with the group as a whole, not between individual members. Sometimes it is difficult to determine who should be credited with an idea—"It just developed out of the group discussion." The solution is unknown at the start and is sought from whatever source it may develop.

4. A fourth danger to be avoided in the group process is allowing the discussion to develop into an argument, so that the goal becomes winning a point rather than finding the best all-around decision. Individuals tend to present alternative views and then spend the rest of the discussion defending their position. The idea-gathering stage is cut off too soon, and pro and con analysis starts too early. This is one of the most common faults of brainstorming sessions. Instead of allowing the creative process to fully develop, individuals begin to challenge each others' contributions before enough different thoughts have been laid out on the table.

It is quite natural for this "argument" type of discussion to develop because of the way we pin labels of authorship on every idea presented. Mr. A will make a suggestion and right away Mrs. B will say, "I agree with A for the following reason . . ." or "I disagree with A because . . ." The agreement or disagreement ought to be directed at the *idea* of A, not to A himself. If we keep talking about A and B and C instead of their respective ideas, we run the risk of turning to personalities, or we at least encourage A and B and C to defend their views as originally presented—to win an argument.

One helpful technique for avoiding this danger is to conduct the meeting in such a way that ideas are focused upon rather than their authors. Use a chalkboard or a flip-chart. As ideas are mentioned, write these in view of everyone, but without labeling the authors. After enough different ideas are posted, look for combinations and restatements, so that in reality the final versions are the cooperative, creative output of group interaction, rather than someone's in particular.

The same approach can be used in bringing to a discussion a prepared-in-advance written statement of a proposal or suggestion for discussion. Why must this type of proposal always be presented as Bob's idea or Mary's idea? We only invite bias by doing this. If the architect of the proposal is someone (or group) whom we trust highly, we are likely to overlook defects in it. If the author(s) is someone we have misgivings about, we are likely to transfer our mistrust to the ideas without giving an objective evaluation. Some managers refuse to even consider a proposal seriously until knowing "the type of people who put it together." Why not evaluate the worth of the idea instead of worrying about where it came from?

5. Finally, avoid adopting the same discursive posture in all group situations. Figure 8-1 suggests four basic communications approaches you might wish to take in working with the group. You will probably wish to use all of them at one time or another. They hardly need explanation, as the four

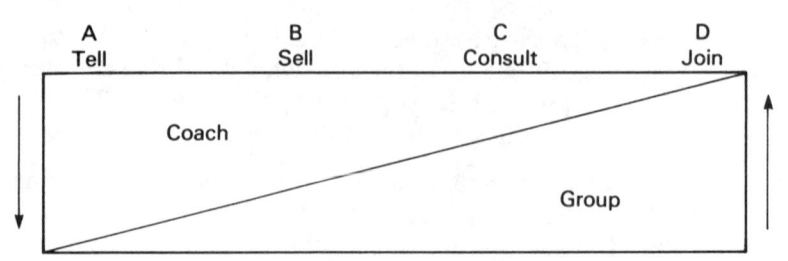

Figure 8-1 Varying Communications Flow in Group Work

words at points A, B, C, and D rather succinctly identify the varying roles you are playing. Going from A to D there is less downward flow of messages from you and more upward flow from the group.

One of the most important skills that the coach of today must acquire is the ability to work creatively with others for solutions to problems which successfully combine the inputs of all members of the group.

As a kind of blueprint for action in doing this, the following might be the manager's mental attitude: "Whenever a difference of opinion arises (and I should actively be looking for varying points of view), my role ought to be to determine the reasons why dissenting individuals view the issues differently and get these reasons verbalized. The more we try to understand why an individual feels the way he or she does, the more likely it will be that we can understand his or her side and reevaluate our own judgment in this light, all for the purpose of maximizing the potential for good results that exists in all of us."

SUMMARY

When you give instructions to others, correct their mistakes, delegate responsibilities to them, or lead a group discussion, you can do so in such a way as to impress your people with your knowledge, skill, and authority, reinforcing in their minds that you are the boss and they are the subordinates. Or, you can see each of these, and a host of other situations which occur in the course of day-to-day work relationships, as opportunities for developing your people, as occasions for unleashing their potential for growth. The suggestions and warnings reviewed here reflect a conscious attempt to foster a constant posture of encouraging maximum development of your human resources.

9 TRANSACTIONAL ANALYSIS FOR THE COACH

Child rearing may be considered as an educational process in which the child is taught what games to play and how to play them.

ERIC BERNE
Games People Play

The previous two chapters have reviewed the desirable traits and behavior characteristics of an effective coach and set forth a series of suggestions for a variety of coaching situations which you are likely to face routinely. The review probably did not reveal much startling new information. As we think of the way we *ought* to behave there is little convincing to be done. We know what we want to do. Then why is it that we so often fail to operate in that way? What prompts us to behave the way we actually do?

A recent school of behaviorists suggests the roots of our actions and reactions are developed from three different parts of our personalities, called *ego states,* and the different feelings we have of being either OK or not OK. Whenever we act, we do so from one of these states, manifesting one or another type of behavior. This in turn prompts a reaction on the part of someone else, so that the action and reaction together now make a transaction. The study or analysis of the varying possible kinds of transactions and what prompts them is called Transactional Analysis.

Our purpose in this chapter will be to try to understand the three ego states in order to understand and handle better the motivations and sources of our behavior and that of John and Jane Doe. We hope, thereby, to create healthier organizational and interpersonal relationships and improve the climate of growth and development. We will learn in turn:

1. to identify the three ego states and the transactions caused by each;

2. to see the productive and nonproductive in each ego state;

3. to choose the appropriate ego state;

4. to diagram transactions;

5. to develop people through stroking;

6. to handle games people play.

THE THREE EGO STATES

Dr. Eric Berne, author of *Games People Play* and other best sellers, made popular the realization that our personalities include three separate and distinct sources of behavior: the parent ego state, the adult ego state, and the child ego state. His theories were made more scientifically reliable by the work of Wilder Penfield, a Canadian neuro-surgeon whose probing of certain parts of the brain was able to recall feelings and events of patients' past lives.

According to Berne and those who have followed him, each of us has these three parts of our personalities present at all times, and we come and go from one to the other, sometimes in rather rapid succession. Suppose you are working very hard on a project in the office, but you're having difficulty completing it because you lack certain statistical information. You begin to get angry at those who you think should have provided the information to you, so you start criticizing these individuals to your associates. This is coming from your parent state, which we will see is the judgmental part of your personality. Then, realizing that the only way to get the project completed is to get on the phone and request the data you need from the persons who have the figures, you more calmly and straightforwardly ask for the needed facts. This is coming from your adult ego state, which is the part of us that gathers analytical information in a rational manner. But you're told on the phone that someone else already obtained the information and completed the report you were working on, so you don't have to do anything more with the project. Hearing this, you whoop for joy, see there's only a half-hour left in the day anyway, and decide to knock off early and have a couple extra martinis on the way home. This is coming from your child state, which is the part of us that gives in to emotional outbursts. In a very brief time you have moved from your parent to your adult to your child. Now let's look at each of them in turn.

The parent ego state

As can be seen from Figure 9-1, this is the part of our personality that causes us to act the way we saw our parents act. Imagine yourself growing up with a tape recorder or movie camera strapped to your back, capturing all the training and information you were getting from the senior, important people in your life (relatives, superiors, teachers, religious leaders, heroes, police officials, etc.). During this time you learned a memory bank full of slogans, maxims, axioms, traditions; all the sacred cows of social, technical, professional, civil, and religious life. You acquired many habits and procedures in all walks of life simply because "That's the way we've always done it." You learned to believe things on faith. You respected arguments from authority whether or not supported by reasoning. You became superstitious.

The words and catch phrases which spring from our mouths so readily because we've heard them ourselves so often are indicative of the tape that is still being played: How could you? It's about time! Where have you been? If I were you . . . It's all right now. Let mommy kiss it. Included here are also all the sayings that as a child you committed to memory without ever trying: Don't play with matches. Don't walk under a ladder. A stitch in time saves nine. A bird in the hand is worth two in the bush.

The body language of the parent includes those things you see acted out so well by children who are "playing house," imitating their parents: planting both feet firmly apart, shaking the head from side to side, waving around a rolling pin, looking over the rims of glasses. This is the part of us that wants to be critical or protective.

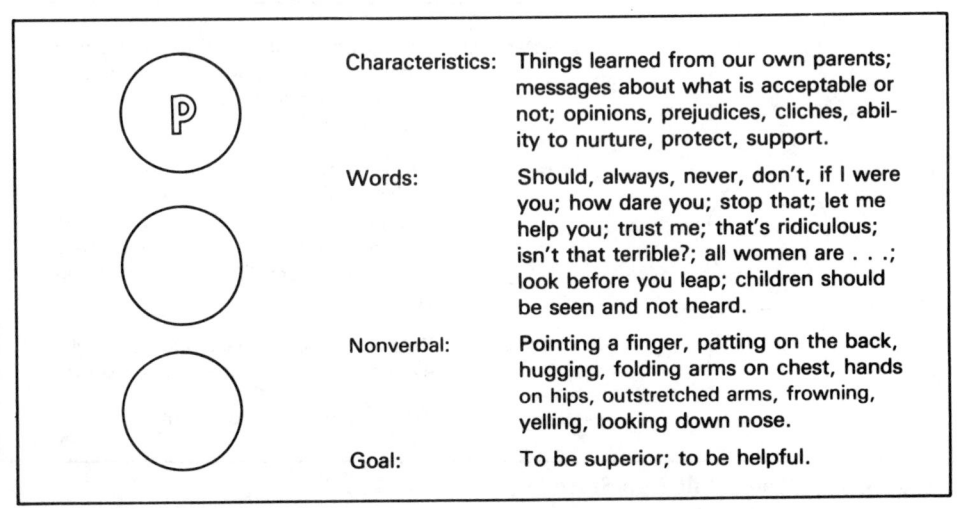

ⓟ	Characteristics:	Things learned from our own parents; messages about what is acceptable or not; opinions, prejudices, cliches, ability to nurture, protect, support.
◯	Words:	Should, always, never, don't, if I were you; how dare you; stop that; let me help you; trust me; that's ridiculous; isn't that terrible?; all women are . . .; look before you leap; children should be seen and not heard.
◯	Nonverbal:	Pointing a finger, patting on the back, hugging, folding arms on chest, hands on hips, outstretched arms, frowning, yelling, looking down nose.
	Goal:	To be superior; to be helpful.

Figure 9-1 The Parent Ego State

The adult ego state

Figure 9-2 summarizes the main features of the adult ego state. This is the part of us that wants nothing but the facts. Think of the efforts you make to remain with specifics, weighing alternatives, considering pros and cons, drawing up a scheduled approach to work; making lists of things to be done; asking for verification; seeking to be realistic; wanting to be prepared at all times; providing solid, tangible, practical, compelling evidence for your position on a matter; willing to offer guarantees; being serious and business-like in approach; avoiding gimmicks, manipulation, or "hard sell"; being logical; refusing to take things for granted.

People in their adult state are always asking: How does that compute? Have you checked that out? What are the probabilities? Where does it fit on a scale of one to ten? Is it based on experience?

Nonverbal signs include gestures which invite openness, honesty, and objectivity, such as standing to greet a person on equal terms, arranging comparable chairs and sitting arrangements, having a firm grip, or sitting forward a little bit (not charging over the desk). This is the part of us that wants to be competent, on top of things.

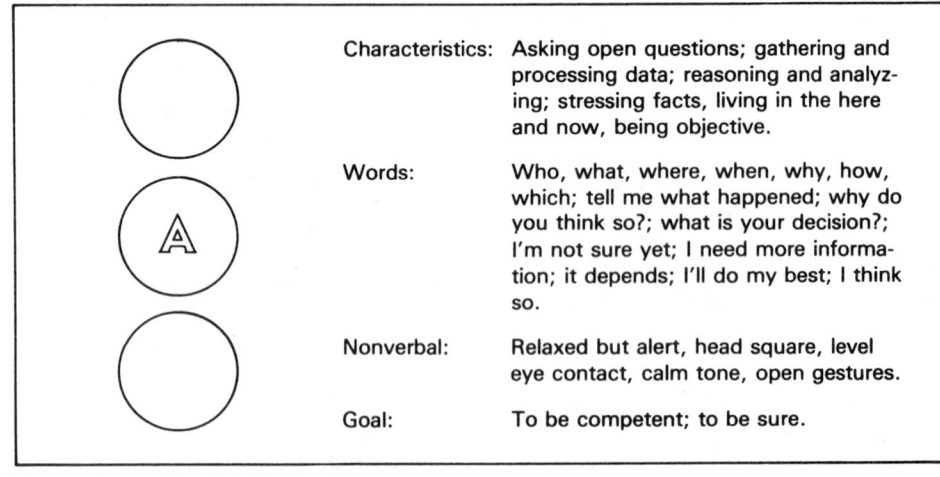

	Characteristics:	Asking open questions; gathering and processing data; reasoning and analyzing; stressing facts, living in the here and now, being objective.
	Words:	Who, what, where, when, why, how, which; tell me what happened; why do you think so?; what is your decision?; I'm not sure yet; I need more information; it depends; I'll do my best; I think so.
	Nonverbal:	Relaxed but alert, head square, level eye contact, calm tone, open gestures.
	Goal:	To be competent; to be sure.

Figure 9-2 The Adult Ego State

The child ego state

As summarized in Figure 9-3, this is the part of our personality which tells how much insecurity and dependence we have. The child needs a lot of attention, leaves things half completed, cannot concentrate on anything for too long a time, loses things, remains in a state of uncertainty, and refuses responsibility. It is also the inquisitive, questioning, searching, creating, wondering, peering into new territories part of us which dreams new dreams.

Words typifying the child state include: I wish...; It's not my fault. He told me to. Watch me. Common gestures and postures of the child include joyful jumping, skipping, hopping, clapping hands; and the uncertain being late all the time, never knowing what time it is, throwing things, stamping the foot petulantly, etc. This is the part of our personality that wishes to be liked and cared for, or that doesn't give a damn, or that wants what it wants and now!

It should be noted that in this system the word *childish* is never used. Rather, the word is *child-like*. Similarly there is no such thing as an immature person; there are only people in whom the child ego state has taken over inappropriately or unproductively.

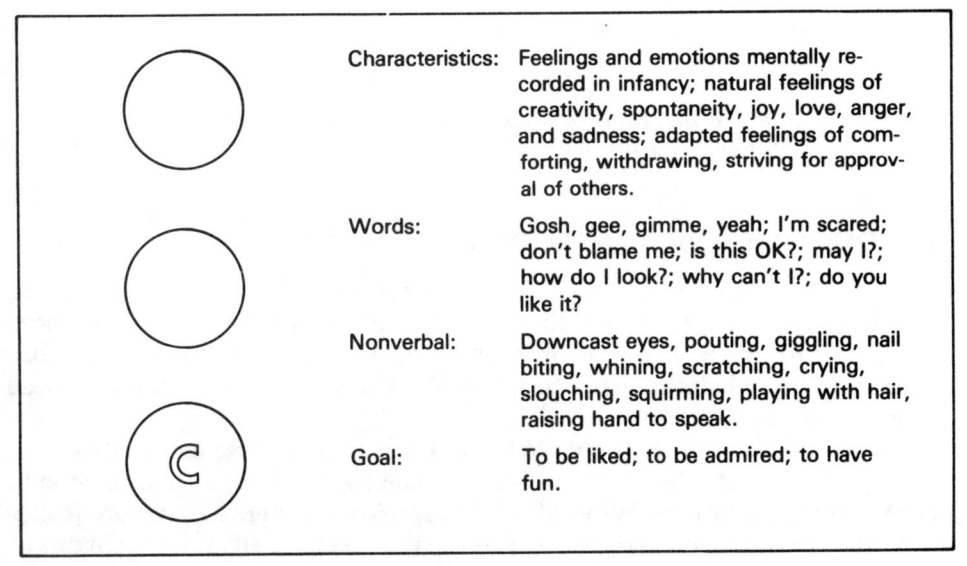

	Characteristics:	Feelings and emotions mentally recorded in infancy; natural feelings of creativity, spontaneity, joy, love, anger, and sadness; adapted feelings of comforting, withdrawing, striving for approval of others.
	Words:	Gosh, gee, gimme, yeah; I'm scared; don't blame me; is this OK?; may I?; how do I look?; why can't I?; do you like it?
	Nonverbal:	Downcast eyes, pouting, giggling, nail biting, whining, scratching, crying, slouching, squirming, playing with hair, raising hand to speak.
	Goal:	To be liked; to be admired; to have fun.

Figure 9-3 The Child Ego State

To summarize, you are in your parent state when you act the way you saw your parents act; you are in your adult state when you deal only with the facts of the here and now; you are in your child state when you act the way you did as a child.

To be sure you can distinguish the three basic ego states, here is a simple exercise to aid in recognition of each.

> ⊚ Circle the letter to the left of each statement in order to identify the ego state the words seem to be expressing. (Gestures and tone of voice would accentuate each of these, so you might like to try them aloud.)
>
> Ⓐ P A C 1. If you can't do something right, don't bother doing it at all.
>
> P A C 2. Don't blame me! I don't make the rules around here.
>
> P A C 3. I really don't know what to do. Can you give me more information?
>
> P A C 4. Believe me, I know what's best for you.
>
> P A C 5. Woman driver, eh? It figures.
>
> P A C 6. What kind of performance did *they* turn in?
>
> P A C 7. What kind of performance *did* they turn in?
>
> P A C 8. What kind of performance did they turn in?

PRODUCTIVE AND NONPRODUCTIVE ELEMENTS

No inference should be made from the previous descriptions regarding which is good, better, or best. Each state has its productive and nonproductive parts. Figure 9-4 shows how each of the ego states is a mixture of more helpful and less helpful characteristics. We want to understand all of these so as to be able to choose at will.

Because we wish to be able to select from among these facets of each of the ego states, let's begin to see how we use them all from time to time in our coaching situations. While all of this applies to others in our work group as well as to the coach, let's focus on ourselves exclusively, mindful of one of our basic suggestions in this text, namely that it is easier to change our own behavior than to change someone else's.

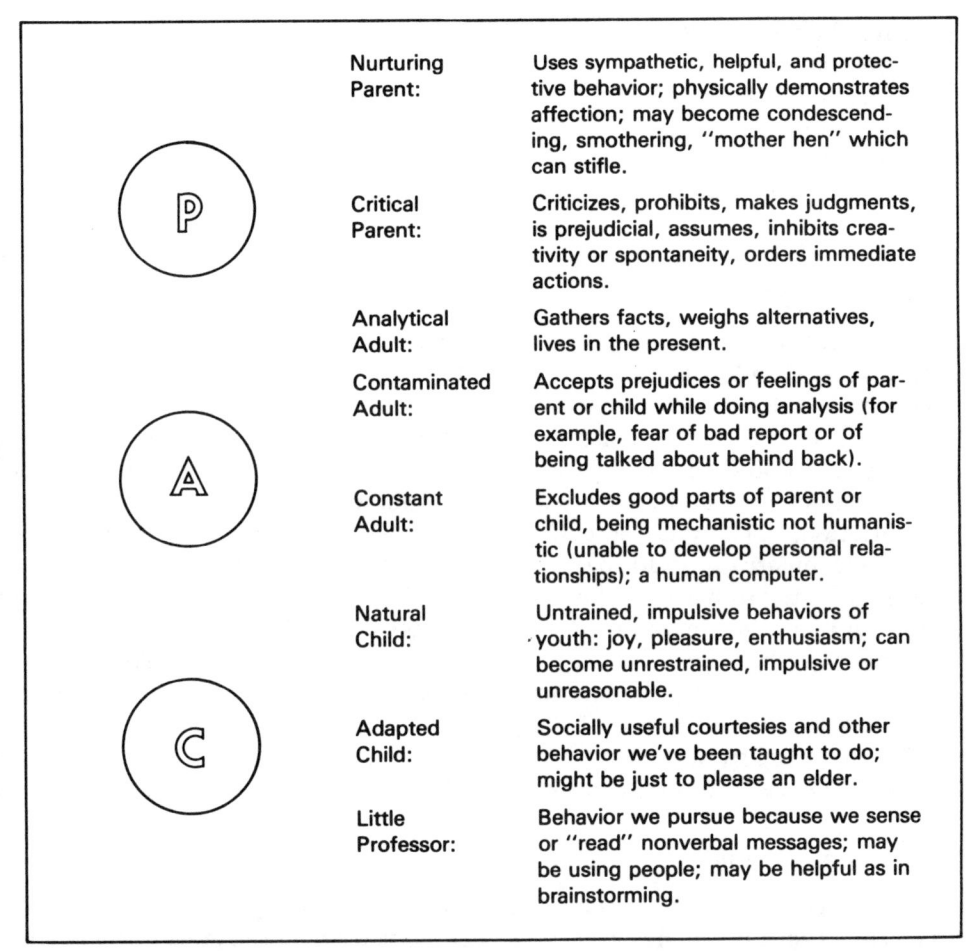

(P)	Nurturing Parent:	Uses sympathetic, helpful, and protective behavior; physically demonstrates affection; may become condescending, smothering, "mother hen" which can stifle.
	Critical Parent:	Criticizes, prohibits, makes judgments, is prejudicial, assumes, inhibits creativity or spontaneity, orders immediate actions.
(A)	Analytical Adult:	Gathers facts, weighs alternatives, lives in the present.
	Contaminated Adult:	Accepts prejudices or feelings of parent or child while doing analysis (for example, fear of bad report or of being talked about behind back).
	Constant Adult:	Excludes good parts of parent or child, being mechanistic not humanistic (unable to develop personal relationships); a human computer.
(C)	Natural Child:	Untrained, impulsive behaviors of youth: joy, pleasure, enthusiasm; can become unrestrained, impulsive or unreasonable.
	Adapted Child:	Socially useful courtesies and other behavior we've been taught to do; might be just to please an elder.
	Little Professor:	Behavior we pursue because we sense or "read" nonverbal messages; may be using people; may be helpful as in brainstorming.

Figure 9-4 Three Ego States: Productive and Nonproductive Areas

The nurturing parent

The nurturing parent has much the same desires as the coach. This is the part of us that wishes to protect from harm, sorrow, and failure. You are applying the lessons of history and personal experience to the protection of those you are trying to develop. We need to be reminded to look both ways before crossing the street and to be cautioned that playing with matches could be dangerous. So on the job we want to provide safety cautions and to spell out procedures that will lead to successful accomplishment of a task, and to recommend developmental plans based on years of experience and tradition and a higher perspective in the organization. Two things to watch out for, however, are: (1) the temptation to be a "know-it-all" (which will infuriate the less experienced who soon tire of being told, "I told you so."); and (2) the danger of never untying the umbilical cord (which will keep you in a position of superiority, but never get the junior to stand on his or her own two feet on the job). Productive nurturing eventually yields to self-sufficiency on the part of the young who must take their place in the adult world.

The critical parent

The critical parent is that part of us which comes to conclusions because of prejudicial standards, mostly arbitrarily applied. It's what often makes us act with a "hair-trigger" reaction to circumstances. The coach is expected to be able to make judgments about how things are done. But to be helpful, judgments should be accompanied by reasons. When the coach barks orders or corrections or appraisals without supporting information by way of explanation, nothing constructive is accomplished. The ability to tell correct from incorrect performance puts the coach in a position of authority and allows him or her to make judgments. It is when the criteria for making the judgments are explained and preferably mutually accepted by coach and trainee ahead of time that the ability is gradually transferred to the junior so that the latter begins to make judgments about his or her own performance without the need of the parent to render the evaluation. In time, self correcting or adjusting mechanisms are applied, and development begins because the learner knows when the job is done well or not.

The analytical adult

The analytical adult is the straightforward, hard-hitting, firm but fair coach who calls the shots as he or she sees them, but with all the good parts of the parent or the child. Factual analysis draws upon the experience and the righteousness of knowing what has worked in the past. It also arrays facts so as to stimulate moving on to more creative (nontraditional) synthesis. When you ask for all the facts before laying blame, when you ask why people do things before judging their intent, when you talk your subordinates through the decision-making process instead of answering questions for them all the time, when you focus on results and leave the freedom for people to choose their own method of getting those results even if different from your way, then you are coming from your analytical adult.

The contaminated adult

You are in your contaminated adult when the analytical process is manipulated for some parental or child-like purpose. Screening facts and admitting only those which support your predetermined position is being a contaminated (with parent) adult. Challenging every fact adduced as though it is an attempt to show you in a bad light is contaminating the adult (with the child). If you have ever seen anyone "black-balled" or "railroaded," then you have seen contaminated adults at work. They know how to twist facts to benefit their own purposes. If you have ever rigged a meeting by getting all the votes you needed lined up ahead of time, if you have ever suggested to a subordinate that he or she "play his cards right" and support your position, if you have ever displayed statistics on a chart in a way that omitted figures counterproductive to your proposal, then you were coming from your contaminated adult.

The constant adult

The constant adult is the person without feelings at all. Making assignments exclusively for the greatest profit and without consideration at all of the natural feelings of the people involved, never being able to smile or tolerate a little levity at a meeting, insisting on use of titles and the formalities of protocol—these are the marks of a constant adult. The individual who cannot go on a family outing without repeatedly checking weather, maps, road conditions, traffic patterns, safety reports, and the like, is a bit of a bore. The harried executive who comes home to be greeted by a loving child exclaiming, "Daddy, I love you" would be a constant adult if he responded, "Oh, that's interesting." The manager who announces at an orientation meeting for new employees, "Now we expect you to leave your personal problems at home" seems to be lacking a little in human compassion.

The natural child

The natural child part of your personality prompts the unfettered emotional response to circumstances. Spontaneous applause when hearing good news, slapping someone on the back in congratulations for a job well done, overindulging at a company picnic, are all reminiscent of childhood behavior patterns. The danger here is the possibility of these impulsive actions to be completely unrestricted. The manager who wants his or her own way all the time, the supervisor who is unwilling to share the limelight with coworkers, the conference leader who insists on simply telling stories all through the meeting, are examples of allowing the natural child to be out of bounds. One workshop participant said in confidence after a session that he thought the reason he reached retirement age without ever getting higher than first level supervision was simply his over-developed child, for he had the reputation of constantly telling jokes and not being able to be serious or face any degree of tension in a discussion at all.

The adapted child

When you are in your adapted child, you are polishing the apple. You've learned the niceties that are expected by society of superiors, but only as an accommodation to them, so they come off a little phoney. The natural child digs into a piece of cake with both hands; whereas the adapted child has learned to use a fork. Any time you catch yourself going through the motions, as it were, you are probably coming from your adapted child. You've been complaining for quite some time about the old fasioned performance evaluation forms used in your company, and now you get a couple more in the company mail to be filled out for your subordinates. Your natural child wants to send them back with one word scrawled across them: "Bullshit." Your adult wants to return them completed as best as possible with several pages of substantiating background information to explain the ratings given more objectively and with a request that something be done to improve the official forms. But your adapted child has learned that if you want a raise for your people, you play the game and rate your folks at least as high as everyone else is getting rated, smile to your boss when you turn in the forms, and continue to complain to your peers.

The little professor

The little professor in you likes to intuit the response others are expecting and behave exactly that way. This is mind-reading or making inferences from the nonverbal communicating going on around you. The military aide-de-camp probably has this down to a science, trying to stay one jump ahead of his senior officer (and at the same time expecting to be treated exactly the same way when his turn comes). An assistant who becomes a perfect "yes-man" is coming from his little professor. The danger is in becoming a con-artist. Too big a little professor can really use people—to make a sale, to get a promotion, or to talk a subordinate into an assignment for one's own personal gain.

All these parts of our personality are mixed up in each of us in different proportions. While one may predominate, we will find all of them to some degree. The particular combination that is present leads to our personal profile. Figure 9-5 shows the four more common profiles. In A, we find a highly-developed child part of the personality, with a smaller amount of the adult, and a still smaller part of the parent. This combination is called the *Snowman* because this individual will tend to melt on you due to highly-developed emotions. B is the reverse, with a highly-developed parent, smaller adult, and even smaller child. This is the *Rocky Road* because it's likely to tumble over from the weighty things on top. The configuration in C is called the *Dumbbell* because of the heavy proportions of prejudices and

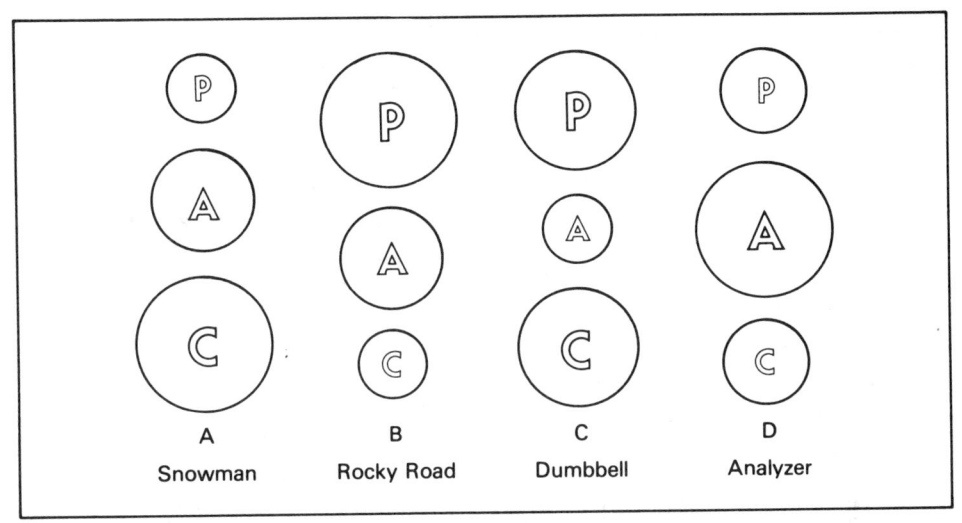

Figure 9-5 Some Common Profiles

A Snowman   B Rocky Road   C Dumbbell   D Analyzer

feelings to the detriment of factual knowledge. And D is the one with most adult and smaller amounts of parent and child, showing a predominant pattern of fact gathering and analyzing.

SUPERVISORY BEHAVIOR

We saw in studying the profile of an effective people developer that there are many traits and behavior patterns we can imitate in those coaches we have known and esteem. Chances are the parent part of us already does a lot of this without our realizing it. Remember, we come from our parent when we do things we learned by observing our parents. Think back to when you were a youngster. Is there something in your early family life which you remember fondly . . . something which was done by one or the other of your parents . . . something which you always felt was nurturing, protective, supportive? Perhaps a parent always read a little story to you before turning out the lights at night? Perhaps your parents insisted on everyone in the family being at home for a big dinner whenever it was someone's birthday? Perhaps a parent made it a point to accompany each child to school on that first dreadful day of becoming a student? And now do you find yourself doing exactly the same thing in your family? Do you read a story to the children at night because that's the way to put children to bed? Do you insist on a big dinner on birthdays because that's the way to celebrate a birthday? Do you go to school with the children on their first day because that's what every considerate parent does?

This time, recall something from your early life that you didn't really appreciate at the time. Is there some behavior of one of your parents that you can remember as a child that made you uncomfortable? Were you made to sit at the table until every morsel from your plate was cleaned off? Were you slapped by your father if you ever raised your voice to your mother? Were you taught that piano lessons were more important than playing baseball? And now do you find yourself with exactly the same rules or values in your family? Children must clean off everything on their plates. Children don't dare raise their voice in disrespect or they will get cuffed. Piano lessons are more important than playing baseball. The obvious lesson is that you recorded the behavior of your parents and learned that this was appropriate parent behavior. So, when it became your turn to be a parent, you put into practice the things you saw in your parents.

The same is true on the job. You were treated by your early supervisors in a certain way. Some of the things you observed in their behavior you can recall with satisfaction; others with less comfort. But chances are that you have unwittingly recorded all that behavior on your little tape recorder and are now living out some of the behavior patterns of your own previous supervisors. This next exercise consists of trying to think of some of these actions which are strictly a matter of unconscious imitation.

> Q What particular habit did your previous supervisor have which you feel was supportive, nurturing, developmental? Would it be helpful if you treated your subordinates the same way?
>
> A
>
> Q What particular habit did your previous supervisor have which you feel was uncomfortable, harmful, disruptive? Is it possible you are doing the same?
>
> A

Giving advice

One of the more common roles in being a coach is giving advice to those who ask for it. Depending on which part of our personality guides our behavior on these occasions, we can be more or less productive in those instances. Let us hypothesize such an occasion, and then we'll see the different kind of reactions we are likely to have, depending on which of our ego states we choose to come from.

Situation: Frank has been offered a promotion. It includes an average raise, but involves moving to a small town in another state and taking over a plant that is marginal at the moment. Frank knows that the plant must become profitable or he will be replaced and hurt in his career. He also knows that the General Manager of the Division wants the plant to become profitable soon, as it has been one of his "pet projects." Frank is 38, married, and has children aged 10 and 11. You are an associate of Frank's—not his supervisor—so you have nothing to do with his job offer. But he relies on your advice, and has asked for help in making this decision.

Q How would you advise Frank if you were a critical parent?

A

If you're catching on, you probably would say something like the following to Frank as a critical parent: "Frank, I don't know what you're hesitating for. This is a chance you only get once. A young man like you getting a chance to turn around a plant which the G/M has had his eye on for ages. Why, you can become a hero in his eyes. Where's your self-confidence? And you ought to know it isn't the possibility of failure that might hurt you—it's turning down an offer like this. You know they only give you one chance. If you disappoint them by refusing, you'll be on their black list forever."

In such a response, you are speaking prejudicially of the way offers are made, of the way heroes are made, of the way G/M's behave, and of the career path opportunities "young men" must follow. Most of all, you were a critical parent in that you really didn't help Frank grow through your discourse with him because you didn't help him make the decision; you made it for him. (You could have come up with the exact opposite advice: namely, not to touch the job with a ten-foot pole, for a similar list of prejudicial reasons.)

Now, let's try it from a different vantage point:

> **Q** How would you advise Frank in the same situation if you were a nurturing parent?
>
> **A**

The nurturing parent would probably say something like this: "Frank, you really better think twice before accepting that offer. You've been moving right along in this company, and now they're going to put you with that lemon. Do you know what five years of no upward movement will make in your career? The G/M wants profit fast, and that plant isn't going to be profitable fast for anyone. Besides, what is your wife going to do in that hick town? Believe me, I've been in those small towns—even your kids will have a tough time finding friends their age. For your own good and that of your family, don't accept, Frank."

All the judgments in such an answer are based on a desire to protect from harm. There is nothing necessarily bad about that, but what makes this unproductive coaching is not the advice to turn down the offer, but the fact that once again Frank is not being helped to think through anything on his own. You are making the decision for him still, and the only justification for your judgment is, "Believe me. . . ." If he takes everything on faith, he'll never stand on his own feet.

(Again, you could have given the opposite advice—to take the job in order to protect his future, etc., in a protective manner, and still not let him make his own decision.)

> **Q** Now how would you advise Frank, coming from your adult?
>
> **A**

Hopefully, this time you said something like, "Frank, I agree that this is a tough decision to make. I appreciate your confidence in coming to me, but I cannot make up your mind for you. About all I can do is remind you of some of the things you had best consider before coming to your decision. For example, have you checked out the availability of schools and suitable playmates for your youngsters? Have you discussed with your wife her ability to cope with a small town? Have you figured out what the raise will mean in terms of spendable income and compared prices of things here with prices there? And about the plant itself—do you know how soon you're expected to turn a profit? How will the G/M back you in changes you might have to make? Will you have a free hand? Did you or will you and he mutually set objectives for the plant that you can live with? If you've gotten answers to those questions and others, and check the risk compared with what you and your family can afford at this state in your life, then I guess you will know how to make your decision. Is there anything I can help you look into?"

Q. How would you advise Frank from your adapted child?

A.

Remembering the adapted child does what other people expect, principally to please them or, so as not to violate the book of etiquette, you might have said something like, "Frank, I sure admire you—only 38 and being given an offer like that. The G/M sure must have you as the apple of his eye. I heard you tell the other guys that you're all set to take the job, and I sure think that's the right thing to do. You're a lucky fellow, Frank." This reply was strictly going through the motions; no advice really, just a "yes-man."

Q. If you come from your little professor, how would you advise Frank?

A.

The little professor would probably say, "Frank, that's a real cool move you're making. When you've made the plant a big success and get appointed General Manager yourself, I hope you'll remember those of us who helped you back here. And, by the way, when you get ready to sell your house, don't give it to a realtor, I'd love to buy it, and maybe we can talk without getting an agent's commission in the price...."

Understanding transactions

Any time we send a message to another person and receive a response, we are involved in a transaction, whether spoken, written, or nonverbal. We now have two persons: an actor and a reactor. Each comes from one of the ego states, so at least two ego states are involved in a transaction, the sender's and the responder's. But there could be more than two because while the sender may be trying to hook onto a certain ego state of the responder, the latter may choose to come back from a different ego state.

To understand better what happens during a transaction, we illustrate which ego states are involved by diagramming the communications as they go from one to another and back again by the use of arrows. The arrow will go from the ego state of the sender to the ego state the sender expects or wants the responder to use. By analyzing the communication with the help of these arrows, we can gain useful information about why communication breaks down. We can also learn ways to interrupt nonproductive transactions and increase productive communications.

Transactions are said to be *complementary* when both participants receive the expected response from each other. The arrows will be parallel, which suggests the channels are open and this sort of exchange could continue all day long. Whether you want it to continue or not will depend on whether it is productive or unproductive. For example, in Figure 9-6, messages 1 and 2 are complementary, one critical parent complaining to another and getting the same kind of response. They could continue in this vein forever, but the interchange is not very productive because they are simply being judgmental, so you would want to stop it somehow. Messages 3 and 4 are also complementary, one adult asking straightforward questions of another and getting a factual answer. This is productive and you would want that kind of interchange to continue.

When one participant receives a response from an unexpected or undesired ego state, the transaction is said to be *crossed* and further communications will be blocked, or at least difficult. This sometimes occurs by accident. Or, you may deliberately cross a transaction because you do not wish a nonproductive exchange to continue. In Figure 9-6, messages 5 and 6 make a crossed transaction because the respondent refused to be treated as a child and came back one adult to another. The same thing occurs in messages 7 and 8 as a way of interrupting the original nonproductive comment from parent to child.

SUPERVISORY BEHAVIOR   185

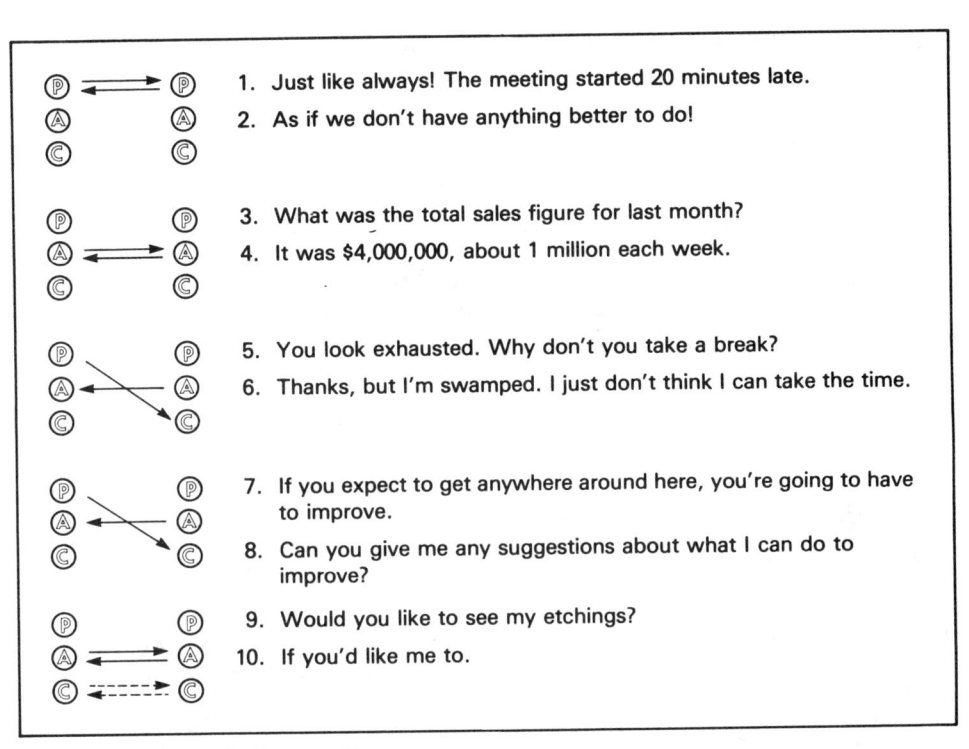

```
 P ←——→ P    1. Just like always! The meeting started 20 minutes late.
 A      A    2. As if we don't have anything better to do!
 C      C

 P      P    3. What was the total sales figure for last month?
 A ←——→ A    4. It was $4,000,000, about 1 million each week.
 C      C

 P      P    5. You look exhausted. Why don't you take a break?
 A ←  ↗ A    6. Thanks, but I'm swamped. I just don't think I can take the time.
 C   ↘  C

 P      P    7. If you expect to get anywhere around here, you're going to have
 A ←  ↗ A       to improve.
 C   ↘  C    8. Can you give me any suggestions about what I can do to
                improve?

 P      P    9. Would you like to see my etchings?
 A ←——→ A   10. If you'd like me to.
 C ←----→ C
```

Figure 9-6 Sample Transactions

Finally, we have *ulterior* transactions, which are distinguished from *surface* transactions. The surface ones are the outward, obvious unmistaken messages. But sometimes there are hidden messages which come from the use of double meaning words, or nonverbal expressions that accompany the words. In Figure 9-6, messages 9 and 10 are surface adult words, but the ulterior message is an invitation to some hanky-panky. Sarcasm is a common use of the ulterior message. If a subordinate comes in late to a morning staff meeting and you say, "Good afternoon, John," you are giving an ulterior message about being late. If you see a salesperson idly sitting on a piece of furniture and make the remark, "When you finish dusting that piece, there are a few more over on the wall!" you are giving another ulterior message. The trouble with ulterior messages is that we have so much difficulty getting clear and concise information imparted with our surface communications, that we only obscure things with ulterior transactions.

When you sense that a sender is attempting to hook onto a part of your personality and expects a reply which you feel will only lead to nonproductive communicating, the only way to get out of it is to attempt to cross the transaction by responding from a different ego state. Sometimes it takes

TRANSACTIONAL ANALYSIS FOR THE COACH

two or three attempts before you can get the conversation turned around to a more productive vein. Here are some initial messages you might receive in your role as coach. Record answers coming from all three of your ego states and then decide which response would be more productive in the given instance.

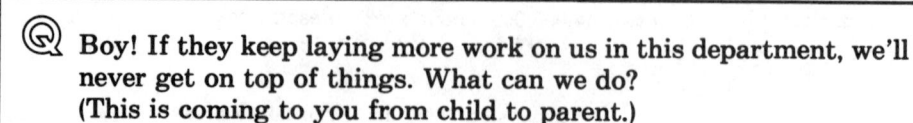

> **Q** Boy! If they keep laying more work on us in this department, we'll never get on top of things. What can we do?
> (This is coming to you from child to parent.)
>
> **A** Parent to child:
>
> Adult to adult:
>
> Child to parent:
>
> **Q** How do you expect me to finish this report when your group doesn't give us the information we need? You'll have to finish it yourself.
> (This is coming from parent to child.)
>
> **A** Parent to child:
>
> Adult to adult:
>
> Child to parent:
>
> **Q** You know, every time anyone talks to your department, they get the run around. Don't your people know what they're doing?
> (This is parent to child.)
>
> **A** Parent to child:
>
> Adult to adult:
>
> Child to parent:

> **Q** Harry's home sick today and he had an appointment at 2:00 to explain our new sales campaign to the people from the field. Can you handle it for him?
> (This is coming adult to adult.)
>
> **A** Parent to child:
>
> Adult to adult:
>
> Child to parent:

Stroking

Stroking refers initially to any form of direct physical contact. It is thought of with reference to patting a baby, though the pat can take the form of anything from tickling to rubbing to slapping. It has been proven scientifically that infants can actually die without some form of stroke from time to time. By extension, the word *stroking* refers to any act of recognition of another individual; hence, a *stroke* is the fundamental unit of social interaction. Psychologically, we can shrivel up if we do not have some form of interpersonal recognition from time to time. And the interesting thing is that it doesn't make much difference whether the strokes are playful caresses or abusive diatribes, as long as we get attention. This is shown in lab experiments with rats. It was found that the animals needed handling from time to time, whether it was gentle petting or painful electric shocks.

We become creatures of the strokes we receive through life, some of which will be positive and some negative. We bring our childhood patterns of stroking and being stroked to school, to marriage, and to the job, where we seek the same predictable strokes we learned to get long ago. That means that you, as a manager, and the people whom you manage have built up a lifelong pattern of giving and getting strokes. If there is a match, things can be productive; but if you and your people have different stroking patterns and stroking expectations, you may have to work at developing productive stroking as you coach them. You may have to work at avoiding unproductive stroking expected by your subordinates just for the purpose of getting attention.

Here are some common behavior patterns of people at work and what you might want to practice as a coach in order to give more productive strokes as part of the developmental effort:

1. Suppose you wish your John Doe would do more thinking for himself instead of asking you to make all his decisions. It could be that he got strokes for being a "pleaser" in the past. Maybe all he's doing is working eagerly to do whatever you tell him because he expects you to give him strokes for pleasing you. You have to make him see that he is more of a pleaser if he thinks through his own decisions and give him recognition for that—not for simply doing what he's told.

2. What if your John Doe needs to learn to work more cooperatively with others? Possibly, he got strokes for being strong and independent. This has taught him to continue to work alone and not to ask for help or even accept help when offered. You have to place greater recognition on teamwork than on independent action.

3. Perhaps your Jane Doe is one of those people who works fast and furious, but not painstakingly enough. You therefore have to spend a lot of time checking her work for errors. It might be that she got strokes for hurrying, so she learned to always be in a rush. If you continue to stroke her flurry of activity, she will continue at that pace. You probably want to break that pattern and start stroking her for being patient and accurate instead.

4. Perhaps your Jane Doe is the opposite; she got strokes for being slow. Don't be surprised if she is repeatedly late for meetings and misses deadlines. You have to start a pattern of stroking promptness.

5. Sometimes John Doe will get strokes for acting stupid. He might carry that over to work where you find he is not using the intelligence he has, so that you have to explain things to him several times, for example. Your challenge here is to draw out the intelligence he does have by reversing the stroking pattern away from being stupid to being smart.

6. Possibly you have a Jane Doe who got strokes for trying hard all the time. If that is leading her to nonproductive busy work in the expectation of getting more strokes, you must show her the danger of being passed up for promotion unless that energy is put into meaningful developmental effort.

7. Maybe your John Doe is an arguer. Trying to have a discussion with him is like going into a bull fight. Chances are he got strokes for being tough, so he still tries not to let anyone get the better of him. This is another unproductive pattern, so you would want to recognize a more malleable John.

To summarize, you get what you stroke. If you constantly point out problems, mistakes, bad decisions, or unproductive work habits to your people, you may be feeding a habit rather than improving their behavior. Such negative strokes are at least recognition, and if that's the only time they get recognition, they are going to continue that behavior since they know it brings attention. The result will be that their job performance is unlikely to improve.

Conversely, if you have workers whose performance has always been productive but who start slipping for no apparent reason, it could be that you were not stroking their productive effort. So, to get some kind of attention, they began to perform negatively.

There is also the matter of which ego state we stroke. We want to develop a healthy stroking climate by a balance of all the ego states, especially the productive characteristics of each. To stroke one of them too much runs the risk of overdeveloping that ego state. To compliment a woman, for example, on her dress, her looks, her perfume, etc., is to stroke the child in her and may leave the adult behavior (her skills and work performance) unappreciated and, hence, underdeveloped.

You may want to build a supportive relationship as a coach, and one very valuable tool for that is the skill of positive stroking. The more you can increase the exchange of genuine positive strokes within your work unit, the more productive will be the environment in which your people will have a chance to grow, because they feel more secure and confident.

Games

In transactional analysis, a game is a series of transactions which appear to be productive on the surface, but which have a hidden agenda carried out by repetitious, complementary, ulterior messages. The essential ingredients, then, are the ulterior nature of what is really intended by at least one of the participants, and some kind of psychological payoff. People play games in order to avoid getting too close to someone, in order to get strokes, or to reinforce psychological positions. At root, they are not honest or authentic. Therefore, you want to learn how to get out of the games people play.

Recognize first of all that the word *game* does not mean having fun or even engaging in a form of escapism. The distinguishing characteristic of any human game people play is the attempt to regulate emotions. A person is seeking strokes, so he or she engages in a series of ulterior transactions geared to getting attention. The payoff in this case is the recognition you unwittingly give by continuing to play the game. Or the individual wants to collect stamps. (*Stamps* are feelings that are collected, saved up, and then cashed in the way we collect and redeem grocery store stamps.) This person involves you in a game in order to get feelings of inadequacy, anger, purity, depression, and so on—another bad habit being fed.

The transactions in a game are complementary, and we learned earlier that to get out of unproductive complementary transactions, we want to cross the transaction. This also holds true in games: the best way to get out of a game is to interrupt the flow of the messages. To illustrate, let's use the popular game, *Yes, but*.... You approach John Doe about some assignment which is not up to your expectation and offer a suggestion on how it could be handled:

You: John, I see that the machine was not set up for the first shift as we had planned when making out the week's production schedule.

He: Yes, because we didn't have the manual from engineering to show us how to hook it up.

You: Well, couldn't you have called Engineering and gotten one?

He: Yes, but they said they were too busy to find it if we didn't have it with the machine.

You: What about going down there and getting it yourself if they were too busy?

He: Yes, but they wouldn't let us in the files.

You: Then why not get the one from XYZ Department because they have the same kind machine?

He: Yes, but that's an earlier model and things would be different.

You: Couldn't you call the supplier and get another copy or some instructions over the phone?

He: Yes, but they'd make us wait for our account rep to come over and see us.

This kind of exchange can go on indefinitely. On the surface it looks as though the two of you are engaging in adult-to-adult "operations," a set of transactions to accomplish some stated purpose: to get the machine set up. But the ulterior transaction is his parent-to-child discounting of you by knocking every suggestion you come up with. He's telling you that you're not OK. And you're feeding his psychological feeling of superiority over you as he persecutes you by valiantly trying to come back with something which will prove you are OK, child to parent. We would diagram it thus:

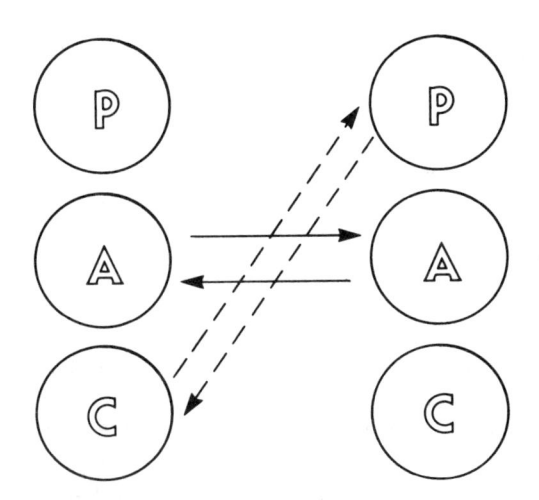

The only way you are going to get out of this is by crossing the transaction, no longer trying to prove anything to him, but asking him what he would suggest. Stop giving him a chance to tell you that your ideas will not work. Let him know on the surface and with no other possible ulterior meaning that it is up to him to live up to the responsibility of setting up the machine. So, you would say, "What do you think we can do about it since the machine must be set up at once?"

As a coach trying to help your people maximize their potential, you want to help them break the habit of playing games, which are always destructive rather than constructive. There are much more productive ways of getting strokes, which you will be trying to develop. So you want to be on the look out for the many games that people play at work. In general, these fall into four main categories depending on the ulterior payoff being sought:

1. When the individual plays the part of a *victim,* he or she is seeking negative strokes and the inadequacy stamps that come from a feeling of "I'm not OK." So there is Kick Me, Wooden Leg, Harried Executive, Poor Me, Ain't It Awful, See How Hard I Try, and others.

2. When the person wants to share misery about being not OK with you, there will be a *blaming* game that says "You're not OK." Also, there is If It Weren't For You, See What You Made Me Do, and so on.

3. *Persecutor* games are those in which the individual is reinforcing that you're not OK principally. They include Blemish; Now I've Got You, You S.O.B.; RAPO; I Told You So; Yes, But; Mine is Better Than Yours; and Uproar.

4. The other kind of "You're not OK" game is where the other person wants to come off as a *Rescuer*. Games include I'm Only Trying to Help You and Let Me Do It For You.

When you notice any one of these games being played, remember to cross the transaction. Respond from an ego state different from the one expected by the game player.

SUMMARY

This has been a very cursory introduction/review of the basic ideas of transactional analysis in the hope that you will be aware of how actions and interactions can be made more developmental. You are encouraged to do more indepth reading; for example, Eric Berne's *Games People Play,* Thomas A. Harris' *I'm OK—You're OK,* Muriel James and Dorothy Jongeward's *Born to Win,* and Muriel James' *The OK Boss in All of Us.*

10 PRACTICE CASES

Having reviewed the traits and behavior characteristics of an effective people developer, you may now wish to practice preparing for a developmental interview and communicating developmental ideas before you actually try your hand at some of these skills with your John or Jane Doe. We hope you have been applying the techniques presented in this text to your subordinates, especially in working out the exercises. But now it is important for you to get a feel for what it's like to pull them all together and use them in a coaching situation.

This chapter consists of a series of cases used with a number of clients and in public workshops on Coaching. They are arranged in order of simplicity. First are five vignettes, hypothetical short situations described in the third person, which you might wish to study by yourself for the purpose of analyzing the situation and preparing an interview based on the Interview Checkpoints to be found after this brief introduction. Next are three cases written for role play in which two individuals are given insights into the situation from their own perspective, one as superior and one as subordinate. These you may wish to try to act out with someone. Finally there is a single more lengthy case offered for you to handle according to the case study method.

If you role play, you may find it useful to ask someone to fill the position of Observer and make notes on the Observer's Checklist (Figure 10-1) and the Parent/Adult/Child Checklist (Figure 10-2) to aid in reviewing how you conducted the interview.

The following is a proposed list of things you should specifically prepare for in conducting your interviews. They can be used as items to write down as you formally plan an interview. They can also be used as a frame of reference for a discussion with anyone who might be able to observe you in action.

1. How will I establish rapport with this particular person?
2. What is my overall game plan, the thing(s) I wish to accomplish during this interview?

194 PRACTICE CASES

Figure 10-1 Observer's Checklist

Instructions: In order to help the interviewer (ER) improve skills and techniques, you are asked to indicate strong and weak points below. Check the word or phrase that best describes the ER's handling of the interview. After this has been done for all the items, go through the items again in order to evaluate the contribution of each item to the interview as a whole. Note there is a box at the far right of each item. If you interpret the item as being a good aspect of the interview, put a (X) in the box. If you feel that it is a poor aspect, put a (—) in the box. If it had no direct bearing on the employee (EE), favorable or unfavorable, put a (0) in the box.

1. The purpose of the talk was
   ___clear to the EE
   ___somewhat ambiguous to the EE
   ___unclear to the EE
   ☐ 1.

2. The ER's lead-off question encouraged EE to talk about things important to
   ___the EE
   ___the ER
   ___unclear which
   ☐ 2.

3. Who spoke most of the time during the interview as a whole?
   ___the ER
   ___the EE
   ___about 50-50
   ☐ 3.

4. The ER interrupted the EE
   ___not at all
   ___a few times
   ___a great many times
   ☐ 4.

5. The interview was centered around
   ___the ER most
   ___the ER more than EE
   ___the EE more than ER
   ___the EE most
   ☐ 5.

6. Leading questions were used
   ___not at all
   ___a few times
   ___a great many times
   ☐ 6.

7. The ER's prejudices and biases were
   ___very apparent
   ___somewhat apparent
   ___not at all apparent
   ☐ 7.

8. The ER gave advice and/or suggestions
   ___never
   ___occasionally
   ___frequently
   ☐ 8.

9. Eye contact was maintained by ER
   ___not at all
   ___at times
   ___most of the time
   ☐ 9.

Figure 10-1 continued

10. The listening responses were	___never used ___used occasionally ___main technique used	☐ 10.
11. Probing was	___always followed up ___sometimes missed ___poorly done	☐ 11.
12. The ER used closed questions	___often ___occasionally ___never	☐ 12.
13. Did ER put EE in stress situation?	___never ___occasionally ___frequently	☐ 13.
14. Pace of the interview was	___too fast ___about right ___too slow	☐ 14.
15. Was closure satisfying to EE?	___yes ___no	☐ 15.

3. How will I state the central issue to this individual?
4. Are there specific items of knowledge, skill, or attitudinal change that I want to draw attention to?
5. What do I know about the background of this person?
   a. What type is he or she (Type I, II, or III)?
   b. Is the person one of our not so rare birds?
   c. Have I reviewed physical, intellectual, emotional, work background, and goals information?
6. What kind of questions can I use to open the person up?
7. What listening skills might I use as I go along?
8. Do I have any suggestions to offer, if needed, in terms of developmental activities?
9. Are there any transactional analysis behaviors I can watch?
10. What commitment do I wish to get from this person?
11. Can I close with a time and action plan?
12. How might I assess the overall satisfaction with the interview?

PRACTICE CASES

Figure 10-2 Parent/Adult/Child Checklist

Instructions: When you observe a particular ego state in action, please jot a note in the appropriate column and provide feedback on this after the interview is over.

Ego State	Words/Phrases	Tone of Voice	Facial Expressions	Gestures	Posture
Critical Parent					
Nurturing Parent					
Adult					
Natural Free Child					
Adaptive Child					
Little Professor					

I'M DIFFERENT

John, 20, is a very aggressive young buyer in the Purchasing Department. He has been with the company for six months and has a strong desire to move into a management position as fast as possible. He has completed two years of college and is now attending night school in hopes of finishing his degree.

John knows that one must have a degree to enter the company's management training program. He is also aware, however, that exceptions are made to this degree requirement from time to time. The present Director of Purchasing, because of his marked aptitude in his earlier assignments, got into the training program without the degree.

You are Assistant Director of Purchasing in charge of some items kept in inventory and John is one of your buyers. You were personally involved in interviewing John before he came to the department and told him when he mentioned his desire to get into management soon that he looked like he had the stuff to move ahead fast.

All of the managers involved in career planning agree that John has potential as a management candidate some time in the future, but, at age 20 and with only six months experience, John's application for management training has been turned down for the present, with a notation that he is not an exception to the rule.

John feels strongly that he is an exception. When told he will not enter this year's training group, but that he might transfer to production control for a period of time to get some "seasoning," he refused.

John then went into a slump. Work that once was done meticulously is now done incompletely and begrudgingly. His attitude has become negative about everything. You don't want to lose John and yet you cannot put up with inadequate work performance either.

THE SAFETY GOGGLES RULE

You have been foreman of the maintenance crew in the plant for the past two years. There are twelve men in this crew and they usually work alone or in pairs. The work involves maintenance and repairs of a variety of machines in the factory, and entails use of standard tools and equipment. It is your responsibility to assign men from the crew to different jobs as repair orders come in and to visit them at the repair locations to give such supervision and assistance as might be needed.

As supervisor, you are also responsible for the safety of your men. This is an important function. As the crew members move from section to section of the plant, they must not only know and follow proper safety rules about their own equipment, but also adhere to special safety requirements of the different sections where they are on temporary assignment.

The company's safety record has not been too good overall, and recently there have been installed very strict safety rules. As part of the safety program, a method has been devised concerning penalties up to three weeks layoff for anyone caught violating safety practices. The slogan is, "No job is so important that it cannot be done safely."

Today you are on your way to check out a repair job being done by Bill Smith, one of your best workers who has been with the company for twenty years. You have had no complaint about his work because he is skilled; but you know he believes you supervise too closely, especially for someone like him with his seniority and proven ability.

As you round the corner to the area where Bill is supposed to be working, you remember to put on your safety goggles as required of anyone entering the area due to constant flying sparks. The machine Bill is repairing is in the middle of this spark area, and as you approach, you are certain you just saw Bill whip his goggles out of his pocket and hurriedly place them on as he spotted you coming.

SEVENTEEN

Ann was an hourly employee who was just recently promoted to a more responsible non-exempt but salaried position involving managerial functions and requiring managerial talents. She is a college graduate and has held several different jobs since graduating six years ago. She left her last position where she was earning more than she is now. Her reason for doing so was to get into engineering. When approached for this new assignment she was extremely eager and enthusiastic, again explaining her desire to get into management. Because of Ann's background, education, enthusiasm, and ability to "sell herself," she was moved into the position with great expectations from you as her supervisor.

You had only two weeks to introduce Ann to her new job and train her in certain responsibilities as you would then be on a vacation for two weeks. However, the training and explanations were complete, thorough, and documented and she seemed to understand and grasp her responsibilities with complete self-assurance. Before leaving, you wrote up a complete list of seventeen things to be accomplished in your absence. This list was prioritized and the timing of each task was outlined for the entire two-week period. Furthermore, each item on the list was explained and discussed before you left.

As soon as you left, Ann seemed to have undergone a complete character change. She immediately jumped into the role of "boss" and made the fact very clear to the others who resented the attitude. When approached by several other workers urging her to assist on a project they felt she could help complete for the department, she refused. When you returned, you found only three items on the list of seventeen had been done, and those three were of the last priorities and the easiest to do.

THE MORNING AFTER

You are the supervisor of a division employing seventy-five men and women and six first line supervisors. You like your job and the supervisors and employees who work for you, and you feel that they cooperate with you.

This morning you noticed that one of the supervisors, Bob Jackson, was rather late in getting to work. Since Bob is very conscientious and was working on a rush job, you wondered what happened. Bob is thorough and dependable; when something delays him, he always phones you. For this reason, you were concerned. You were about to call his home when one of Bob's men, a young fellow named Joe Blake, came in. Joe is a good-natured kid, just out of high school, but this morning he was obviously angry and said he was not going to work for Bob another minute and was going to quit unless you got him another assignment. Evidently Bob had come in, started to work, and then lost his temper completely when young Joe didn't do something right.

Although Bob occasionally has bad moods, it is unlike him to lose his temper that way. This latest rush job may have put him under too much pressure, but even so, his outburst this morning seems difficult to explain. You think something must be wrong and want to get Bob to talk about it. Is there more to this than meets the eye?

You talked with Joe for several minutes and when he felt better and was ready to go back to work, he left. You have just phoned Bob and asked him to drop around when he has a chance. He said he wanted to stop by the first aid station and get something for his splitting headache. He also mumbled something about being up all night, about just chewing out one of his young squirts, and about another change in that rush job.

ALICE IN SLUMBERLAND

Alice works in the bedding department. She has been with the store for twenty years. Fifteen of these years have been in the bedding area as a regular. She is married and has grown children. Working is not a necessity now but she enjoys it. Her education consists of completing high school. She has been a dependable employee and her sales, while not the highest in the area, are still fairly good. Normally, she is third best of a group of six people.

Recently, a program was introduced in the bedding area, as well as three other areas, which involved refinement of the goal setting, training, and review process. Alice has always had an hourly production goal but now she has had to take part in the goal setting and come up with specific sales dollars broken by month and merchandise category. She has been told she will be getting reviewed monthly to determine weak spots. Alice now has to write up and keep records of all cash and charge sales as well as fill out a daily and monthly tally of her sales. She feels this involves a lot of time and effort. She sees no real reward for doing this either, even though a pay-off in yearly raise had been explained. Competition is much keener on the floor and she feels there is now a cut-throat attitude among her coworkers. She is also being asked to keep card files of good customer prospects and, following a major purchase, to make "thank you" calls. All of this, she feels, is time consuming and some duplication of what is already being done on cards. She feels customers do not want calls at home.

When you wanted to discuss the program, she refused to discuss it. She says her job was fine until a month ago when all this started and she does not want to talk about it as she probably will quit.

THE NONSUPERVISING SUPERVISOR

General Information

Many changes have taken place recently in the credit and billing operation of the Exceptionale Company. New systems and procedures, flexible budgeting credit programs, expansion of credit files, new reporting requirements, and reevaluation of time standards have all caused disruption of the normal work load of the Credit Department.

As Section Head of the Accounts Receivable Billing and Mailing area, Ruthie Garcia has her hands full. She is very conscientious about her work and has a sincere desire to do a good job. However, billing has remained constantly behind schedule, which reflects poor planning in personnel requirements and in knowing and correcting problem areas. She used to rely on the position of Accounts Receivable Supervisor for help in her planning. This position was eliminated in the economy moves of last year and Ruthie has not been able to pick up the ball and run with it.

Last week the Industrial Engineering Department reviewed the situation. The engineer suggested some short interval scheduling techniques which would give her better utilization of available manhours of work without increasing payroll costs. Apparently she would have no part of this newfangled system and told the engineer as much.

Accounts Receivable Manager Role (Thomas Green)

Miss Garcia must recognize that the planning of work schedules and the efficient utilization of available working time is the supervisor's responsibility. If she is only there to keep peace in the family and to help input document keypunch operators decipher unintelligible records, she is not managing.

You are going to have a meeting with her this afternoon. Your objective is to convince Miss Garcia that it is to her advantage to accept the unconventional time scheduling of her people to meet the bulges of work load as suggested by the Industrial Engineer.

Perhaps she doesn't understand the system as proposed, its importance to the success of the credit operation as proposed, its importance to the success of the credit operation as a whole, or the possibility that many of her input keypunchers might look with favor on irregular working hours. Perhaps you can get her to see the advantages rather than the disadvantages of the new system.

Section Head's Role (Ruthie Garcia)

You are going to have a meeting with the Accounts Receivable Manager this afternoon. You assume he is going to play the same song again about the bottleneck in your section.

You know you have a lot of work to do. You and the other girls are working as hard as you can. If they would only give you two more girls. Why, your girls are taking coffee breaks at their desks in order to get fifteen minutes more of work done each afternoon. Some of those secretaries spend half an hour or more in the cafeteria at coffee time—they don't know what it's like to work hard.

You are sure going to remember to tell Mr. Green that you would appreciate his keeping those smart alecks from Industrial Engineering out of your area. The last time they were in they caused more trouble and wasted more time. All their ridiculous questions and those silly stop watches got the girls all upset. They think management doesn't think they are working hard enough. You had to talk fast to prevent a slowdown strike after their first day in the department. And then that red headed guy who was the boss, not even dry behind the ears yet, who carried a pocket calculator with his MIT locker number still written on it, tried to sell you some new-fangled scheduling system. Why, he used words you never heard before. You sure put him in his place when you asked if this system had ever been used in a billing department before. He didn't know!

TIRED TIRES

General Information

The Zorro Tire Company has always operated an automobile service garage as a customer service. It has proven to be a valuable asset to merchandising its accessories, tires, batteries, and other related car owner needs. The volume of business of the service department has dropped 14.2 percent this year to date as compared to last year.

There seem to be two explanations for this: (1) the storage space for cars awaiting repairs has been reduced by the expansion of the auto accessories selling area; and (2) there seems to be a lack of real leadership on the part of Carl Ryan, the department manager. Everyone seems to be going his own way. A customer might be treated well on one visit, shabbily on the next.

Carl Ryan started as a mechanic in the auto service garage seven years ago. He handled customers extremely well. His work was of a high quality and repeat customers always asked for him to work on their cars. When the former manager of the auto service garage had to retire for poor health three years ago, Carl was asked to take over.

For awhile things continued as before. However, with changes in personnel, the old methods are not well understood and followed and practices are somewhat slipshod in many instances. New employees are not getting the training they should. There is a lack of planning and scheduling of workloads. Some of the old hands are grumbling and longing for the good old days before old Mike took sick.

Carl seems to think it is easier to do something himself than teach the other guy how to do it. When problems occur, he solves them. Customers like him and he can easily handle any mechanical problem on which less experienced personnel get into trouble. But he is a poor planner and doesn't see his job as a trainer.

General Manager Role (Charley Fisk)

This morning your boss suggested you ask Carl Ryan to look for another job. You got him to agree to give you six months to work with Carl to develop some leadership potential which might be there.

Now you want to do some coaching with Carl. You have to impress him with the need to improve his management skills. There are three areas you have to work on to improve his performance: (1) developing skills in planning and organizing work, his own as well as subordinates; (2) understanding the needs of his subordinates to gain satisfaction from their jobs and the effect his "taking over" has on their morale; and (3) his responsibility to train others and how this in the long run will save him time as compared to doing it himself.

You decide you are only going to tackle one of three areas in your meeting this afternoon.

Auto Service Manager Role (Carl Ryan)

So Charley's going to have me on the carpet this afternoon. I wonder what he wants to talk about? I bet it's income level. That report that came out last week shows we're 14 percent or so behind last year. Small wonder. They take half your storage space to add more tire display area—radial tires, studded tires, snow tires, rain tires, regular tires—next thing you know, they will make different tires to use if you're going to take a trip on concrete freeways as compared to using scenic tar paved roads. All it does is make us store our customers' cars out in the open. Who wants his car to stand out in below-zero weather when another garage will keep it warm, inside all day? It's bound to affect business.

You know these new mechanics Personnel has hired for us are something else too. None of them know how to handle any real tough mechanical problems. Anything that goes beyond Basic Mechanics taught at Industrial High School and they throw up their hands. Then I have to come in and finish the job for them. Well, you can only cover for so many of these dodos—sometimes the customer finds out we ain't hiring master mechanics so they take their business elsewhere.

ON AGAIN—OFF AGAIN FINNEGAN

General Information

There's an old joke about the salesman named Finnegan who was criticized for making his weekly reports too lengthy. It seems he could never be brief enough to satisfy his sales manager who personally hated the paper work connected with his job. Finally the epitome of brevity was reached with the following report: "On again—out again—gone again—Finnegan."

There was no joking among top management of the Eastern Region concerning John Finnegan's management of the Middle Atlantic zone. John knew his merchandise very well. Prior to joining the sales organization he had five years experience in the design part of the business. He even had done a stint in the credit department of a competitor before that.

During the five years he has served as zone manager, John has had a highly erratic performance record. One year he would exceed quota and profit goals. The next year he would rest on his laurels and have an off year. Management would really lay it on the line; give him a "shape up or ship out" challenge and he would have another good year. Alternating between "off years" and "on years," management wondered if you could employ him only every other year.

Last year he broke the pattern—it should have been one of his off years, but surprisingly enough he exceeded quota.

Regional Manager Role (Tom Atlas)

As you prepare for his appraisal interview session, you realize John Finnegan will feel proud of his accomplishment. Not only did he exceed his quota, but for the first time in five years, he has broken the cycle—he had two good years in a row.

Unfortunately, this has been an unusually good year for the entire industry. While most zones made their quota, we are still in eighth place among our competitors. It is nice to see John made his quota, but he should have aimed higher. Basic quotas were made by some kind of windfall all around the country. You have to condition him to view his performance as something less than that with which he should be satisfied. He should be prepared to expect a critical rather than a laudatory interview session.

Zone Manager Role (John Finnegan)

As you prepare for your appraisal interview session, you are feeling pretty smug. They have never called you the "on again—off again manager" to your face, but the grapevine has fed back to you the fact that your boss refers to you in this manner. Well, you sure showed him—for two years in a row, you exceeded the quota.

It is your chance to speak up and pat yourself on the back, and you are going to take advantage of it. You have finally overcome the cycle. Next year you're going to make quota too. It's a good thing you were conservative on your planning. It sure feels good to know you won't be chewed out as a failure and a possible termination this year after the warning you got last year.

HOW TO FACE THE MUSIC

Instructions: You should read this entire case with a view to being asked to play the role of any one of the characters mentioned: the Division Manager, the Department Manager, the Assistant Buyer, the Trainee, or the Salesperson.

Tom Martin chewed the end of his pencil pensively. He had been trying all morning to zero in on the reason his department has been having problems. Tom's superior, Fred Bellows, Divisional Merchandise Manager, has called Tom to have lunch today—a rare occurrence. Tom is convinced it will also be a business discussion. Things have not been going too well in general, but they have taken a sharp downturn in the last two months. Mr. Bellows has just returned from a six-week foreign trip. Tom feels he wants an accounting for the bad times and a plan of attack. For the first time in the four years he has been with the company, Tom was apprehensive about his forthcoming meeting.

Until now, his track record showed him to be one of those young, dynamic men who can develop and be developed, the type that contributed much to making the company one of the most progressive, growth-oriented, and profitable national retail outlets in the country. A graduate from a small mid-western college with a B.A. degree in English literature, he heard the company's recruiter say, "We want above-average people . . . for above-average pay . . . and we want to give them a chance to learn and grow and move with the organization." This had appealed to Tom who turned down several opportunities to go to work for firms where it was well-known that you could stay on board by "keeping your nose clean" and could sit and wait until it was your turn to reach divisional level. A real "star" in the eyes of those who guided his introduction into the business world, he tackled his first position of responsibility with zest, as Assistant Buyer in men's sportswear. Eighteen months ago he became Buyer in the same department, exceeded plans, and surpassed sales and profit goals substantially.

During these earlier assignments he had actually enjoyed his performance appraisals, and found that he was doing even better than his predecessors in each capacity. Once he was sure he was going to make it in business, he took the big plunge and married one of the fashion models who worked parttime at the store. Everything had seemed to be going beautifully for the 25-year-old couple. Their little girl was now two years old and a second child was expected in another month. They were just getting used to the suburban home they had bought using last year's bonus as a down payment.

But now Tom began to feel the walls closing in on him. Would he be able to keep up the pace? What would happen as a result of his forthcoming meeting? Things aren't going as well in his new department, Junior Dresses, where he had been transferred after his earlier successes. He had been there four months now. During the year just ended, sales in the store had increased an average 4 percent. How is he going to explain to Mr. Bellows his department's unsatisfactory performance?

As he perused his year-end Operating Statement (see Appendix A), he wondered what his justifications would be. He was safe in the area of markups, having exceeded plan. But gross margin was down, stock shortages were way over plan because of a theft problem everyone was well aware of, and the department was $150,000 below planned sales.

As he searched for some of the causes of his poor record, he recalled his last conversation with Milicent Sharpe, trainee in the department. Tom was convinced she wanted to be a buyer and that she probably could be a good one in time. She might need a little seasoning, but she seemed to have real talent. Their talk had been prompted by her request to Mr. Bellows for a transfer. Tom had had no idea that she was that dissatisfied. Of course, he was away at market 50 percent of the time, like most buyers, and so he had delegated to his assistant, Chuck Scobie, the prime responsibility to teach Milly about the operation.

Anyway, Milly had accused Chuck of being very unfriendly and reticent in discussing her questions. It seemed to her that he was almost hoarding his knowledge. He gave her one- or two-word answers, she said. He never gave her anything to do. When she inquired as to why they always seemed to run out of stock on lines that were in demand all over the city, Chuck's reply was an acid reminder that in trend merchandising you cannot stay too long with sellers, but must be ahead of the market in testing new trends. High turnover was the name of the game.

Tom had tried to reassure his trainee, but didn't sound convincing even to himself, so he then decided to speak to Chuck about the situation. The Assistant Buyer presented a somewhat different version of what was going on.

"Leave it to Miss Smarty-pants to blame someone else," Chuck said. "The truth is, every time I want to show her something, she's busy selling. If you ask me, her level of aspiration is too high. Her own behavior shows she is more comfortable with the other females around here, out on the floor."

"But she does have a college degree," Tom pointed out. "Hers was a small school, it is true, but she was a retailing major and was head and shoulders above the rest of her class. Don't you think she deserves a chance to learn, the way the rest of us did?"

"I just don't think she can cut it. Take the time I sent her to the receiving dock to get the Valentine's Day special up here in time for the ad we had in the paper. If I hadn't gone down myself to verify her report that the stuff was on the way, we wouldn't have gotten it until Easter."

Tom really wasn't sure who was right. And discussing it further with Chuck didn't seem to get him anywhere. Poor Chuck sure was up to his ears in his people problems. It was his job to supervise the sales force and he wasn't enjoying it. There were six full time regulars, three of whom were rather new, and eight extras, six of whom were new.

As Chuck put it, the regulars had a total of 98 years of service, but didn't show it. They certainly had been selling long enough to know how to handle customers, but constantly complained about the younger generation they were now called upon to serve. Even the extras had noticed the disrespect of the teen-age customers. As one of the sales clerks put it, "When I was their age, my mother bought most of my clothes, or at least accompanied me to the store to be sure I behaved myself like a lady. Why, even the way these young girls look today is a disgrace. They come in here looking absolutely unclean. Then they expect you to find things for them at the same time; a body has all she can do to understand their language, much less keep up with them as they dart from one rack to the next."

Tom had to smile, despite himself, as he recalled this description of customer relations in his department. But he sobered quickly as he also remembered that it was this same clerk who had come to him on one of the rare occasions he stayed late one evening to see how the late shopping hours were working out. Elsie Hubbard—or "Mother Hubbard" as she was not so affectionately dubbed by Chuck—had come in as a sort of emissary from the other regulars to say that because of the demands of the "younger generation," as she called the Junior Misses, there ought to be additional pay. While the store didn't really compete with industry in the metropolitan labor market, the somewhat lower wages had always been taken for granted by the sales personnel as endemic to the retailing field. And with his own department's gross margin down the way it was, Tom didn't feel he was in a position to push for higher wages even if he should want to do so with the Wage and Salary office.

It was all becoming a jumbled mess in Tom's reverie. Milly complaining about Chuck; Chuck complaining about Elsie; Elsie complaining about her pay and the customers; customers complaining about not being able to get the dress they had heard so much about; Mr. Bellows sure to complain about the department's overall performance. About all he could be sure of was that nationwide it looked like a market trend for youthful styles, and he had better do something to get his high volume department in step with the other youth areas in the store.

As if all this wasn't enough to keep anyone occupied twenty hours a day, Tom also had to find time to figure out how he is possibly going to keep tabs on Junior Dresses in the new branch store due to open in six months. It was his responsibility to come up with personnel, inventory, shelf display, delivery orders, and so on, for the new store. Since he had never done this before he really didn't know where to begin and had been putting off these plans.

Tom began to make quick notes on things to discuss with Mr. Bellows.

Appendix A Excerpts from Year-end Operating Statement
Junior Dresses Department

Mark-up	Previous Year	49.8%
	Plan	51.0%
	Actual	52.5%
Sales	Previous Year	$1,200,000
	Plan	1,300,000
	Actual	1,150,000
Stock Shortages	Previous Year	9.8%
	Plan	7%
	Actual	23%
Gross Margin	Previous Year	12%
	Plan	13%
	Actual	10%
Merchandise Turnover	Previous Year	9.5%
	Plan	9%
	Actual	12%

REFERENCES AND RESOURCES

Barnard, Chester I. *The Functions of the Executive.* Cambridge, Mass.: Harvard University Press, 1938.
Bavelas, Alexander. "Communications Patterns in Task-Oriented Groups." *Journal of the Acoustical Society of America* 22 (1950).
Berne, Eric. *Games People Play.* New York: Ballantine Books Edition, 1973.
Boulding, Kenneth E. *The Organizational Revolution.* New York: Harper and Row, 1953.
Browne, C. G. "Study of Executive Leadership in Business, IV." Sociometric Pattern." *Journal of Applied Psychology* 35 (1951).
Drucker, Peter F. *Technology, Management and Society.* New York: Harper and Row, 1967.
Haire, Mason. *Modern Organization Theory.* New York: John Wiley and Sons, 1959.
Harris, Thomas A. *I'm OK—You're OK.* New York: Harper & Row, 1967.
James, Muriel. *The OK Boss in All of Us.* Reading, Mass.: Addison-Wesley, 1975.
James, Muriel and Jongeward, Dorothy. *Born to Win.* Reading, Mass.: Addison-Wesley, 1971.
Leavitt, Harold J. *Managerial Psychology,* 2nd ed. Chicago: University of Chicago Press, 1964.
Lewin, Kurt. *Field Theory in Social Science.* New York: Harper and Brother, 1951.
Likert, Rensis. *The Human Organization.* New York: McGraw-Hill, 1967.
McMurray, Robert N. "The Case for Benevolent Autocracy." *Harvard Business Review* 36 (1958).
Moreno, J. L. Various articles in *Sociometry, Group Psychotherapy,* and *Human Relations.*
Nichols, Ralph J. "Listening: What Price Inefficiency?" *Office Executive* 34 (1959).
Peter, Lawrence. *The Peter Principle.* New York: Morrow, 1969.
Roethlisberger, F. J. and Dickson, William J. *Management and the Worker.* Cambridge, Mass.: Harvard University Press, 1950.
Scott, William G. *The Management of Conflict.* Homewood, Ill.: Richard D. Irwin and the Dorsey Press, 1965.
Simon, Herbert A. *Administrative Behavior.* New York: Macmillan, 1957.
Townsend, Robert. *Up the Organization.* New York: Knopf, 1970.